Speak No Evil

Speak No Evil

The Triumph of Hate Speech Regulation

Jon B. Gould

The University of Chicago Press
Chicago & London

Jon B. Gould is assistant professor in the Department of Public and International Affairs and visiting assistant professor in the School of Law at George Mason University, where he serves as assistant director of the Administration of Justice Program.

The University of Chicago Press, Chicago 60637
The University of Chicago Press, Ltd., London

Printed in the United States of America

14 13 12 11 10 09 08 07 06 05   1 2 3 4 5

ISBN: 0-226-30553-8 (cloth)
ISBN: 0-226-30554-6 (paper)

Library of Congress Cataloging-in-Publication Data

Gould, Jon B.
Speak no evil : the triumph of hate speech regulation / Jon B. Gould.
p. cm.
Includes bibliographical references and indcx.
ISBN 0-226-30553-8 (cloth : alk. paper)—ISBN 0-226-30554-6 (pbk. : alk. paper)
1. Hate speech—United States—History. 2. Race discrimination—Law and legislation—United States. 3. Freedom of speech—United States. I. Title.
KF9345.G68 2005
345.73′0256—dc22

2004025707

∞ The paper used in this publication meets the minimum requirements of the American National Standard for Information Sciences—Permanence of Paper for Printed Library Materials, ANSI Z39.4-1992.

For my parents, and, as always, for Ann

Contents

Acknowledgments

In the many years that I have been reading academic books, I have seen only one other that thanks people in the proper order of contribution. For if we are truly honest, it is our family and friends who make these kinds of ventures possible. They stand with us day to day and provide the kind of support (in all its various forms) that sustains researchers through a laborious project.

In this case, primary thanks go to my wife, Ann. She more than anyone has lived the book start to finish. I cannot count the number of dinner conversations she has patiently sat through while I thought out loud about the project or fretted about completing it. She has never wavered with her confidence in me, and many of the ideas in this book reflect her careful feedback, editing, and suggestions. I cannot thank her enough for the support that allowed me to complete this undertaking. I will always be grateful for those three little words, "yes, of course."

Thanks also go to my family—to my children Michael and Emily, who are now able to report accurately that "Daddy writes books"; to my parents, brothers, and sisters-in-law, who cheered me along the way even as they wondered if this project would ever be completed; and to my in-laws, whose own academic careers allowed for special support and understanding.

Countless friends have supported me, expressed interest in the book (or feigned it well), and shared in the celebration when the manuscript was completed. Many of them find their names woven into the book as monikers for the participants who must remain anonymous. They all have my deepest thanks and enduring loyalty. A few deserve special mention: Nancy Crowe, my former classmate and new neighbor, who has lived this project with me since our days at the University of Chicago. I definitely owe you another round of beer and french fries; Sharon Goodie, one of my oldest friends and current "writing buddy," whose pleasant goading helped to complete the final draft; and Barry McCarthy, whose insights have helped to guide me.

I hesitate to say that this book began nearly a decade ago, but its inception has spawned one of the most important and professionally rewarding relationships I have had. I remember sitting in the office of Gerry Rosenberg at the University of Chicago, whining that I could not pick an appropriate dissertation topic. Gerry and I had already been around the block a few times by then. I had arrived at the University of Chicago, a headstrong former lawyer intent on gaining my doctorate as quickly as possible. In my path stood Gerry, a straight-talking New Yorker who insisted that I earn my stripes. What was a tumultuous first meeting, however, has turned into a wonderful friendship. As I sat whimpering in Gerry's office, he cut right to the quick. "What do you care about?" he asked. "Tolerance," I said. "Well, then, how about hate speech?" he offered. From there a dissertation and eventually this book were born. That is not to say the path has been easy. To the contrary, this has been the most difficult professional project I have ever undertaken. It has been confusing, frustrating, and isolating along the way, but in the end it has been worthwhile. For helping me to make it to the finish line—and for his continuing advice and mentoring—I owe Gerry a debt of thanks. I can only hope that my career lives up to the standards set by Gerry.

If, as the adage goes, it takes a village to raise a child, then in my case it has taken a national collective to produce a book. Many fine scholars have generously assisted me in the project. In addition to Gerry, thanks go to the other members of my dissertation committee, Mark Hansen, Lynn Sanders, and Cass Sunstein. They were enthusiastic about the topic and provided the kind of careful feedback and constructive criticism that improved my ideas along the way. Several other superb scholars have generously offered their time and suggestions. Avern Cohn, Patricia Ewick, Roger Hartley, Lisa Holmes, Tim Johnson, Michael McCann, Christine Nemacheck, Laura Beth Nielsen, and Susan Silbey have all helped to strengthen the book, although, of course, the errors and limitations are mine. I am also grateful to the anonymous reviewers from the *Law and Society Review* and the University of Chicago Press, whose detailed and careful evaluations gave me much to consider and improve at different stages of this project.

This book was composed over several years, some of it spent at the Institute of Governmental Studies (IGS) at the University of California, Berkeley, where I was a visiting scholar, and the remainder at George Mason University (GMU), where I am a faculty member. I am grateful to Nelson Polsby, past director of IGS, as well as to the staff and other visiting scholars at IGS, who made me feel at home and provided a supportive environment in which to work. At GMU, Scott Keeter, Steve Mastrofski, and Daniele Struppa have quite literally invested in my work and me. They are part of what brought me to George Mason, and I feel fortunate to have such talented, engaging, and personable colleagues. I am also grateful to George Mason University and the Mellon Foundation for financial support to undertake the research and complete the writing.

The research itself relied on the good will and participation of countless faculty, staff, and administrators at the one hundred schools in the study sample, as well as several knowledgeable observers. Although too numerous to thank here individually, I deeply appreciate their willingness to share insights, campus history, and college policy. The research could not have been completed without their cooperation.

In my family February 25 will be remembered well, the day that John Tryneski phoned to say that the University of Chicago Press would be publishing this book. John and his capable assistant, Rodney Powell, have been a dream to work with, even if John and I share competing loyalties to Chicago baseball teams. I am also grateful to Dawn Hall and to Leslie Keros, Ashley Cave, and Ryan Li at the University of Chicago Press, who have helped to shepherd the manuscript to publication.

Hate speech is a problem that continues to vex America and other democratic societies. Although reasonable people can certainly disagree about the appropriate response to such expression, let us never forget that hate speech is fundamentally based in bigotry. Like the many others who work for social justice, I long for the day in which we triumph over prejudice and intolerance. Doubtful, yes, but it doesn't hurt to dream.

Introduction

In September 1997, Professor Don Staples shocked an audience at the University of North Texas when he seemed to single out minority students as ignorant and uninterested. Staples, a tenured professor of film studies, had been participating in a campus forum to "discuss ways of improving the college experience."[1] When asked about the failure of many professors to weave African American contributions into course work, Staples responded that minority students at North Texas would appreciate their courses better if they stopped skipping class. Almost as soon as the remark left his lips Staples realized that he had "made a big mistake,"[2] an "unfair generalization"[3] as it were, but the immediate uproar drowned out Staples's attempts to explain his comment or apologize.[4] Staples soon found himself on leave from the university, the administration having concluded that the professor had engaged in hate speech. As the university's chancellor, Alfred Hurley, wrote in a campus memorandum, "free speech will be defended," but "racism will not be tolerated."[5]

A few weeks earlier, Professor Lino Graglia of the University of Texas Law School appeared at a press conference in Austin to announce the creation of Students for Equal Opportunity, a new organization that welcomed "diversity but not affirmative action" on campus. In the course of his remarks Graglia criticized preferential admissions programs for minorities, claiming remarkably that "blacks and Mexican-Americans can't compete academically with whites" because they come from cultures in which "failure is not looked upon with disgrace."[6] By themselves, Graglia's comments would be controversial, but they became a lightning rod throughout the state coming on the heels of *Hopwood v. Texas*.[7] In *Hopwood* the U.S. Court of Appeals for the Fifth Circuit had ordered the University of Texas (UT) to dismantle its affirmative action programs, and many feared that Graglia's remarks would lead minority students to believe that UT was "not hospitable" for them. The Reverend Jesse Jackson came to Austin to lead protests against Graglia; top UT officials, including its chancellor, labeled Graglia's comments "abhorrent";[8] and a member of the board of regents urged that the law professor be fired.[9] But for all of the talk and threats, Graglia kept his position without penalty or charge. As UT law dean Michael Sharlot explained, "'given applicable First Amendment protections,' there would be no disciplinary action."[10] In fact, UT would later revise the harassment policy that Graglia had been accused of violating, university officials having concluded that its sanctions were unconstitutional.[11]

How is it that the University of North Texas and the University of Texas would reach such different results? Both are public schools in the same state, administered by identical regents and answerable to the same elected officials. They are less than two hundred miles apart. Opponents of Staples's treatment, and those who worried about Graglia, would say that the professors were victims of a "progressive political ideology" in American academe,[12] an orthodoxy that few campus leaders were able to resist. Also called political correctness or "PC," many critics see the embodiment of such "thought reform"[13] in college policies prohibiting hate speech.

THE CONVENTIONAL STORY OF MODERN HATE SPEECH REGULATION

The story of hate speech regulation in America stretches back almost a century, although it has received its greatest attention over the last fifteen years as several colleges and universities adopted policies prohibiting hate speech by faculty, staff, or students. The debate has been heated and intense, with many commentators offering editorials, articles, and books about the merits of hate speech regulation.[14] But as important as that discussion has been, there have been few serious attempts to understand why hate speech regulation developed when it did, not to mention what its rise says about American legal, political, and social processes.

Of course, many have attempted to address this topic. In their books and articles about hate speech regulation, the opponents of speech codes decry a vast movement of political correctness in which a postmodern army of liberal academics arose to advance their political manifesto on as many college campuses as possible. Even if this depiction is a bit tongue in cheek, opponents have largely viewed the speech codes through the rubric of political mobilization. A cohort of liberal academicians—those raised on the civil rights and women's rights movements—were said to be extending the civil rights laws by punishing discriminatory words as well as deeds. However, because their views had little support in the political or legal processes of the Reagan administration, activists allegedly retreated behind the gates of their ivory towers to enact on campuses what they could not accomplish in wider society. Indeed, most descriptions of the hate speech "movement" reflect concern that a rising "totalitarian mindset"[15] on campus would spill over into larger society and champion politically correct dogma.

The opposition to speech codes attracted an unusual mix of activists, including representatives from the civil libertarian left and the socially conservative right. One saw Nat Hentoff and George Will joining sides, just as the American Civil Liberties Union and the Individual Rights Foundation litigated together against college hate speech policies. By and large these groups have successfully challenged hate speech regulation in the courts. In 2003 a federal judge in Pennsylvania overturned Shippensburg University's student code of conduct because it violated "students' First Amendment rights to free speech."[16] Coming nearly eight years after the last major college hate speech case, this decision seemed to reiterate what five other courts had said before it—that hate speech regulation is unconstitutional. Courts in California, Michigan, Wisconsin, and Ohio[17] have considered college hate speech policies, finding them vague, overbroad, and ultimately illegal. These decisions were confirmed by the U.S. Supreme Court in 1992, which ruled that public institutions may not pick and choose among hateful messages when regulating speech.[18]

The courts' decisions have been hailed by the opponents of college hate speech policies, who see these precedents as the welcome death knell of hate speech regulation. Although the Foundation for Individual Rights in Education (FIRE) continues to agitate against college hate speech regulation, the bulk of opposition quieted down in the late 1990s. After a short victory lap of editorials, opinion pieces, and the occasional law review article, the issue has receded from its heights in public consciousness.

THE TRADITIONAL EXPLANATION IS WRONG

If academe were Hollywood, the speech codes might make a good screenplay. A band of liberal activists arose to threaten free speech under the mantle of political correctness. They were met and ultimately defeated in court by a broad coalition of civil libertarians and social conservatives, all of whom were concerned with the preservation of open discourse and free expression. In the end, the camera would close on the occasional skirmish at a rebel campus with the protectors of free speech ever vigilant and firmly in control of legal and political processes.

The problem with this account is that it is wrong, substituting a simple story for a complex tale. To be sure, some hate speech policies may owe their enactment to the conventional story line, and some elements of this depiction are true. Critical race theory arose in the mid-1980s, both as an ideological heir of the civil rights movement and to argue that historic legal victories had yet to achieve racial equality. Minority groups, and in particular African Americans, were increasingly demanding their full "membership rights" within society, including challenges to the "soft racism" of jeers, affronts, and slights. And, of course, academe contains a disproportionally liberal membership, at least when compared to American society as a whole. But to lay the speech codes at the feet of a collegiate PC movement is to miscalculate the political acumen of progressive activists. It also misses the varied, utilitarian, and almost cynical rise of college hate speech policies.

One of the difficulties in the popular depiction of speech codes is that its authors argue from anecdote. When Dinesh D'Souza wrote his 1992 book, *Illiberal Education,* he relied considerably on five campuses to reach his sweeping conclusion that a "revolution [was afoot] on behalf of minority victims."[19] George Will's many columns about hate speech name only ten schools as offenders.[20] Even FIRE's founders, Alan Kors and Harvey Silverglate, who have done a commendable job of compiling examples of due process violations on American campuses, fail to describe their method for selecting examples. Claiming that their book, *The Shadow University,* exposes a "widespread reliance on kangaroo courts and arbitrary punishment to coerce students and faculty into conformity," the reader is left to wonder whether the cases they cite are typical or attention-getting aberrations. Indeed, Avern Cohn, the judge who overturned the University of Michigan's speech code, has said of the book, "if one is confined to a single word to describe [Kors and Silverglate's work], the choice would fall somewhere among diatribe, jeremiad, philippic, and polemic. If one takes a good look at *The Shadow University*'s Web site, the word would be self-aggrandizement."[21]

Why have the opponents of speech codes relied so heavily on anecdotal reports? Do they have a political message to sell, or are they largely political commentators and lawyers, activists who while well intentioned are largely untrained in (and may lack the patience for) empirical research? To be fair, this charge is hardly limited to the codes' opponents, for others too have failed to understand the rise of speech policies. But the codes' proponents were hardly as vocal as their antagonists, nor did they fear the lasting influence of such policies.

This book takes a different path in the hate speech controversy, tracking the rise of campus speech policies through an empirical study of multiple methods. Drawing from a random sample of colleges and universities from across the country, the book estimates that nearly one-third of American schools developed hate speech policies by 1992. Although this figure is sizeable, the severity of the policies varied, with less than 10 percent of schools adopting policies that challenged existing First Amendment principles. More significantly, the research fails to link the speech codes to an organized movement of identity politics. Based on quantitative research at one hundred schools and in-depth interviews and archival research at several institutions, the book instead identifies three distinct motives for the speech codes. In each case relativist or multicultural theory spurred the speech policies, but the pivotal actors were top collegiate administrators acting on instrumental motives. In many cases, officials crafted speech codes as symbolic responses to racial incidents on campus, seeing the policies as a sop of sorts to assure campus constituencies that action had been taken against intolerance. Another set of schools engaged in normative isomorphism—an academic version of "keeping up with the Joneses"—crafting hate speech codes to remain within what top officials saw as the mainstream of higher education administration. At a final, much smaller group of schools, speech policies were developed by student services administrators who legitimately believed in the merits of the codes. These were probably the closest model to the traditional explanation offered by speech code opponents, although they are but a small percentage of the schools. Even more, the speech codes in these cases were proposed and adopted by administrators, not the student or faculty activists envisioned by the anti-PC crowd. If anything, minority groups on campus were largely agitating for more tangible measures, including increased minority hiring and additional funding for scholarships, fellowships, and salaries. Few were outspoken advocates for hate speech policies.

THE TRIUMPH OF HATE SPEECH REGULATION

The conventional explanation also misconceives the afterlife of hate speech regulation. By 1997, five years after the Supreme Court spoke on hate speech regulation, almost half of American colleges and universities had hate speech policies on the books, a rise of nearly 30 percent from the time of the Court's opinion. The rate was even higher for those schools that adopted the most constitutionally suspect policies—codes that banned offensive speech—where numbers had tripled. Nor was this rise restricted to private schools, those institutions not covered by the First Amendment and the relevant court cases.[22] Public schools reflected the same increase. Rather than settling the matter of college hate speech regulation, the court decisions were ignored, evaded, and resisted.

This point would sit well with Kors and Silverglate, who contend that colleges and universities are still "enforcing their own politically correct worldview through censorship, double standards, and a judicial system without due process."[23] But Kors and Silverglate's claim is by turns both too broad and too narrow. While many school administrators have failed to enforce their speech policies explicitly or punitively—in part because they are hesitant to create controversy or to run afoul of the court decisions—the policies continue to wield great power. Even if these policies sport few actual teeth, their symbolic power has flourished as student services staff and other college officials continue to advance the underlying message of the speech policies, mainly that hate speech has real and harmful effects and that it should be purged wherever possible.

If the speech codes' opponents believe this message is limited to colleges and universities they misunderstand its reach, for the conceptual kernel has taken root in American society, bringing with it greater acceptance of hate speech regulation. Public opinion increasingly favors the informal prohibition of racist and sexist speech,[24] newspapers and other media have eschewed expressions that vilify a racial, ethnic, or sexual group, and many Internet service providers have voluntarily removed or banned postings that malign another's race, gender, ethnicity, or sexual orientation. For that matter, existing law reflects the tenets of hate speech regulation, albeit through a slightly different lens. Although addressed to action and not speech, the penalty enhancement provisions of hate crime legislation can be traced back to college speech codes. Moreover, sexual harassment law has expanded to punish employers when workplace speech denies employees equal opportunity. While some try to explain away this doctrine as an exception in which a "subcategory" of "proscribable speech" is "swept up incidentally within the reach of a statute directed at conduct rather than speech,"[25] the hostile environment prong of sexual harassment law rests on the same basis as does hate speech regulation: Words not only wound, but severe or pervasive messages may also discriminate. Whether they have recognized it or not, hate speech regulation has quietly surpassed the wildest fears of its opponents to become an accepted norm in American society.

THE MEANING OF FREE SPEECH AND THE FIRST AMENDMENT

The hate speech controversy is not simply a story of who wins and loses in restricting hateful speech. It also addresses the basis and reach of American law, particularly the First Amendment and freedom of speech. The First Amendment, of course, is no simple doctrine. In many ways it forms the centerpiece of American legal, political, and cultural life; people say they want to follow it, and are guided by its terms in their daily lives, regardless of whether they are formally required to do so. For years legal scholars have debated the basis of free speech law. Is it morally based, does it flow from notions of natural law, democracy, or self-actualization? The hate speech controversy shows many of these rationales to be equivocal, for proponents and opponents of the policies borrowed from the same bases to stake their claims. But at a larger level the controversy suggests that such musings are unnecessarily myopic, focusing as they do so often on the ducking, weaving, and eventual decisions of judges. Courts are only a starting point in establishing the meaning of rights and law, for the concept of free speech is by far one of the most socially constructed notions in American law and culture.

Over the last half-century both scholars and practitioners have come to recognize that judges construct constitutional law, that they apply their "experiences and world view"[26] when establishing legal doctrine, creating rules that are not so much "natural" as reflections of the "power relationships in society."[27] More recently, researchers have suggested that other governmental branches, in this case Congress, construct constitutional meaning along with the courts.[28] Even so, these interpretations still rest the Constitution's meaning on governmental institutions. This book takes a step further, joining those commentators who argue that constitutional construction occurs in civil society among other influential yet nongovernmental institutions. Certainly, we have seen elements of this before in public law scholarship. Researchers have examined the public's acceptance or rejection of court decisions, they have unpacked the public's understanding of judicial rules, and they have chronicled the role of law in everyday life.[29] Still, many seem reluctant to make the ultimate claim—that the Constitution and related court decisions are but one (and perhaps not even the most important) part of the legal meaning-making function. The essential arbiter for legal meaning is civil society and its institutions, which themselves construct constitutional law.

In advancing this point the book distinguishes between the Constitution and mass constitutionalism. The former refers to formal and legally enforceable interpretations of the U.S. Constitution and its amendments, while the latter represents the practical understanding and meaning of constitutional norms in civil society. Of course, the line between constructed constitutional principles and simple social norms may be a fine line, especially when the subject is free speech. For example, a parent's hush of her child fails to implicate the First Amendment, whereas prior restraint of news coverage quite clearly does. Nonetheless, the two are much closer than often realized. In the case of hate speech regulation, opponents did not simply criticize public institutions for violating the First Amendment, they denounced all who would limit open discourse. Yet their arguments were premised on many of the same justifications that undergird the First Amendment. In a sense, the constitutional principles and social norms overlapped, premising popular interpretations of free expression on notions of what the more formal constitutional right implies.

Constitutionalism is often dependent on formal, governmental constructions of the Constitution to create public understandings, but the hate speech debate shows that the bounds of a constitutional right may be reinterpreted without the courts or governmental institutions giving their blessing. This supposition suggests other strategies for those who seek to bring about legal or social change. Rather than relying on legal mobilization to influence the courts or political organizing to change legislation, there is power in co-opting other institutions within civil society to spread one's view of mass constitutionalism. Even if the ultimate goal is formal legal change—if only because recognizable rights are enforceable in court—the practical effect of altered constitutionalism is the tantamount recognition of rights in day-to-day life. The hate speech codes have shown as much, as the prevailing norm now is to quash hate speech, even if in an extra-judicial setting. There may be other examples, especially where formal political processes are closed. Among other things, the gay rights movement has found success in cultivating the media and academe to recast public perceptions of their cause even if formal legal recognition of gay rights has been slower to advance.

Ultimately, then, this book brings together three debates in the public law field—the basis of free speech and the First Amendment, the social construction of law, and the creation of social or legal change—to argue that the real power in legal meaning-making is found outside of formal governmental institutions. To be sure, institutions form the building blocks—being either a formal instigator of legal meaning or serving as a vehicle to introduce new ideas about law and rights—but ultimately we miss the true power of rights construction if we focus so narrowly on government and especially the courts.

HOW TO READ THIS BOOK

This book is actually a lesson in two parts. In one respect it is a story about a social and legal controversy, a grand firestorm that enveloped American society and its opinion leaders for the better part of a decade. Calling into question past explanations of hate speech regulation, the book tells a different tale, one that is based in empirical study. The story is the ultimate "whodunit," piecing together varied elements that almost backhandedly advanced a doctrine: philosophical priming from the civil rights and women's rights movements, instrumental adoption to quell racial unrest, supposed silencing by the courts, rejection or evasion of judicial precedent, and eventually a sub rosa triumph of hate speech regulation within civil society. When compared to the acceptance of sexual harassment law and its hostile work environment test, it is fascinating how related doctrines get treated differently yet reach similar points in civic culture.

This book is also about the social construction of law and the meaning and influence of free speech norms in America. It joins the burgeoning debate about the mechanisms of legal and social change and argues that legal change comes as much from altering the understanding of legal norms in civil society as it does from changing the law itself. Ultimately, the book advances a model of extra-judicial legal meaning-making, proposing routes through both diffusion and mobilization that advance mass constitutionalism over formal, codified law.

In doing so, the book is divided into six chapters. Chapter 1 provides a history of contemporary hate speech regulation, a study that traces itself back to the civil rights era and continues forward to this day. Chapter 2 ties this controversy to three fundamental debates in law: (1) What is the basis for free speech and the First Amendment? (2) Where does legal meaning lie—in judicial doctrine or in the "shadow of law"? (3) How is legal or social change created? Chapter 2 also presents a theory of extra-judicial law and legal meaning-making and connects this theory with the narrower hypothesis of the codes' critics, who argued (perhaps unwittingly) that legal mobilization explained the rise of "politically correct" speech policies.

Chapter 3 tests the critics' hypothesis for the rise of college hate speech codes, concluding that speech policies were largely an instrumental creation of top-level college administrators and not the result of legal or political mobilization as advanced by others. The chapter is empirically based, relying on both quantitative and qualitative research at one hundred colleges and universities. Of particular interest is the comparison between hate speech codes and their intellectual cousin, sexual harassment law and its hostile work environment (HWE) test. Where HWE was advanced directly and deliberately in the courts, hate speech codes arose circuitously as defensive measures.

Chapter 4 evaluates the formal legal rules that faced colleges with speech codes, describing how the courts have dealt with hate speech regulation and contrasting these rulings with those of sexual harassment law. While acknowledging that there were sound bases for the courts to have treated individual cases differently, this chapter suggests that the difference in the two doctrines' fates lies less in their individual merits than in other nonlegal forces. Where HWE has had strong advocates, hate speech codes have had but tepid supporters and a powerful opposition. The two doctrines have also been framed differently, one as sexist action the other as thought control. Ultimately, this chapter rejects the notion that sexual harassment law is easily distinguished from hate speech codes or that the courts have done an adequate job of explaining their divergent decisions.

Chapter 5 is likely to be unsettling to the many opponents of hate speech regulation. Reexamining the prevalence of college speech codes in light of the courts' holdings, this chapter finds colleges not only declined to follow the courts' decisions, but they also adopted new and more extensive speech policies in the face of contrary precedent. This paradox—between court decisions and public behavior—illustrates the power of extra-judicial legal meaning-making, for the resistance of college administrators served to redefine the meaning of the underlying constitutional norm.

A final chapter expands the inquiry from college campuses to civil society, concluding that hate speech regulation has permeated other elite institutions like the media and has trickled down to influence mass opinion and common understandings of constitutional norms. This chapter reconnects the hate speech story to extra-judicial law and the power of legal meaning-making, arguing that informal law or mass constitutionalism is as powerful as the formal Constitution, providing vehicles for change that exist without the intervention of courts. Contemporary hate speech regulation arose almost from happenstance, but the lesson remains true for those who seek legal change: Although the courts help to establish legal meaning with their decisions, it is just as important to win the battle in civil society by influencing the public's construction of legal and constitutional norms.

The book is based on empirical research, but there are few tables, equations, or logarithms in the text to confuse the lay reader. The arguments and results are made in prose. For those who would like to examine the research method, an appendix explains the quantitative and qualitative research involved along with results from the quantitative tests on which some of the conclusions are based.

A DISCLAIMER

Let me assure the reader at the start that this is not another book about the legitimacy of hate speech prohibition. Undoubtedly, the merits of speech regulation have been well debated over the last fifteen years. This book asks different questions, queries quite frankly that should have been answered years earlier. Why did hate speech regulation arise in the late 1980s? Why at colleges and universities, those institutions most closely connected to academic freedom and free speech? How have these measures prospered in the face of contrary legal precedent to the point where hate speech prohibition has become the accepted norm in American society? Most importantly, what does this process say about the basis of constitutional law and the meaning of free speech in America? Many authors have examined the speech codes, some more thoroughly than others. But even a decade following the first major hate speech codes, we are still missing a full, fair account of their development and meaning.

On a topic so heated, I suppose it is only fair that the reader should know where I stand. In truth, I have struggled with the question of hate speech regulation, for I am sympathetic to the arguments behind hate speech codes but believe that they were applied too broadly. We have already decided as a society that there are some areas in which it is inappropriate, indeed illegal, to deny individuals certain benefits on the basis of their immutable characteristics. Education must be among those. The law has been willing to acknowledge, at least in the realm of sexual harassment, that speech can deny those benefits as much as action. To refuse this point is to live in a land of make-believe, for persistent or severe epithets can cause real physiological or psychological harm.[30] The key question, then, is not whether public bodies *can* restrict speech in the interests of preserving equal opportunity, but rather what *test* should be used to distinguish proscribable speech or conduct from the acceptable. In this respect sexual harassment law seems to have the threshold right: severe or pervasive speech directed against a subject who cannot avoid it, when the speech is both objectively discriminatory and subjectively objectionable to its target.[31]

This definition would weed out almost all of the cases that were prosecuted by colleges and universities as hate speech, and it should. The point is not to prohibit speech that is merely objectionable—for a point of college is to learn to deal with objectionable speech—but to punish expressive conduct that truly denies equal educational opportunity. Cases such as *Rubin v. Ikenberry* reach this level, where a professor repeatedly berated female students with comments like, “The problem in schools is uppity, greedy women. . . . If I were king, all women teachers would have to spend fifteen minutes on a moonlit night, in a canoe, on a lake with a drunken sailor."[32] Speech like this serves no value except to marginalize individuals on the basis of their immutable characteristics, a problem all the greater given the power differential between faculty members and their students.

Speech rules need not reach public demonstrations or rallies, for a student's education is hardly threatened when he can walk away, but they should cover classroom speech where the audience is in some sense captive. True, this practice may seem to threaten academic freedom, but no right is absolute, and academic freedom itself presumes that expression will be educationally appropriate. Moreover, the encroachment here is minimal, since the number of applicable cases is likely to be small.[33] In fact, the better objection to hate speech regulation is its limited reach, for a speech rule of these proportions is likely to be more symbolic than operative. Nonetheless, as the findings of this book suggest, it would be a mistake to confuse symbolism with impotence. Symbols reflect society's values and concerns and offer support (even if primarily moral) to those individuals a community aims to protect. Indeed, the hate speech codes prove this very point. Created primarily as symbolic measures, they have had larger and lasting societal influence.

The prior discussion notwithstanding, this is not a book about the merits of hate speech regulation. Nor is it a polemic, although it takes to task several others who have used the speech codes as their patsy to attack political correctness and identity politics. Like many others I believe in liberty and free speech, but there is a fair debate to be had on the limits of expression, especially when poisonous speech arguably threatens the equality rights of others. Hate speech challenges democratic nations, requiring societies to stake out the relationships between citizen and government and citizen and citizen, particularly when some groups in society have been historically more privileged than others. I respect those who would rule for unrestrained speech (including Nat Hentoff, Dinesh D'Souza, Nadine Strossen, and George Will, all of whom were interviewed for this book), just as I admire those who claim that free speech must bend to achieve equality (Mari Matsuda, Richard Delgado, and Charles Lawrence, with whom I am familiar). But up to now we have largely been treated to advocacy on hate speech rather than analysis.[34] The present inquiry is different, not only addressing the forces behind hate speech regulation but also unmasking the legal and political myths our society creates about legal development. Ultimately, the book explores the ways that laws and constitutions, that legality and constitutionalism, shape the meaning and effects of rights and law.

Background and Chronology

On May 13, 1991, ABC's *Nightline* joined other national media in reporting that 125 colleges and universities had adopted so-called hate speech codes.[1] Although the program failed to define speech codes, media reports suggest that the policies at issue sought to punish students (and in some cases faculty and staff) for uttering offensive comments about another's race or ethnicity. One of the most famous policies was adopted at the University of Michigan, which prohibited:

> Verbal or physical behavior . . . that stigmatizes or victimizes an individual on the basis of race, ethnicity, religion, sex, sexual orientation, creed, national origin, ancestry, age, marital status, handicap or Vietnam-era veteran status . . . and that creates an intimidating, hostile or demeaning environment for educational pursuits, employment or participation in University sponsored extra-curricular activities.[2]

WHAT IS HATE SPEECH?

It is interesting that Michigan's policy was dubbed a "hate speech code," for at no point did the policy mention the term "hate speech," nor does American law provide a ready definition. "Hate speech" is a creation of commentators and opponents of the speech policies, although the expression has become commonplace in everyday society. Its bounds are difficult to determine, for, like former Justice Potter Stewart's famous quotation about pornography ("I shall not today attempt further to define the material . . . [b]ut I know it when I see it"),[3] hate speech is fuzzy in the abstract but more apparent when confronted in person.[4] The term "hate" is also a misnomer of sorts. I may hate my neighbor, and I may tell him so, but vitriol alone does not make an argument "hate speech." Hate speech is generally reserved for verbal attacks that target people on the basis of their immutable characteristics, or any form of "speech attacks based on race, ethnicity, religion, and sexual orientation or preference."[5] It may be easiest to think of hate speech on a continuum. Certainly, the term includes racist, ethnic, religious, and sexist slurs, words like "spic," "kike," "cunt," or "towel head." It is difficult to imagine situations in which these terms are not meant as verbal attacks. Hate speech is closely connected to the Supreme Court's category of fighting words—those expressions that by their very nature are likely to bring people to blows[6]—but the two are not completely analogous. Where a nasty insult, say like "motherfucker," might well precipitate a brawl, the jeer would not rise to the level of hate speech, which implies some sort of attack against an individual's immutable characteristics. Termed "race hate" in the 1920s and 1930s and "group libel" in the 1940s, "hate speech" or "racist speech" became the common terms in the 1980s as other characteristics, including sexual orientation, were included within its bounds.[7]

That hate speech usually involves immutable characteristics is but part of the definition, for the term also connotes an attack against minority status. Although an African American might contemptuously call a white person a "dumb honky," there is debate about whether the epithet counts as hate speech. Certainly, the attack marks the target's race, but there can be little doubt that whites remain a majority in this country, whether by absolute numbers or by measures of political or social power. Absent some other threat, no reasonable recipient of the slur would believe himself in danger of marginalization or worse. Richard Delgado and Jean Stefancic, two of the most notable proponents of hate speech regulation, have gone so far as to claim that "hate speech directed against blacks and other minority groups has no ready analog in speech against whites."[8]

Context matters in hate speech, not only the relative power differential between perpetrator and target but also the speaker's intent. Consider the terms "nigger" or "faggot." For years these have been among the worst slurs that whites could utter against blacks or heterosexuals could fling at gays and lesbians. But over the last fifteen years some minorities have begun to reappropriate the terms, stripping the words of their ugly and debilitating connotations. One now hears rap albums in which African Americans gamely call each other "nigger." The rap group N.W.A., a.k.a. Niggers With Attitude, is one of the most notable examples of African Americans redefining the "N word" as a badge of honor. In its 1991 single, "Niggaz 4 Life," N.W.A. sang:

> Why Do I Call Myself a Nigger, You Ask Me?
> I Guess It's the Way Shit Has to Be
> Back When I Was Young Gettin A Job Was Murder
> Fuck Flippin Burgers
> 'Cause I Deserve A Nine-to-Five I Can Be Proud Of
> That I Can Speak Loud Of[9]

So too some gays have begun to use "faggot" when talking about one another. Dan Savage, a sex columnist for many urban, alternative newspapers, explained his use of the slur when he sat for a 1995 interview. Said Savage, who is gay:

> When [my] column started in 1990 or 1991—when we first started talking about [faggot]—that was during ACT UP and Queer Nation's Ascendancy. And that's when the whole reclamation movement started taking back hate words. . . . Faggot is what my gay friends call each other: That's how we talk to each other. And inviting . . . people to use that term when they address me sort of strips the word of its hate, or demonstrates a way it can be stripped of its hate.[10]

Savage is more accepting of "reclaimed" slurs than are others, for whites and heterosexuals often court trouble if they try to use the same terms in conversation with blacks or homosexuals. There the power differential between social groups—the fact that whites and straights are in the majority and blacks and gays are not—embeds the speaker's words with a different and disturbing message. Explains Savage, "some gay people get *very* upset when they see . . . straight people using [faggot]. It's okay for us to use it amongst ourselves, but it's not okay for me to give permission for straight people to call me that word."[11] Even well-meaning people have found this out the hard way. At Central Michigan University a white basketball coach uttered the word "nigger" when conducting a pep talk for his team, the majority of whom were black. According to the coach, he used the term like his players did, in a "positive and reinforcing" way "to connote someone who is 'fearless, mentally strong, and tough.'" Although the players generally failed to take offense, news of the incident soon spread through the campus community. A student demonstration was staged, unfavorable news stories were written about the university, and the coach soon found himself out of a job.[12]

There are some who find this "double-standard" unfair,[13] that minority groups can use certain terms among themselves without criticism but that if "outsiders" seek to apply the same words for similar purposes they are assailed.[14] However, the key elements at work here are the historic power differences between social groups and the fact that certain words are associated with the exclusion of minority groups by others. The dynamic is more prevalent than some might initially realize. Jews freely tell Jewish jokes about themselves, but if a Christian is caught doing the same the prat falls flat. The Irish can spin yarns about the drinking capers of their countrymen, but a Brit who attempts to tell the same joke faces disapproving glares, at best. Years ago the television show Seinfeld satirized this dynamic when its character Jerry, a Jewish comedian, took umbrage at his dentist who converted to Judaism and immediately began telling Jewish jokes. Visiting a priest to complain about the dentist's sham conversion, Jerry told the priest that he believed the dentist converted "just for the jokes." "And this offends you as Jewish person?" the priest asked Jerry. "No," said Jerry, "as a comedian."[15]

Of course, there is nothing funny about hate speech, although it can be difficult at times to disentangle slurs from seriously intended conversation. Just as context matters, so does the standard for measuring offense. Should hate speech be judged by the intent of the speaker or the feelings of the recipient? In the case of *Doe v. University of Michigan,* the plaintiff feared that he might be punished under a hate speech code for suggesting that women are biologically programmed to be caregivers. To some, this view would smack of sexism, the speaker insinuating that women should remain at home tending to babies and baking cookies. Yet the speaker might claim a legitimate interest in examining the biological basis of gender definition, a point of academic debate worthy of consideration. Whose view should win here? What about the case where a speaker questions the determinants of sexual orientation, claiming that homosexuality is an "ungodly lifestyle" because "people choose to be gay."[16] This message would undoubtedly be an affront to the many gays and lesbians who only recently have felt free to "come out" without serious social stigma. But should the speaker be punished for raising an idea, even one that is offensive to its target?

These are central questions in the hate speech debate, ones that do not have easy answers. Among those who have written on hate speech, the prevailing view is that hate speech turns on the intent of the speaker.[17] Where an individual seeks a legitimate debate, even on controversial questions, his message should not count as hate speech. But when the purpose is to offend, to silence, to marginalize, then speech becomes hateful. Admittedly, these lines are malleable, but the principle is worth considering. When someone criticizes what she sees as a double standard in the use of the word "nigger," her purpose presumably is to question the differential use of a historical epithet, not to denigrate a minority group.[18] Even if the audience thinks her insensitive or unreasonably provocative, her message is not itself intended as an attack. By contrast, the person who decries "the niggers on campus," arguing they should "go back to Africa,"[19] is clearly attacking African Americans on the basis of their race. Whether, in fact, this speaker should be permitted to make his remarks unchecked is another question—and one that forms the heart of the hate speech debate in America—but it is impossible to ignore his prejudice and the despicable meaning of his words. His speech is hateful and directed against a group because of its race.

The more difficult cases are those in which a speaker makes indirect, presumptive, and prejudicial comments about a group. In the summer of 2002 the famous Hollywood agent-turned-studio-head Michael Ovitz gave an interview in which he attributed his fall from grace to the "gay mafia" in Hollywood.[20] Did Ovitz intend to impugn a group on the basis of its immutable characteristics? Perhaps, if as most experts now recognize, homosexuality is biologically determined. Ovitz clearly saw a conspiracy among gay studio executives to sink his career, but was this an attack on their sexual orientation or Ovitz's uncovering of a cabal that was linked by sexual orientation? Another way to ask this question is how would we react if the criticism had been of "Jewish bankers" who controlled Hollywood? Most studio veterans acknowledge that Hollywood employs a larger percentage of Jews and gays than does American industry as a whole, but what is the point of highlighting a target's religious or sexual identity in criticizing certain individuals? Imbedded in the message is a reflection of prejudice, an attempt to denigrate a person's actions because of his membership in a historically marginalized group. Should it matter that Ovitz's comments were quoted in a magazine, not spoken directly to his enemies? Even the proponents of hate speech regulation differ. Some see a threat whenever prejudice is expounded; others would limit sanctions to personally delivered vitriol. Richard Delgado has himself changed his approach over time. Where Delgado once attacked general messages of racial inferiority,[21] his more recent proposals call for tort penalties when a speaker directly addresses his target.[22]

Were we in Canada or Europe, Ovitz's comment might implicate the criminal law, since the United States is virtually alone among Western democracies in refusing to sanction hate speech per se under the law. Both the International Convention on the Elimination of All Forms of Racial Discrimination and the International Covenant on Civil and Political Rights[23] prohibit the advocacy of hatred and link it to discrimination. German law punishes expression that incites racial hatred,[24] and the Canadian Supreme Court has upheld prohibitions on hate speech directed against groups who have faced "historical and social prejudice."[25] To be sure, Ovitz was hardly attempting to incite a mob; rather, he sought to explain away his own poor performance. But the irony of America's attention to hate speech is that there is no comparable legal standard against which to measure the misdeed. By and large, we address the subject through academic writings and social commentary, for there are neither criminal nor civil statutes that define the terms of hate speech. Certain states now punish hate crimes, but for most of America's history both law and society tolerated conduct that is only now being labeled by observers as hate speech.

HATE SPEECH AND THE COURTS

In truth, hate speech has been with us for years, almost from the moment that the first "others" got off the boat to a chilly reception. For centuries African Americans have endured vindictive slurs—and much worse—from white Americans, and Jews too have suffered through several periods in which anti-Semitism was not only accepted but also fashionable.[26] Anti-Catholic prejudice followed the arrival of Catholic immigrants in the mid-1800s, and a general anti-immigrant fervor took over the nation in the late nineteenth and early twentieth centuries. Few, however, would ever have thought to label such treatment as "hate speech" at the time. Prejudice was openly spoken, especially among so-called polite society, and the courts were rarely asked to intervene because the lines had already been drawn in civil society.

For that matter, free speech and open discourse are privileged rights under the First Amendment. According to the courts the First Amendment applies to "expression," a term that is generally considered to mean speech. Certainly, some actions can be expressive, including the burning of the flag, a draft card, or the donning of offensive apparel,[27] but for the most part the courts have distinguished between speech, which is expressive and thus constitutionally protected,[28] and actions, which are neither.

Historically, there have been only five bases under which the courts are willing to restrict speech: obscenity; libel; time, place, and manner regulations; the clear and present danger test; and fighting words. Obscenity law probably traces back to our Puritan past, reflecting the notion that some expression is so carnal and salacious that it may be regulated.[29] Libel is a branch of defamation law, allowing individuals to sue those who knowingly malign their reputations. Time, place, and manner restrictions are just as they sound, permitting public bodies to place reasonable limits on the way in which expression is delivered, rather than its content. A protestor may not blare his message outside your bedroom window at two in the morning, although he is free to express his views at a more reasonable time and place. Similarly, under the clear and present danger test, courts have been willing to punish expression that imminently incites others to criminal or dangerous activity.[30] The classic example is yelling "fire" in a crowded theater, where the speaker's interest in expression is overwhelmed by the threat of people being trampled on the way out. Courts interpret this test very narrowly, with only the most egregious speech qualifying as dangerous. Finally, fighting words statutes are said to protect the public peace. First recognized by the Supreme Court in the 1942 case of *Chaplinsky v. New Hampshire,* the term was initially defined as words that "by their very utterance inflict injury" and "tend to incite an immediate breach of the peace." However, over time this definition has been winnowed so that by the mid-1960s it included only the latter half—speech that incites an immediate breach of the peace.[31]

At one point in the 1950s the Supreme Court toyed with a constitutional claim against group libel. In *Beauharnais v. Illinois* the Court considered the case of an Illinois segregationist who had been convicted under a statute that made it unlawful for anyone to "publish, present or exhibit in a public place . . . [anything that] portrays depravity, criminality, unchastity, or lack of virtue in a class of citizens of any race, color or creed [when such presentation would expose] the citizen of any race, color, creed, or religion to contempt, derision, or obloquy."[32] In this case the Court upheld the appellant's conviction and with it statutes like Illinois' law that punished offensive expression against particular groups. The decision is significant for its expansion of the harms that justified speech restrictions. Until *Beauharnais* the courts had only looked at the immediate effects of a message's impact—its ability to initiate a fight or create dangerous conditions—but in this case the Supreme Court seemed willing to ban expression that denigrated minorities or advanced racism. Where Justice Brandeis had previously intimated that the answer to unpleasant speech was to oppose it with more speech, the courts seemed to be saying that the response to racist or hateful speech was to quash it.

The *Beauharnais* era, however, lasted less than a decade. By 1961 Illinois had repealed its group libel law, and the Supreme Court in its civil rights decisions of the Warren and Burger eras essentially overturned *Beauharnais,* limiting the case essentially to those utterances that create violence and disorder. In a sweeping blow to those who would punish group libel, the U.S. Court of Appeals for the Seventh Circuit permitted the American Nazi Party to demonstrate in Skokie, Illinois in the late 1970s. Skokie is a suburb of Chicago, and at the time it had a large Jewish population, many of whom were Holocaust survivors. If there ever were a case in which a group libel law should apply, this was it. Not only were the Nazis prepared to "exhibit contempt to citizens of a religion or creed," but they were also likely to use fighting words in their march. Indeed, it seemed quite clear that the Nazis intended to inflict psychic injury on the residents of Skokie. Had group libel still been good law, or if the *Chaplinsky* test still encompassed hurtful words, the Seventh Circuit presumably would have enjoined the Nazis' rally. But the court let the march proceed and in *Collins v. Smith* ruled that the Village of Skokie could only restrain the Nazis if the marchers themselves were intent on violence and disorder. Speech, even the most hateful speech, said the court, could not in itself justify restraint.[33]

COLLEGE HATE SPEECH CODES

If the first wave of American hate speech regulation had flamed out by the 1960s and 1970s, a second wave was poised to begin. Following on Title VII of the Civil Rights Acts and the concomitant drive by feminists to eradicate sexist and hostile work environments, the second, or modern-day hate speech movement is closely tied to the development of so-called college hate speech codes. Crafted in the late 1980s and early 1990s, hate speech policies were said to have swept American academe like a wildfire.

When asked to conjure up a vision of collegiate hate speech, many observers of the time would likely cite controversial incidents at Brown University or the University of Pennsylvania that drew national attention. The Brown example happened first, when, in 1990, junior Douglas Hann engaged in a hate-filled diatribe while stumbling home following his twenty-first birthday celebration. In what would become perhaps the most consequential five minutes of his young life, Hann got into a verbal exchange with Brown freshmen, managing to disparage "niggers," "faggot[s]" and "fucking Jew[s]" all in one fell swoop.[34] Hann's identity was later discovered with the help of enterprising campus and national journalists, and his classmates soon filed a complaint against him with the student disciplinary council. Eventually, Hann was convicted of harassment, and in a first for the school, was expelled. Initially Brown managed to keep the Hann case quiet, but as soon as the *New York Times* got hold of the story, the matter flared like a bonfire. National headlines portrayed the case as "Student . . . Expelled under a Rule Barring 'Hate Speech,'"[35] although Brown's then-President, Vartan Gregorian, claimed that the decision reflected Brown's hard line against "abusive, threatening, or demeaning actions."[36]

Three years later, Penn freshman Eden Jacobowitz was studying when members of an African American sorority began celebrating their founders' day outside his dormitory. At first Jacobowitz asked the students to keep quiet so he could concentrate on his studies, but on being ignored the freshman eventually shouted at the women, "Shut up, you water buffalo! If you want a party, there's a zoo a mile from here." Jacobowitz was not the only student to yell at the sorority members, nor did he expressly swear at the women as some others had. He was, however, the only student to fess up to his comment. As a graduate of a yeshiva, or religious Jewish school, Jacobowitz had used the English translation of the Hebrew word behema, which roughly means rowdy person, or even water buffalo. But water buffalo also denotes an African or Asian animal, and in urging that a group of black women belong in a zoo, Jacobowitz had ventured near the line of a racist insult.

Jacobowitz was brought up on charges at the University of Pennsylvania, accused of violating the university's policy against insulting or demeaning a person on the basis of race. Although Penn's policy required an affirmative intention by the speaker to "direct injury," the university's Judicial Inquiry Officer recommended that Jacobowitz either "plead" to an offense and rehabilitate himself or face a judicial hearing with the prospects of suspension or expulsion. Jacobowitz would have none of it, and in selecting leading conservative historian Alan Kors as his judicial advisor, a mere college freshmen set in motion a public-relations nightmare for Penn. Jacobowitz's team of defenders regularly funneled embarrassing details about the university's disciplinary procedure to the press, finally reaching the point where officials were willing to settle. Four months after Jacobowitz first uttered the term water buffalo, Penn dropped all charges and Jacobowitz apologized for his choice of words. Two years later the university abolished its hate speech policy.

Brown and Penn became the poster examples of college hate speech codes, but they were hardly the only universities to adopt and enforce such policies. According to reports in the popular media, between 137 and 140 schools adopted hate speech codes from 1987 to 1992, applying either to students or to the campus community as a whole.[37] A number of schools modeled their policies after Michigan's code, one of the most contentious and widely publicized in the country. Kansas State, for example, proscribed "verbal, physical or written behavior directed toward or relating to an individual or group on the basis of race, ethnicity or racial affiliation and [that] has the purpose or effect of . . . creating an intimidating, hostile, or offensive work or educational environment."[38]

Other schools, like Stanford, narrowed their focus to "fighting words,"[39] prohibiting expressions "intended to insult or stigmatize an individual or a small number of individuals on the basis of their sex, race, color, handicap, religion, sexual orientation, or national and ethnic origin." There was a wide variety in approaches. Emory University, while borrowing from Michigan's code, addressed its policy to discriminatory "oral conduct" that creates "an offensive, demeaning, intimidating or hostile environment . . . [for] any person or group."[40]

The distinction between policies like Michigan's and those closer to Emory's is important, for on their face they appear directed to different expression. By incorporating minority status into its rule, Michigan's policy appeared to offer special protection to disempowered groups.[41] Admittedly, the policy did not single out a particular race, gender, or ethnicity as deserving special protection over others, but by incorporating these terms in the first place the rule seemed concerned about harassment of minorities.[42] This is particularly noticeable when one considers that policies like Emory's cover any offensive or demeaning expression and not simply that based on race, ethnicity, or the like.

TITLE VII AND SEXUAL HARASSMENT

On their face the speech codes appeared to rewrite free speech norms to grant racial minorities special protections, but one of the ironies of the collegiate hate speech codes, not to mention the controversy they generated, is that they were intellectual cousins of sexual harassment policies that had been on the books for several years. Both prohibitions were or seem to be premised on Title VII of the Civil Rights Acts, which prevents employers from "discriminat[ing] against any individual with respect to his . . . conditions or privileges of employment because of such individual's race, color, religion, sex or national origin."[43] Originally, this language was used to bring suits challenging wages and promotions, but over time courts have recognized that harassment can become "so severe and pervasive that it affects the conditions of employment" and thus violates Title VII's prohibition of workplace discrimination.[44]

Sexual harassment has two bases, quid-pro-quo harassment and the creation of a hostile, intimidating, or offensive workplace. The former generally covers sexual advances or requests for sexual favors when presented as a condition of employment, but it is hostile workplace harassment (also called hostile work environment or HWE) that is most relevant to the speech policies. That tort has five elements:

- Verbal or physical conduct of a sexual or sex-based nature.
- That is unwelcome.
- That is directed against an individual because of her (or his) sex.
- That has the purpose or effect of unreasonably interfering with an indi-

vidual's work performance or creating an intimidating, hostile or offensive working environment.

- That an employer knew or should have known of and did not take adequate action to stop or prevent.[45]

When compared to the terms of HWE, many of the campus speech codes look remarkably similar. Just as sexual harassment law singles out an immutable characteristic—sex—as the basis for protection, several speech codes offered protection on the basis of race, ethnicity, and the like. Both rules also cover unwelcome verbal or physical conduct. Although the hate speech codes did not define "unwelcome" explicitly, their requirement that conduct demean or stigmatize another presumed that an attack would be unwelcome. Finally, the hate speech codes used the same standard as HWE for triggering liability. Although occurring in an educational setting and not at the workplace, the requirement that conduct create an intimidating, hostile, or demeaning environment for educational pursuits is taken entirely from the law of sexual harassment.

When first acknowledging the legitimacy of an HWE action, the courts were silent about the claim's application to expression. In the 1986 case of *Meritor Savings Bank v. Vinson,* for example, the United States Supreme Court ruled that the defendant's actions alone were sufficient to find liability under HWE apart from the invectives he spewed at the plaintiff. Since that time the Court has had two other opportunities to rule on the sufficiency of expression to trigger Title VII. In *R. A. V. v. City of St. Paul,* the Court sidestepped this precise question, essentially creating an exemption under the First Amendment for sexual harassment claims based on expression. Similarly, in *Harris v. Forklift Systems* the Court failed "to mention the First Amendment objections to Title VII's harassment law" even though that case was based largely on misogynist speech. The Court's silence has left the law courts to finagle the issue; without contrary precedent from the Supreme Court, "most courts adjudicating harassment suits either avoid the issue [of verbal harassment] or assume that the speech allegedly contributing to a hostile environment is unprotected."[46]

But if speech restrictions are permitted in the workplace under Title VII, the courts have been much less sympathetic to measures that extend to the classroom or other parts of campus. As one judge has said, "Title VII addresses employment settings, not educational settings" and is thus inapplicable in the classroom.[47] So too the Supreme Court has ruled that a college campus, "at least for its students, possesses many of the characteristics of a public forum."[48] But perhaps the biggest legal obstacle to collegiate speech codes has been the courts' belief that academic speech deserves constitutional deference.[49] As one scholar suggests, the "academy is so central [to the system of freedom of expression] that it claims its own branch of First Amendment doctrine: academic freedom."[50] This perspective is often shared by the courts, where judges have overturned rules that allegedly restrict "the diversity of ideas among students and thereby prevent[] the 'robust exchange of ideas' which intellectually diverse campuses provide."[51]

Given such precedent, the college hate speech codes were seen by many as a bold attempt to reformulate First Amendment norms. Several policies, including those from Michigan and Wisconsin, seemed to fly directly in the face of *Collins* and other free speech rulings of the 1960s and 1970s. In fact, the codes almost read like the group libel law from *Beauharnais,* with students subject to punishment if their conduct stigmatized or demeaned another on the basis of race, ethnicity, or the like. Other policies like Stanford's appeared to take a more moderate approach by limiting their reach to fighting words. But even here, some rules exceeded common understandings of the term by defining fighting words to reach not only expressions that "incite a breach of the peace" but also those that "by their very utterance inflict injury." These definitions had not been seen in constitutional law since the 1950s. In fact, taken as a whole, one might have concluded that the speech code "movement" was attempting to return First Amendment law to its prior status.

The rise of campus speech codes would have tied a First Amendment absolutist in knots. If one accepted the Supreme Court's view that expression should be as open as possible, then the speech policies were a serious threat. And the threat came from a variety of schools, both public and private. This alone may be surprising, since as a matter of law only public institutions are bound by the First Amendment.[52] Private schools were free to experiment with whatever speech restrictions they wished—even those that challenged then-accepted notions of First Amendment law. But public schools too seemed willing to defy the constitutional line. In fact, some of the first (and most famous) speech policies were developed at the Universities of Michigan and Wisconsin, with similar rules adopted at many more public schools.

RACIAL INCIDENTS

At the time they were initiated, the speech codes were linked to a number of social and political phenomena. Whether any of these were truly causal we'll leave to chapter 3, but to understand the hate speech controversy it is important to appreciate the influences that were associated with the codes' rise in popular debate. Foremost among these was a perceived "epidemic" of racial harassment and violence on the nation's campuses. Indeed, many of the popular explanations of the hate speech codes see them as a reaction to racial tensions on campus.[53] Michigan's policy, for example, was preceded by a period of racial turmoil in which a campus DJ told racist jokes on-air, racist graffiti appeared across buildings, and minority students took over an administration building to protest the racial climate on campus. But Michigan's controversy was preceded over a year earlier by what arguably became the bellwether incident across the nation. Following the sixth game of the 1986 World Series, a racial brawl took place at the University of Massachusetts–Amherst between white students who supported the Boston Red Sox and black students who were fans of the New York Mets. What might have been an isolated campus incident took on a life of its own, becoming symptomatic for a souring racial climate among college students.

About six months before the U Mass incident, the national media had begun to discover racial tensions among college students as reporters covered campus rallies against apartheid and the reaction of many white students to the protest. The U Mass story thus provided the hook to "uncover" what appeared to be a rising trend. In the year preceding the racial brawl, national newspapers and magazines ran eight stories about growing racial unrest at colleges.[54] This number more than tripled in the two months following the U Mass incident, with racial violence breaking out at the Citadel and the University of Alabama, to be followed by incidents at the University of Connecticut, Stanford, University of Wisconsin, Northern Illinois University, and other schools. Coverage snowballed for the next three years, with publications like *Time* reporting on "Bigots in the Ivory Tower," the *Washington Post* covering "Civil Rights and Wrongs" on campus, and the *New York Times* reporting that "Campus Racial Tensions—and Violence—Appear on Rise."[55] In fact, the trend continued until 1989 or 1990 when the focus seemed to change to the several schools that responded with speech codes. From 1987 to 1991 media coverage of racial incidents dropped by over 80 percent.[56]

It is unclear whether the spate of stories reflected a new epidemic of racial violence on campus or just a tendency by reporters to join a bandwagon of coverage. But if it is the latter it would not be a new dynamic. As a commentator explained, "Every so often Americans stumble upon some unpleasant fact of life and call it a new phenomenon in need of prompt treatment. There was the new poverty in the early 1960s, the new interventionism in Indochina, the new drug abuse last summer, and now the new racism."[57]

Journalists seized onto the incidents as indicative of larger trends in American social and political life. Some were taken by the inherent contradiction of racist incidents occurring at what had traditionally been considered "liberal bastions." Explained a Minnesota human rights commissioner, "It's disturbing because [the incidents are] occurring on campuses. . . . One would hope that you'd have a more enlightened environment."[58]

Others seemed intent on blaming "the Ronald Reagan years" for racist violence, which they claimed "were marked by less emphasis on affirmative action and traditional civil rights goals."[59] Said a writer for *The Nation:*

> When Reagan was elected in 1980, this year's freshman class was 10 years old. Their political consciousness was formed while the White House used potent code words and attacked social programs to legitimize a subtle racism. [And don't forget George Bush's campaign which portrayed blacks as] criminals, drug addicts and welfare cheats. . . . Undergraduate viewers may have been even more vulnerable to the Horton propaganda than was the rest of the TV audience, because most of them lacked the experience and knowledge required to challenge racist imagery, especially after eight years of Ronald Reagan.[60]

Of course, reporters and editors may have been taking their cues from advocates in the civil rights community—those who had an interest in attracting the public's attention to racial incidents—but the question still stands: Did these collegiate incidents reflect a new and alarming dynamic, or did they just generate significant press coverage? In 1989 the American Council on Education conducted a survey of administrators to assess the state of race and ethnic relations at American's colleges. According to the study, 83 percent of officials at baccalaureate institutions reported little or no racial or ethnic tension on campus. The same was true for 68 percent of administrators at comprehensive universities and 59 percent of officials at doctoral and research universities.[61] Nevertheless, 27 percent of administrators, representing over 370 four-year institutions, reported racial or ethnic tensions on their campuses. As sizeable as these numbers may seem, there are no comparative data available to deduce whether these conditions were better or worse than in the past.

Throughout the 1980s and early 1990s the National Institute Against Prejudice and Violence compiled reports of racial violence on campus and conducted studies about ethnoviolence.[62] Howard Ehrlich was the research director of the Institute, and he regularly fielded calls from reporters covering the racial incidents. Ehrlich argues that the 1980s did *not* see an appreciable rise in the number of racial incidents nationally, a conclusion he says he could rarely convince reporters to accept.[63] Racial violence had occurred on college campuses for decades. "Talk to any black student who attended college in the 1950s," he explains. "They will tell you that they faced harassment from the beginning. . . . The incidents haven't changed much since then. The difference is that they suddenly got more attention." Ehrlich cites three factors for the heightened coverage: First, a number of national newspapers, including the *New York Times, Washington Post,* and *Boston Globe,* had student stringers at many of the schools that experienced racial violence, so when a fight broke out it was likely to be covered. Second, minority students and faculty had gained considerable political and social power since the 1950s, to the point that they were unwilling to endure insults, harassment, and violence. When incidents occurred, minority students and faculty responded with protests, which themselves begat news coverage. Third, many journalists believed that the conservative policies of the Reagan and Bush administrations were rubbing off on college students, and they latched onto reports of racial incidents as proof of this perspective. At the same time, Ehrlich says, a smaller group of reporters, including one notable representative from the *New York Times,* thought this storyline was bunk and criticized the work of the Institute, which it fingered as the source for the deluge of stories.[64]

Other observers claimed that racial incidents were really on the rise, or that they had at least changed in severity. Reginald Wilson, director of Minority Concerns for the American Council on Education, said, "I cannot remember a year prior to 1986 when as many incidents were reported."[65] Michael Olivas, a law professor at the University of Houston who chronicled reports of racial violence, agreed. According to Olivas, "Not only [was] there more careful reporting about incidents of racial harassment, but it is quite clear from the data that there are more incidents as well."[66]

It is unclear from what sources Olivas made his claim, for at the time neither colleges nor law enforcement bodies had uniform standards for the reporting of racial harassment or violence. Some advocacy organizations had compiled data prior to Olivas's work, including the Anti-Defamation League, the Southern Christian Leadership Conference, and even a few national, black fraternities. Yet, none of these groups used common standards in reporting. By the early 1990s Congress had ordered the collection of hate crime data, requiring colleges and universities to compile reports on campus crime. However, the definition of hate crime would have screened out all but the most serious incidents of violence. While U Mass would probably have been required to report the racial brawl, the incidents at Michigan, Wisconsin, Stanford, and many other schools could have gone unreported.

What, then, should we make of the presumed "epidemic of hate" that was said to be sweeping America's campuses? The best answer seems to come from Sherwood Thompson, a veteran minority affairs officer who served at the University of Kansas and the University of Massachusetts–Amherst. Thompson claims that the civil rights movement had succeeded in quieting racial incidents on campus. "We still experienced racial harassment, but they were more minor matters, not the violence and attacks we had seen before," he says. The racism of the late 1980s was more subtle: white students who would not sit near minorities in class, the epithets uttered under one's breath, the assumption that minorities were admitted because of affirmative action. So, he says, when racial brawls broke out at U Mass–Amherst, or when black cadets were attacked at the Citadel, the reaction was stronger. "It was kind of like a wake-up call. 'Hey,' we thought those days were over," Thompson says. Whether these blatant incidents represented an epidemic is unclear, but more to the point it is almost irrelevant if they did. With the national media and opinion leaders convinced that the pendulum had swung back on racial progress, campus incidents would have a substantial bearing on the development of college hate speech codes.

NATIONAL CIVIL RIGHTS POLICY

Whether press reports were correct in linking campus racism to policies of the Reagan and Bush administrations, national civil rights policy saw several changes under both presidents. Ronald Reagan vetoed the Civil Rights Restoration bill, replaced commissioners of the U.S. Commission on Civil Rights "with people more in line with his conservative philosophy," and used the bully pulpit of the presidency to denounce racial quotas in hiring.[67]

Reagan's policies antagonized the civil rights community, putting many on edge at the prospect of backsliding. Said John Jacob, president of the National Urban League, "It is hard to avoid the conclusion that the continuation of illegal discrimination and the resurgence of racist feelings are fostered by the [Reagan] administration's refusal to admit that racism may still be a problem." Jacob cited the Department of Justice's "war on affirmative action" as well as the administration's inactivity in the face of rising black poverty.[68]

The Reagan administration's influence extended also to the federal judiciary where Reagan, and to a lesser extent President Bush, "focussed on the courts and the judicial system to institutionalize further [their] New Rightist and neo-conservative policies." In the case of Reagan, he "appointed more than half of the 743 federal judges then seated, more appointments than any [ ] predecessor" since FDR.[69] The judges were chosen only after "close ideological inspection," a fact that Edwin Meese, Reagan's former Attorney General and Counsellor, confirms in his memoirs. Says Meese, "since the problems we confronted [from the "modern liberal mind set"] had come about because of judges, then something had to be done about the judges. . . . Accordingly, the selection of judicial personnel and reform of the judiciary became and remained important priorities of the administration."[70] Their faith in the judiciary was well placed, for the newly appointed Supreme Court justices were instrumental in the Court's treatment of affirmative action and other civil rights issues. In 1989 the Supreme Court increased the plaintiff's burden of proof in civil rights cases, and the same year it declared minority set-aside programs to be constitutionally questionable.[71]

Many of these policy changes alarmed the civil rights community, but the 1988 presidential race only added fuel to a burning fire. By now the "Willie Horton ad" has become political lore, a television advertisement aired by an independent political committee but informally adopted by the campaign of George Bush. In the ad Bush's opponent, former Massachusetts governor Michael Dukakis, was criticized for a prison furlough program adopted by his predecessor. As the ad made starkly clear, a black felon, the convicted murderer Willie Horton, had terrorized a white couple while out on his "weekend pass." Bush's supporters never came out and said it, but more than a few commentators interpreted the likely subtext of the ad's strategy: scare white voters into voting for Bush. Jesse Jackson attacked the ad, as did a number of national black leaders, with the uproar only confirming the fears of many minorities that Bush was leading a backlash against the policies that benefited minorities. It hardly helped that Bush's campaign tactics took place at the same time that David Duke arrived on the national scene. A former leader of the Ku Klux Klan, Duke secured a seat in the Louisiana legislature before attempting to win office nationally. Although Duke claimed to have repudiated his past, many of his speeches, not to mention his issue positions, seemed to draw on white resentment. The fact that Duke attracted a national following had many within the civil rights community distressed. As a news report explained, "Civil and human rights workers say national events have created a more tolerant atmosphere for racial discrimination. They point to increasingly conservative stands taken by the U.S. Justice Department, and the Supreme Court, and the recent election of a former Ku Klux Klan leader [in] Louisiana as signs."[72]

THE HAVEN OF THE IVORY TOWER

If national political developments worried civil rights activists, they still had academe, an arena presumably open to their interests. Historically, college campuses have been portrayed as liberal bastions, and although a bit legendary, there is some truth to this presumption. As the work of Everett Ladd and Martin Lipset has shown, "American academics have been more liberal than other strata. . . . [T]here can be little doubt that a majority of those associated with universities and other intellectually linked occupations have been liberals or progressives."[73] Thus, if national events were turning against their interests, liberals might have turned their energies to campus events and politics, where the ideological climate was more welcoming.

If progressives retreated to college campuses they would have found an increasingly diverse environment, as schools were working to add women and minorities to positions of leadership. By a 27 to 1 ratio, four-year institutions had increased their hiring of women faculty in the first half of the 1980s, with four times more schools than not expanding their recruitment of minorities.[74] This increase was also felt within administrative ranks and student services staff, where the number of women college presidents rose in the decade ending in 1984. By 1989, 80 percent of institutions reported some activity to increase the number of women and minority faculty, with 50 percent recruiting more women and minority administrators.[75] These efforts coincided with the expansion of university bureaucracies, as more staff were enlisted to handle extracurricular and administrative activities. Assistant academic deans were added, new positions were created in student activities, and women and racial minorities had more opportunities to help lead their institutions.

Many of the new faculty and staff had attended college in the 1960s and had grown up alongside the rights movements. Influenced by the experiences of their "formative school years," this "age cohort" was largely supportive of the civil rights and women's rights movements.[76] This does not mean, as some have suggested, that new faculty and staff were necessarily liberal activists,[77] but rather that they may have been a receptive audience for measures premised on diversity and equal opportunity. If activists were to address intolerance and protect civil rights, college campuses seemed like a natural laboratory.

THE NEW CAMPUS CONSERVATISM

According to some conservative commentators, academicians returned their attention to campus life because they had lost their "political self-confidence" and with it the drive to continue fighting for national civil rights policies.[78] Dinesh D'Souza, in particular, claims that "Ronald Reagan frustrated the Left, and his 1984 election ushered in the sense that the academic left could not compete in national politics."[79] Adds George Will, academicians "became disillusioned because they had lost their permanent hold over D.C. Going back to John Kennedy, the academic intelligentsia had thought they would be incorporated into government, that they had a role to play in developing policy."[80] Having thus lost its influence under Reagan and Bush, both D'Souza and Will hypothesize that the "New Left" retreated to college campuses, using campus politics and academic proposals to advance its political interests.

Even if D'Souza and Will are right, liberal activists would have encountered some of the same national issues on campus. Student attitudes had begun to turn against some civil rights policies, with only a quarter of incoming freshmen identifying themselves as political liberals.[81] There were also new tensions on campus, as white resentment began to build against affirmative action and minority programs at several schools. On some campuses divestment protestors were attacked and their shanties burned or destroyed.[82] Only about half of these incidents were solved, but where perpetrators were identified they included conservative students who objected to the "liberal antics" of their classmates.

On a number of campuses, alternative conservative student newspapers sprang up, funded largely by the Madison Center for Educational Affairs, and dedicated to countering the "liberal agenda" on many colleges campuses.[83] The newspapers were accompanied by such groups as Accuracy in Academia, a self-described conservative watch-dog, and Students for America, a national conservative student group founded in 1984 by activist Ralph Reed and committed to recruiting 10,000 college students.[84] A few schools experienced an even stronger backlash. Students at Temple University, the University of Florida, the University of Southwest Louisiana, and the University of New Orleans established white student unions, with students at the Universities of Minnesota and Nebraska attempting to do the same.[85] "Fed up with what they perceive[d] as favored treatment of blacks," the students organized to fight "prejudice against whites [which they claimed was] much stronger than against blacks." High on their agenda was the elimination of affirmative action and minority scholarships, as well as phasing out new courses on African and Asian culture in order to return to traditional Eurocentric studies.[86]

The supporters of white student unions were hardly among the mainstream of conservative activists, but they were fortified by a growing crop of campus conservatives—including a national collection of faculty. "Outraged by what they [saw] as the 'radicalization' of courses, hiring policies and academic standards," nearly three hundred American faculty formed the National Association of Scholars (NAS) in 1988. Designed to provide a public opposition to liberal, academic "barbarians," NAS members complained that "political objectives, many of them flowing from the affirmative action programs for women and members of minority groups, had contaminated what [had previously been] objectivity on decisions about curriculum, promotion and academic discourse." A number of the NAS members were senior faculty, who they said, had "seen American universities transformed by the ascent of teachers and administrators whose political views were shaped as students in the 1960s."[87] Yet the NAS never really pushed a formal agenda on campus, serving more as a bully pulpit for conservative scholars and providing moral support to conservatives who challenged the "moral orthodoxy" of liberal faculty.

It is difficult to assess the strength of collegiate conservatism. It would be a stretch to say that conservatives dominated campus life, and of course, each school had a different experience. Still, collegiate conservatives were becoming more active and organized in the 1980s. In a sense, this question mirrors the earlier consideration of racial incidents. Indeed, they may well be linked. As a conservative backlash began to rise on campus, certain whites may have felt a greater license to criticize minorities, whom they claimed were admitted because of affirmative action. Granted, this is quite a jump in the argument, and one that unfairly lumps together sincere conservatives with the antagonists who would harass their classmates or colleagues. Certainly, no reasonable leader would advocate such action, but with conservative scholars and politicians questioning the merits of civil rights policies, disingenuous minds might have seen such advocacy as implicit backing for their activities.

A POTENTIAL STORM CLOUD

Whether the objections were scholarly or crude, criticism of affirmative action struck a sensitive chord on several campuses, for black enrollment was at risk during this period. Between 1986 and 1996 the college-age population declined 17 percent. This affected many colleges, where one in four had to resort to a faculty retrenchment program.[88] But the drop in student enrollment was not uniform, coming disproportionally from black students. Beginning in 1960, black college enrollment had grown five times to 1.1 million, but by 1982 the trend had begun to reverse itself. This was particularly troubling to colleges because during the same period other minorities, especially Asian Americans, were applying to college in record numbers. The American Association of State Colleges and Universities found that between 1975 and 1981 the "percentage of college-eligible blacks going to college dropped 11%" even while the number of blacks graduating from high schools increased by 29 percent. By the mid-1980s this trend had become critical, with periodicals like the *Washington Post* reporting on a "'crisis' of decline in black enrollment."[89] The drop was felt precipitously at some of the nation's most prestigious schools, with the University of Michigan seeing its black enrollment drop from a peak of 7.2 percent in 1976 to 4.9 percent in 1983.[90] Similarly, the University of Massachusetts saw its minority enrollment drop 10 percent in the two years following the 1986 brawl.[91]

Those black students who remained reported an increasing sense of isolation on campus—"isolated in an environment where they are not respected or understood by their white peers, and with no one to turn to for help."[92] The problem was even acknowledged in the 1989 American Council on Education (ACE) survey, where only 25 percent of college administrators reported that their schools provided an excellent or very good climate for black students.[93] The response by schools to this problem was mixed. Eighty-three percent of schools reported "some or a lot" of activities to improve the campus climate for minorities.[94] Seventy-five percent of administrators said they sponsored events to celebrate diversity, with 80 percent working on minority recruitment and retention. But even while administrators reported minority outreach, they failed to prioritize these efforts among their other activities. Asked to name what tasks were priorities for their schools in the early 1990s, only 14 percent of administrators at liberal arts colleges and comprehensive universities specified diversity. Thirty-three percent of officials at research/doctoral universities selected diversity, but this placed diversity last among seven challenges, including financial issues, enrollment issues, program quality, faculty issues, facilities and technology, and other issues.[95]

That diversity even appears on the list shows it had a modicum of support, but one might understandably wonder if administrators were only giving lip service to minority recruitment and retention. Administrators may have favored diversity in principle while simultaneously doubting their school's ability (or need) to recruit minority students and faculty. Michigan's liberal arts dean Peter Steiner was among the most direct when he said, "Our challenge is not to change this university into another kind of institution where minorities would naturally flock in much greater numbers. I need not remind you that there are such institutions—including Wayne State and Howard University."[96] Although Steiner was refuted by other administrators at Michigan, "most of the college administrators responding to [the 1989 ACE] survey acknowledged that their institutions were not doing very well in attracting black and Hispanic students."[97]

MULTICULTURALISM AND POLITICAL CORRECTNESS

On the curricular side of campus, though, faculty were pushing proposals to increase multicultural perspectives in course offerings. Criticizing classes that revolved around the work of "dead white men," proponents advocated new courses and assignments that celebrated comparative and multicultural approaches. Over time this move has proven successful, with many colleges now requiring course work in diverse cultures or non-Western civilizations, but it is difficult to say whether multiculturalism itself has helped with minority recruitment and retention. Certainly, its supporters would say that multiculturalism has given racial and ethnic minorities a greater sense of belonging, that their backgrounds and heritage are now respected and validated in class. Others, however, claim that colleges have only given lip service to multiculturalism and that American academe remains as unwelcoming as before to minorities, especially African Americans.[98]

One can hardly utter "multiculturalism" without expecting to hear the charge of political correctness or "PC" from social conservatives and academic traditionalists. Now a routine term in social and cultural debate, political correctness actually has been part of the academic lexicon for some time, referring at different points to Chinese doctrine during the Cultural Revolution as well as the New-Left agenda during the Vietnam War.[99] It came back on the scene in the mid-1980s as feminists and rhetoricians proposed gender-neutral language for terms previously incorporating masculine phrases. In 1986, for example, the Minnesota House debated legislation to change such terms as chairman to chair and sportsmen's clubs to sporting clubs.[100]

A definition of modern-day political correctness depends in large part on the ideology of the person you ask. To some, PC was a "McCarthyism of the left," a frontal assault on time-honored principles of Western Civilization.[101] To others, it represented a healthy questioning of assumed truths, particularly those based on white and/or male perspectives.[102] A Lexis/Nexis search from 1986 to 1992 finds 4,253 articles that addressed political correctness, a distinct sign of its contentiousness. It is hardly an overstatement to say that PC became the conservatives' demon. Columnists like George Will, William Safire, Charles Krauthammer, and radio personality Rush Limbaugh all took aim at the "dangerous PC trend."[103] Public figures like William Bennett, Lynne Cheney, and even President George Bush attacked what they saw as liberal orthodoxy emanating from America's campuses. News articles appeared with titles like "The Academy's New Ayatollahs" and "The Rising Hegemony of the Politically Correct."[104]

Political correctness quickly became associated with the college hate speech codes, with opinion pieces such as the one in the *New York Times* declaring it "distressing that the 'politically correct' view on campus these days seems to favor curtailment of speech."[105] This article was soon joined by the writings of other commentators, the majority of whom attacked political correctness and its perceived embodiment, hate speech codes. The Heritage Foundation produced a report outlining the various policies it claimed represented the PC agenda. Among these were "anti-speech codes; discriminatory admissions criteria [affirmative action]; withholding accreditation of some colleges on political grounds; bans on non-PC speakers; and curricula revision."[106]

In many ways it is understandable that people would link hate speech codes to the political correctness controversy, for the speech policies seemed designed to provide minorities special protection. On their face the policies could have applied to any racially demeaning comment, but their enforcement pattern showed a tendency to apply the policies against white students who attacked minorities. For example, the University of Wisconsin reported nine incidents across the university's several campuses in which its policy was applied. Of these, seven involved racial harassment, in all of which the insults were directed against minorities by white students.[107]

This is not to say that Wisconsin officials were unjustified in their actions, rather to suggest that the speech policies were connected to a cultural shift in progress on American campuses. Where a white/male perspective had been the norm, multiculturalism announced that the views of the previously unempowered needed to be incorporated into academe. Where scholars had previously held up Jefferson, Hobbes, and Dickens as the intellectual ideal, a new wave of academicians endorsed Catharine MacKinnon, Alice Walker, and Derrick Bell. Nor were these advocates afraid to assert their goals. Multiculturalism was not simply about studying new subjects, they said. It was about redirecting American cultural life. Where white heterosexual men had dominated for decades, multiculturalism sought a greater appreciation for minority culture and constituencies.

CRITICAL RACE STUDIES

Among this wave of scholars were proponents of a new legal philosophy called critical race theory. Led by such professors as Mari Matsuda, Richard Delgado, Charles Lawrence, and Kimberle Crenshaw, these scholars called for a reexamination of legal doctrines that disadvantaged people of color, arguing that the "dominant conceptions" of law had become "increasingly incapable of providing any meaningful quantum of racial justice."[108] Among their greatest concerns was the failure of the American legal system to protect racial minorities from harassment and violence, where the "negative effects of hate messages are real and immediate for the victims."[109] Richard Delgado, a colleague of Matsuda and a coauthor of the University of Wisconsin's speech code, described the potential harms in more detail:

> The psychological responses to such stigmatization consist of feelings of humiliation, isolation, and self-hatred. . . . [It] injures its victims' relationships with others . . . [and] may also result in mental illness and psychosomatic disease. . . . The psychological injuries severely handicap the victim's pursuit of a career. The person who is timid, bitter, hypertense, or psychotic will almost certainly fare poorly in employment settings. . . . Finally, and perhaps most disturbing, racism and racial labeling have an even greater impact on children than on adults, [as] minority children [may come to] exhibit self-hatred because of their skin color.[110]

According to critical race theorists, it was time to abandon the ostensible color-blind approach to constitutional law, a tradition that while neutral on the surface had the practical effect of thwarting racial minorities. As Matsuda explained, the First Amendment's sanction of offensive speech failed to acknowledge "the victims' experience of loss of liberty in a society that tolerates racist speech." In turn, Matsuda and her colleagues proposed a frankly "nonneutral, value-laden approach,"[111] criminalizing "a narrow, explicitly defined class of racist hate speech to provide public redress for the most serious harm."[112] As they said, the First Amendment had to give way to the Fourteenth Amendment when the equality rights of minorities were seriously threatened.

To the extent that Matsuda, Delgado, and other leaders within critical race studies were pushing the courts and legislatures to limit racist speech, their approach differed from earlier minority advocates who had calculated that their interests were best protected under the "broadest, most content-neutral protection of speech."[113] Since "those less privileged culturally or more radical politically are likely to use words and phrases that might be judged to impair civil discourse,"[114] earlier activists had pressed for a system of open expression in which "extreme, emotionally loaded words" might "captur[e] attention, dramatiz[e] an issue and mobiliz[e] people for change."[115] During the civil rights movement, advocates got their wish in such cases as *Cohen v. California, Gooding v. Wilson,* and *Edwards v. South Carolina,*[116] where the Supreme Court legitimized boycotts and offensive language as part of political protest. Critical race scholars rejected this approach, however, having concluded that existing doctrine did not protect against the current scrounge of racial harassment and violence. The First Amendment had failed minorities, they said, and in attempting to push constitutional law forward, their proposals broke with the immediate past.

It is interesting to note that Matsuda, Delgado, Lawrence, and Crenshaw are all law professors, as are several others who spoke out in favor of college hate speech regulation. Their interest in speech codes makes sense. On one level the policies read like traditional legislation. The measures defined terms, classified behavior, and sought sanctions. The codes also drew from existing legal standards. Michigan's and Wisconsin's policies mirrored Title VII, with codes at Fitchburg State and Monmouth College adopting the language almost verbatim. Even Stanford's policy borrowed from the constitutional doctrine of fighting words.

On a deeper level, though, the hate speech codes seemed to reflect the natural instincts of legal craftsmen. As Nadine Strossen, a law professor and president of the American Civil Liberties Union (ACLU), said, "if you're a carpenter, the solution to a problem is a nail. If you're a law professor, the solution is a rule." Academicians were facing an intractable problem, she says, and the immediate response was to enact policy to stop the harassment.[117] What Strossen did not add is that law, perhaps more than other disciplines, has been historically concerned about rights—about the rights of individuals against government, of citizen against citizen, and of course, of minorities against the majority's will. Hate speech codes were understood as a trade-off between rights—of free speech and equality, of academic freedom and educational opportunity. It is no wonder, then, that the topic attracted the attention of legal scholars and practitioners.

A GRAND CONTROVERSY

To say that the speech codes were controversial hardly captures the conflagration, for the topic created a firestorm of controversy within social, legal, and political circles. Michigan's policy was first adopted on May 31, 1988, and speech codes at Wisconsin, Emory, and several other schools followed over the next three years. Although it took commentators about a year to discover the new rules, they made up for lost time in their criticism of the policies. More than eight hundred stories about the speech codes appeared in major media over an eight-year period, as the topic became caught up in the larger fight over "political correctness," and with it cultural control.[118]

The rise of college hate speech codes grabbed the nation's attention for a variety of reasons. To many observers the policies appeared to challenge traditional notions of the First Amendment, in which governmental actors were required to remain neutral about a speaker's message even when it included derogatory comments about race, gender, or ethnicity. Unlike past attempts to regulate group libel, proponents of hate speech regulation in the 1980s faced not simply blank law books but a growing First Amendment doctrine that fundamentally opposed speech restrictions. To renew this fight, then, suggested a return to earlier times in which the courts countenanced restrictions on hateful, racist, and inflammatory rhetoric. But opponents did not simply fear a doctrinal shift. Many also resented the likely source—academic elites. To them the intelligentsia were thumbing their noses at the courts, at traditional understandings of the First Amendment and free speech. Others were worried about the potential persuasive power of college speech codes, with academic activists indoctrinating a new generation of youth to ideals that otherwise would not succeed in the political process.

Among the most impassioned were political conservatives, whose concerns focused less on the theoretical rebalancing of constitutional doctrine than on the specter of liberals rewriting the social order in their favor. Once again this was a fear of political correctness. Explained Dinesh D'Souza, hate speech "codes were the soft underbelly of multiculturalism."[119] Added a compatriot:

> A familiar jest—that some liberals do not care what anyone does, so long as it is compulsory—must be revised in light of goings-on on campuses. Today's newfangled liberals, the enforcers of political correctness, care minutely about what people do, say and think. They resort promiscuously to intimidation and coercion. But their curdled liberalism is not just about a political agenda. It is also a program for the personal pleasure of bossing people around.[120]

Even President Bush took the occasion of a commencement speech at the University of Michigan to warn of the dangers that hate speech advocates posed.[121]

At the same time, the speech code controversy provided a very public discussion of the meaning of free speech and the First Amendment. Many legal scholars took up the question in law review articles on the subject,[122] but popular commentators also debated the merits of hate speech regulations.[123] The subject was also a favorite of newspaper editorial boards, who published no fewer than 450 editorials on the subject between 1988 and 1994. Of these, approximately 80 percent opposed the speech codes.[124]

One of the most interesting developments of the speech code controversy was the ideological split between groups on the Left. It was not surprising that conservatives would have opposed the speech policies. Whether political conservatives or legal traditionalists, the Right would naturally have resisted the codes and their presumed attempts to rewrite constitutional norms and social relations. But on the Left the reaction was fractured, splitting former allies into camps advocating either civil rights or civil liberties. On one side were those who emphasized racial equality, arguing that the First Amendment had to give ground to stamp out the kind of hatred and harassment that perpetuated racism. On the opposite side were civil libertarians, trying to uphold unfettered expression while at the same time expressing concern for the plight of harassment's victims. Into the former camp would fall Richard Delgado,

Mari Matsuda, and other supporters of critical race studies; the latter group would include Nat Hentoff, Nadine Strossen, and Robert Post, then professor of law at the University of California–Berkeley.

The divide between these two camps is seen most clearly in the internal deliberations of the American Civil Liberties Union. Shortly after the issue broke, the ACLU's legal director went on record in stating that "too often the First Amendment had been allowed to trump the Fourteenth." He was joined by Mary Ellen Gale, a member of the national board of directors and a leader within the southern California chapters, "who reminded her colleagues that the Fourteenth Amendment is 'no less a part of the Constitution than the First.'"[125] Within California alone, the ACLU's three chapters initially adopted different policy statements on college hate speech codes. Eventually they met and agreed on a joint statement, but even here they seemed to condone restrictions on expression. Their declaration recognized that college and university administrators were "obligated to take all steps necessary within constitutional bounds to minimize and eliminate a hostile educational environment which impairs access of protected minorities to equal educational opportunities." As part of this approach, they approved restrictions on expression that "is specifically intended to and does harass an individual or specific individuals on the basis of their protected status."[126]

The California ACLU policy provoked a strong reaction within the national ACLU, but the larger body moved slowly in developing a policy on the college speech codes. At the organization's biennial conference in 1993, Charles Lawrence and Nadine Strossen debated each other on the subject, and internal deliberations continued. Meanwhile two state affiliates acted on their own, challenging speech policies at the Universities of Michigan and Wisconsin. Finally, in October 1990—two years after Michigan's policy had been adopted—the national ACLU issued a statement declaring its opposition to:

> all campus regulations which interfere with the freedom of professors, students and administrators to teach, learn, discuss and debate or to express ideas, opinions or feelings in classroom, public or private discourse. [T]his policy does not prohibit colleges and universities from enacting disciplinary codes aimed at restricting *acts* of harassment, intimidation and invasion of privacy, [though] the fact that words may be used in connection with otherwise actionable conduct does not immunize such conduct.[127]

LEGISLATIVE PROPOSALS

One of the oddest developments in the fight against college speech codes was the pairing of the ACLU with Republican congressman Henry Hyde, a conservative representative from Illinois who had drafted a bill to prohibit post-secondary institutions from disciplining students for offensive speech.[128] Hyde was joined by the ACLU, a partnership that even he recognized as an unlikely duo.[129] Hyde's bill was introduced in March of 1991. About a year later, Larry Craig, a Republican senator from Idaho, introduced his own legislation called the Freedom of Speech on Campus Act. Under Craig's proposal, private universities would have been prohibited from receiving federal funds if an institution took "any verbal or written action against individuals who [engaged in] offensive speech." According to the Senate Committee Report, the bill would have banned "behavior codes prohibiting racial and sexual harassment on campus."[130] Neither Hyde's nor Craig's bills went anywhere in Congress, although the Senate Labor and Human Resources Committee held a hearing in September 1992 to examine "how American colleges and universities have responded to racial and sexual harassment on campuses."[131] Along with Senator Craig, the Committee heard from witnesses representing the ACLU, the Free Congress Foundation, Towson State University, and St. Olaf College, as well as receiving testimony from Catherine MacKinnon, Charles Lawrence, and three college students. Congress, however, took no further action.

Although Congress demurred, one state passed significant legislation in response to the hate speech codes. In California, state senator Bill Leonard introduced a bill to hold private educational institutions to the standards of the First Amendment. His proposal represented a historic change to constitutional doctrine, since until that time private institutions were exempt from the First Amendment.[132] Leonard was successful in enacting the legislation, prohibiting private colleges and universities in California from disciplining any student "solely on the basis of . . . speech or other communication that when engaged in outside the campus is protected from government restriction by the First Amendment."[133] Church-controlled schools remain exempt from the law, for fear that the statute might conflict with freedom of religion, but the legislation has proven quite effective at achieving its author's aims. As discussed in chapter 4, the popularly called "Leonard Law" provided the basis for overturning the hate speech policy at Stanford University.

PUTTING IT ALL TOGETHER

The initial controversy over college hate speech codes would last less than a decade, from the late 1980s to the mid-1990s, but its influence would be felt longer and more profoundly throughout society. Beginning in 1989, the courts would be called to involve themselves in the matter, and over the next several years every court that considered hate speech regulation found the measures unconstitutional. But anyone who thinks the courts have beaten speech codes "into retreat"[134] has missed the greater ability of public understandings to overcome judicial pronouncements of rights. As the rest of this book describes, hate speech codes owe their rise to a combination of rights priming and utilitarian motives. Enacted largely as defensive measures, they have persevered in the face of contrary judicial precedent, as colleges have evaded, ignored, and resisted the courts. In the end, these policies have taken on a larger meaning, creating symbolic rights that have filtered out to society as a whole. What its opponents could only have feared when the first college speech codes sprouted has become an accepted norm in American civil society. Hate speech regulation not only lives, it has triumphed.

Theoretical Implications

Much has been written about college hate speech codes in both scholarly and popular publications,[1] although the lion's share of commentary falls into one of two camps. Observers tend either to critique the rise of hate speech policies or address the compatibility of speech restrictions with traditional First Amendment case law. On a deeper level, though, the speech codes illustrate law's social construction. They challenge the bases of free speech law as equivocal and call into question the power of the courts to control the meaning of legal norms. As the codes demonstrate, the work of constitutional construction is carried out in civil society among other influential yet nongovernmental institutions.

It is understandable that much scholarly attention about law goes to the formal Constitution—to official and legally enforceable interpretations of the U.S. Constitution and its amendments. But we would do well to focus more closely on the practical understanding and popular meaning of constitutional norms in civil society. Although these informal but recognized norms are often dependent on judicial constructions of the formal Constitution, the hate speech debate shows that the bounds of a constitutional right may be reinterpreted without the courts or other government institutions giving their blessings. Indeed, social activists may find it just as useful to harness the institutions of civil society to advance their agenda as they do to mobilize and petition government actors for new policy. Even if the goal is legal change, there may be greater benefits to establishing rights and norms in daily practice than in securing the courts' approval for formal legal change.

This chapter offers a broad view of constitutional construction, using free speech and the First Amendment as a guide. The discussion begins by examining the theoretical bases behind the First Amendment, arguing not only that free speech law is socially constructed but also that informal understandings of speech rights have as much, if not more, sway in ordering civil speech norms than do judicial interpretations of the First Amendment. In this respect, the chapter distinguishes between the formal Constitution and mass constitutionalism, the latter representing popular practices and understandings of constitutional law. The scope of constitutional rights is greater than the four corners of the Constitution, showering constitutional connotations and constructions on other relationships that are not technically those between citizen and government. In the case of free speech, civil society has extended the reach of the First Amendment by using it as the benchmark for private behavior—thus placing the ultimate power of constitutional construction outside of the courts.

The notion of extra-judicial law finds support from several scholars, most notably Gerald Rosenberg, Patricia Ewick and Susan Silbey, Stuart Scheingold, and Larry Kramer,[2] who have chronicled the role that popular institutions and everyday people have on constitutional construction. But mass constitutionalism is not necessarily antithetical to positivist or court-centered notions of law. Given the low salience of most court decisions and the general respect with which people hold the judiciary, many decrees are likely to be followed. Even when they are not, the courts may still precipitate others' responses.

The courts, then, are *an* important piece of the legal meaning-making function, but they are not *the* central link. Particularly when the issues are highly contentious and morally imbued, the public is willing to substitute its interpretations for those of the courts, but even in "average" cases the courts' decisions do not achieve their legitimacy and meaning until the public is willing to apply and accept these understandings. For that matter, informal or hidden law may exist in civil society even in the absence of the courts' dictates.

According to several scholars, "the bulk of American constitutional development has taken place outside of the courts, largely outside of the federal courts, and largely outside of the Supreme Court of the United States,"[3] a conclusion reinforced by the work of Kramer, who claims that the American people and not the courts have historically had the power to construct the Constitution.[4] This chapter continues that tradition, offering a vision of mass constitutionalism that centers legal-making in extra-judicial sources. It is this point—the fear that constitutional meaning can be constructed outside of the courts—that may have driven the opponents of the college hate speech codes.

THE DEBATABLE BASIS OF FREE SPEECH

For years lawyers and legal scholars have debated the rationale behind the First Amendment. Is free speech so favored in American law because it is necessary to the functioning of democracy, or, conversely, does the First Amendment reign for instrumental purposes? Do we need free speech protection to reach our full potential as individuals, or, as some critics would say, is First Amendment jurisprudence a political calculus, with outcomes driven by the preferences of dominant social groups? Two hundred years after the adoption of the First Amendment we are no closer, it seems, to a resolution of its rationale. Although most commentators acknowledge that free speech is among the tenets that define America, they cannot agree on the genesis of that norm, whether it flows from some understanding of natural law, whether it is endemic as a necessary principle of democracy, or whether it reflects our political history and culture (one not coincidentally dominated by Anglo-Saxon heritage, and white men at that).

According to many scholars, First Amendment jurisprudence is still a relatively new doctrine, having emerged from the courts' cocoon in the early 1900s.[5] Initially, First Amendment case law was justified by what Richard Posner calls a "moral approach"—the notion that there is "an intrinsic value to speech" that reflects "a corollary or implication of a proper moral conception of persons."[6] The moral approach is reflected in the writings of such theorists as John Stuart Mill and Justice Holmes, who saw the First Amendment as protecting a "marketplace of ideas" that aids citizens to "better understand the world in which we live."[7] Others, like Alexander Meiklejohn and Robert Post, would premise free speech protection on "safeguarding of public discourse from regulations that are inconsistent with democratic legitimacy."[8] Still other theorists believe that free speech is central to personal autonomy, self-realization, and the creation of good character.[9]

Those who disagree with the "moral justification" to free speech jurisprudence do not doubt that open discourse and the First Amendment are important. Rather, they claim that First Amendment jurisprudence is instrumental, that free speech is "valued to the extent that it promotes specified goals, such as political stability, economic prosperity, and personal happiness."[10] Surprisingly, the instrumentalists attract two commentators who often find themselves on opposite poles of legal and political debates, Richard Posner and

Stanley Fish. Posner, one of the leading advocates of law and economics, believes that the costs and benefits of free speech can be estimated, and that the courts should adopt rules that create the greatest efficiency. Criticizing the "moralists," Posner says that theorists assign an "intrinsic value to speech, though not necessarily a value that cannot be overridden by other values," yet moralists consistently operate as if the virtue of free speech trumps all opposing interests. As Posner says, "very few Americans believe that the instrumental values and costs of freedom of speech are *irrelevant* to deciding how extensive that freedom of speech should be."[11]

Posner is joined by Fish, a prolific postmodern theorist, who, although an instrumentalist, believes it is impossible to weigh speech interests impartially. Fish is perhaps best known for his proclamation that "there is no such thing as free speech."[12] By that, he means free speech theory inevitably reflects "a substantive political content," making it impossible to base First Amendment jurisprudence on such intrinsic notions as self-governance, self-realization, or autonomy.[13]

Opponents of hate speech regulation are most often linked with the moral approach, arguing that the intrinsic value of free speech commands unrestricted discourse. When critiquing the college hate speech codes, for example, George Will regularly accused university administrators of enshrining particular opinions as "correct" rather than allowing students the freedom to uncover and develop their own views through open discourse. Proponents of speech regulation, by contrast, are frequently depicted as instrumentalists. In advising critical race theorists, Stanley Fish has said, "The correct response to a vision or a morality that you despise is not to try and cure it or to make its adherents sit down and read John Stuart Mill's *On Liberty,* that's not going to do the job. The only way to fight hate speech or racist speech is to recognize it as the speech of your enemy and what you do in response to the speech of your enemy is not prescribe a medication for it but attempt to stamp it out."[14]

That said, the approaches can be flipped to advance the opposing position on hate speech. For example, Meiklejohn's theory of democratic decision-making undergirds some calls for speech regulation. If, as Meiklejohn says, free discourse is designed to advance the goals of democracy, it is not illogical for the state to step in and officiate when speech disparages or excludes members of the polity.[15] On the other side, some instrumentalists have come out against hate speech regulation. Richard Posner, in particular, has applied a cost-benefit analysis to college hate speech codes, claiming that the punishment of fighting words "enlarges the legal rights of those who are thin-skinned and prone to violence and so encourages people to cultivate a reputation for hypersensitivity."[16]

THE SOCIAL CONSTRUCTION OF FREE SPEECH LAW

One of the difficulties of the hate speech debate is that some would like to treat free speech as "a concept that sits above the fray,"[17] an immutable norm of sorts that is separate from the various debates constructing its meaning. However, whether one believes that free speech has intrinsic value in itself or instead serves instrumental purposes, the rules of open discourse are hardly a static concept. Free speech law, and in particular the First Amendment, are socially constructed norms that inevitably must be balanced against—and sometimes give way to—other social needs.

The history of jurisprudence this past century reflects a recognition that law as a broad discipline is socially constructed, obtaining its meaning from the needs of the day and bending to accommodate changed social relationships. Starting with the legal realists of the 1920s, theorists claimed that, far from being immutable, legal norms were set by the idiosyncrasies of judges. In the classic description of this school of thought, Karl Llewellyn postulated that a judge's legal decisions may have as much to do with his individual disposition as with the applicable legal precedent.[18]

Half a century later, critical legal studies (CLS) arrived on the scene, pushing the concept of legal realism even further. Scholars like Duncan Kennedy suggested that it was more than a judge's personal preference or serendipity that explained judicial decisions. Western law reflected a systemic class bias in which vested interests made legal decisions to maintain their privileged status over lower racial, gender, religious or socioeconomic classes.[19] Under CLS, law is anything but an immutable series of norms. To the contrary, law is not just socially constructed but is a politically infused language of power that perpetuates class inequality.

Most students and practitioners of American law have now grown up with at least the tantamount recognition that the law they invoke is influenced by (or suffers from) the social context in which it is used. For example, as Jane Larson explains, business fraud is enforced but sexual fraud is not because we as a society are hesitant to allow the judicial system into our bedrooms, even though we accept it in the workplace.[20] So too, the development of rape shield laws reflects a legal system that has adjusted to the rising social power of women.[21]

But when we talk about constitutional law, and more particularly the First Amendment and freedom of expression, a strange set of intellectual blinders seems to take hold. At times it seems like scholars and practitioners want to believe that the doctrine is not only sacrosanct but also unwavering in meaning and application. Whether one accepts the moral approach or believes that free speech is instrumental, some advocates seem to suggest that First Amendment jurisprudence must continue to mean the same thing. Justice Black was perhaps the most famous of these champions, claiming that the First Amendment has a fixed meaning—Congress shall make *no* law abridging expression.[22] Others have been more delicate in their argument, claiming that the values behind the First Amendment—including self-expression, truth seeking, and self-government among others—require that its doctrine be unwavering.[23]

Yet this very argument shows the First Amendment's meaning to be open to social construction. The fact that we present cultural and political rationales for the norm of free speech means that we determine its importance through social interactions. We use constitutional law to advance certain social values; in turn the meaning of these norms may change as our social, cultural, or legal needs change. As Gerald Rosenberg has said, the "First Amendment is not a substantive force in itself, but instead a forum for substantive arguments about the cultural definitions of liberty" and its relation to equality.[24]

This realization can be a scary proposition. As Stanley Fish explains,

> People cling to First Amendment pieties because they do not wish to face what they correctly take to be the alternative. That alternative is *politics,* the realization that decisions about what is and is not protected in the realm of expression will rest not on principle or firm doctrine but on the ability of some persons to interpret—recharacterize or rewrite—principle and doctrine in ways that lead to the protection of speech they want heard and the regulation of speech they want silenced.[25]

And yet this is exactly what courts do when they consider free speech cases. Regardless of the legal rule they claim to be following, judges implicitly must balance the value of the speech at issue against the potential harm it presents. Justice Stevens has acknowledged as much when, in *R.A.V.,* he said:

> Admittedly, the categorical approach to the First Amendment has some appeal: Either expression is protected or it is not—the categories create safe harbors for governments and speakers alike. But this approach sacrifices subtlety for clarity and is, I am convinced, ultimately unsound. As an initial matter, the concept of "categories" fits poorly with the complex reality of expression. Few dividing lines in First Amendment law are straight and unwavering, and efforts at categorization inevitably give rise only to fuzzy boundaries. . . . Moreover, the categorical approach does not take seriously the importance of context. The meaning of any

> expression and the legitimacy of its regulation can only be determined in context. Whether, for example, a picture or a sentence is obscene cannot be judged in the abstract, but rather only in the context of its setting, its use, and its audience.[26]

We see these kinds of judgments most clearly when the courts approach symbolic acts. Cases like flag burning, the destruction of draft cards, and written epigraphs like "fuck the draft"[27] reach the Supreme Court and have lasting importance because we recognize that they are not simply value-neutral actions being measured against immutable norms but instead represent symbolic ideas being interpreted and weighed by potentially fallible, and even biased, jurists.[28] The Court takes on these cases, and we watch in rapt attention, because we understand that the Court is operating on the very heart of socially constructed behavior. Symbols are a way of socially constructing meanings. As one scholar explains, law "affects us primarily through communication of symbols—by providing threats, promises, models, persuasion, legitimacy, stigma, and so on."[29]

Court decisions also change to fit the times. That "separate but equal" from *Plessy v. Ferguson* was overruled by the integration decisions of *Brown v. Board of Education* and their progeny reflects a view of constitutional equality that is in flux.[30] The same is true for free speech and the First Amendment. Although the Supreme Court's *Beauharnais* decision seemed poised to set a new trend in decades past, it has been replaced by such free speech decisions as *Texas v. Johnson* and *Collins v. Smith.*[31]

Still, if constitutional law is socially constructed, many traditionalists claim that these interpretations are set by judges and that courts control what the Constitution and First Amendment mean. As they point out, courts exist for the very purpose of resolving legal ambiguity and pronouncing what the law means. Judicial decisions translate constitutional provisions into everyday rules, and legal rulings necessarily create adherence from a public that looks to the courts as neutral interpreters and arbiters. Even when judicial decisions bring about social change (whether instantly through an explicit ruling[32] or more indirectly when a decision changes legal expectations[33]), traditionalists would argue that social transformation is led by the courts. The meanings of constitutional norms do not turn on their own, thus precipitating societal change. Rather, the courts' new interpretations filter out to the public, changing popular understandings of constitutional precedent and setting any coming changes in motion.[34]

The traditionalists or positivists raise a good point, for it is true that "court-made constitutionalism" often "structures what others do."[35] Nonetheless, it is myopic to focus on the ducking, weaving, and reasoning of judges, for courts are not the sole, and perhaps not even the most important, arbiters of what constitutional law (or law in general) means. Constitutional construction occurs elsewhere throughout society. Keith Whittington has advanced this point, distinguishing between constitutional interpretation, which "is a process of discovering the meaning of constitutional text," and constitutional construction, in which other branches of government "fill gaps in the text when they act to enforce broader constitutional principles."[36] As Whittington explains:

> The constitutional text itself serves as a nucleus of a set of constitutional requirements. Surrounding this and overlapping it to a greater or lesser extent, is constitutional law, which translates the text into formal rules for decision. Outside this, finally, but interpenetrating it and underlying it is constitutional construction, which serves to extend the application of the text further by mediating between the text itself and an external environment of policy ideas and political principles. Neither interpretation nor construction changes the core nucleus of the text, but they do provide its extensions and points of contact with political practice. Interpretation flows immediately from the text and thus has a limited reach. Construction bears a more tenuous and alloyed connection with the text but as a result can extend constitutional meaning even further before it to exhaust the possibilities of the existing text.[37]

Whittington's argument is both powerful and imaginative, but he limits constitutional construction to the "province of legislative and executive action."[38] Under Whittington's model, constitutional exposition rests with government; the courts interpret the Constitution's text, and the legislative and executive branches construct the Constitution's gaps.

Although it is unclear whether he would see it as such, developments from early 2004 concerning gay marriage would seem to confirm, if not potentially expand, Whittington's theory. Shortly following the decision of the Supreme Judicial Court of Massachusetts establishing the right of gay marriage,[39] local officials in San Francisco began marrying same-sex couples.[40] Although the Massachusetts decision may have set the process in motion, the case did not apply outside of Massachusetts and had no direct precedential effect in California. Rather, as some public law professors have argued, municipal leaders saw a potential, growing gap in the Constitution and stepped in to construct their own interpretation of the Fourteenth Amendment, if only until the California Supreme Court acted and overruled them.[41]

MASS CONSTITUTIONALISM

Constitutional construction, however, is a broader exercise that occurs within civil society as a whole, particularly among influential, nongovernmental institutions. According to Kramer, this has been the practice for centuries, the founding fathers having concluded that "the people themselves . . . can alone declare [the Constitution's] true meaning."[42] The exercise is one of legal meaning-making, a multifaceted process in which judicial interpretations of the Constitution's text and other governmental actions applying those tenets both help to create public understanding and influence actual practice of constitutional norms. The process is not simply top-down, with constitutional meaning dependent on the actions of government actors, be they judicial, legislative, or executive. Constitutional norms are influenced by social practices, and sometimes even created in civil society, as the needs, expectations, and advocacy of social groups change. Indeed, constitutional change can be fomented as much outside of the courts and formal government processes as it can by pressing public institutions for new rights and interpretations. Even while acknowledging that judicial declarations are often influential, constitutional norms created in civil society have strong—and sometimes competing—authority too.

Any distinction between formal constitutional law and social understandings of constitutional norms must begin with judicial impact theory. For years, research has suggested that judicial decisions do not in themselves command adherence or bring about social change. Perhaps the most cited author is Gerald Rosenberg, who argues that the Supreme Court's celebrated civil rights decisions (including, especially, *Brown v. Board of Education*) did not change rights practices on their own. As Rosenberg notes, public opinion had not yet reached a consensus in favor of civil rights at the time of *Brown* (especially in the South), and President Eisenhower was slow to enforce the Court's decisions. It took until the civil rights movement a decade later for political agitation to change attitudes about equality.[43]

Rosenberg is sometimes viewed as a critic of the courts—challenging judges' presumed power to establish rights—but most scholars of judicial impact acknowledge that law on the books is not necessarily law as practiced. Bradley Canon and Charles Johnson, among others, have studied the impact of Supreme Court decisions, and their model provides a useful guide for understanding the process by which judicial decisions attain their meaning. Canon and Johnson distinguish between the implementation of judicial decisions and the impact of those judgments, although as both scholars recognize, the impact of a decision may also depend on the extent to which public and private bodies implement the courts' dictates. If, for example, a politician refuses to enforce a court order prohibiting prayer in school, his inaction may convince others to reject the court's conclusion. Of course, it may also be the other way around, that the politician refuses to act because he understands his constituency is not prepared to accept the court's decision. There are many reasons why individuals or organizations choose to comply (or not) with a judicial decree. They may agree with the court's policy conclusion, trust in the court's legitimacy, weigh the costs and benefits of compliance, respond to the context or explication of the decision, or seek to minimize their cognitive dissonance with an unpopular decision.[44] Many fine scholars have posited these explanations, their findings all centered on a common point: People and organizations do not always comply with judicial decisions; because people are not always familiar with the courts' decisions, and most significantly, because individuals may have differing prior attitudes about the decisions, the courts' decrees may have minimal impact.[45]

The implication from such research is that there are two kinds of law—law as decided by courts, and law as popularly understood and voluntarily practiced within society. To be sure, the two are often the same. Parties to a lawsuit may feel bound to accept the courts' decision, if only because an enforcement action might be pursued with a sheriff's or marshal's office. People may also agree with the substance of a judicial decree. Or, more likely, the public may respect the courts (or at least the Supreme Court) to a certain extent and accept the validity of their decisions.[46] But legitimation is not automatic, nor can it be said that a judicial decree has achieved societal legitimacy until there is sufficient consensus to accept the ruling, or at the very least not to challenge it.

To some this may sound like a tautology, but it is not. Since the courts rely on the public's sense of legitimacy to enforce their rulings, a judicial decision that generates broad-scale defiance is not going to be accepted as a true legal norm. The decision may remain on the books, but until a critical mass of the citizenry accepts the decision as just, fair, or at least tolerable, it will not permeate into the prevailing legal culture.

It is difficult to define critical mass precisely, for there is not an exact threshold of acceptance that signifies legitimacy or acquiescence. Since most Americans are unfamiliar with court decisions (even those of the Supreme Court),[47] legitimacy turns more often on the public's blind willingness to tolerate judicial decrees than on deliberative affirmation. Where individuals are familiar with the Supreme Court's decisions but do not have strong preexisting opinions about the issues involved, they are likely to accede to the Court's decrees.[48] People may even accept decrees with which they disagree because of their larger respect for the judiciary.[49] Small as this effect may be, researchers have documented instances in which the Supreme Court has augmented policy legitimacy by virtue of the public's diffuse support for the Court.[50]

Perhaps a better way to define critical mass, then, is by its opposite, that judicial rulings will be considered legitimate unless a critical mass of opposition arises to a decision. In this respect, opposition can be expressed in two distinct ways—public opinion about formal law and/or behavior in response to it. A public that is knowledgeable about a decision and disagrees with the substantive ruling may refuse to defer to the court's judgment.[51] In addition, individuals or institutions covered under a decree may refuse to comply with a decision. The two modalities—public opinion and personal or institutional behavior—may operate in tandem or even at cross-purposes. As was the case with the initial school prayer decisions, municipalities may track local opinion by ignoring the Supreme Court's ruling.[52] In other examples, however, local governments may disregard the preferences of their constituents by removing state-sponsored Christmas displays. As Canon and Johnson have ably demonstrated, organizational compliance with judicial decrees is influenced by a myriad of factors, not all of them reflective of support for the courts' substantive rulings. In fact, the compliance of influential organizations may well affect public opinion about the substance of a judicial decree. Were public schools uniformly to reject the courts' limitations on school prayer, they might condition succeeding generations of children (and their families) to discredit the case law.

It is difficult to measure critical opposition precisely, for legitimacy likely exists on a continuum with some cases gaining more acceptance than others. For years scholars have compared the public's response to judicial decisions, finding that some cases generated greater acceptance or legitimacy than others. Two of the most famous decisions are *United States v. Nixon* and *Brown v. Board of Education,* both controversial matters involving serious constitutional questions. According to many scholars, *Nixon* achieved greater and more immediate legitimacy than did *Brown.* The public broadly supported the Supreme Court's decree against President Nixon, and the very branch of government that could have contested the decision's legitimacy—Nixon himself—chose to comply. By contrast, much of the public was not yet ready to accept the Court's substantive decree in *Brown,* nor for that matter did many of the affected school districts initially comply.[53]

Although scholars are able to compare the relative acceptance of particular cases, there is little literature that defines the "tipping point"[54] at which societal opposition renders a court decision illegitimate. Again, the likely reason is that critical mass is a continuous, not dichotomous concept, but there are some generalizations that can be ventured about critical opposition to case law, whether as reflected in popular opinion or individual or institutional behavior.

- Legitimacy is lower when public opinion disfavors a decision and compliance is low.

Institutions may react differently to case law than does public opinion, with public officials in particular deciding to comply with a judicial decree (perhaps prohibitions on school prayer) even when public opinion opposes the decision. The opposite may also be true, with the public broadly supportive of a decision but those covered by the decision refusing to implement the ruling (for example, a reporter who refuses to name her sources). Although the courts' decrees are contested in both instances, the legitimacy of judicial decisions is most at risk when both public opinion and those parties covered by a decision oppose its implementation. This was the case in many parts of the United States following *Brown v. Board of Education,* where whole sectors of the country thumbed their noses at the Supreme Court's ruling.

- The more broadly distributed the opposition to a court decision, the less powerful the ruling will be.

Almost any judicial decision is likely to generate opposition, but no serious observer would believe that the courts' legitimacy is threatened if a handful of people refuse to accept a decision. By the same token, few people would consider a decision to be "the law of the land" if sizeable majorities of the public rejected a decision. But it is not simply the absolute size of the opposition that matters; its breadth and depth are also influential. To the extent that opposition is broadly distributed and not confined to a particular region of the country or a limited demographic (e.g., conservatives, the poor, trade workers), defiance is a greater threat to the courts. This axiom reflects a basic premise of diffusion theory: that social ideas—in this case opposition to court decisions—are spread through interpersonal networks.[55] Thus, the more networks of people who object to a court decision, the less controlling the ruling will be.

- The courts' decisions are under greater threat when the opposition reflects a potential political constituency.

Even if the critics of a ruling are limited in number, they can augment their power by courting political patrons, be they elected officials or others influential in the political process. Consider the response to *Boy Scouts of America v. Dale,* the Supreme Court's 2000 decision that permitted the Boy Scouts to exclude homosexuals from its membership.[56] In the wake of the ruling, 56 percent of respondents in a national poll agreed that "the Boy Scouts of America have a constitutional right to block gay men from becoming troop leaders." Only one-third of respondents opposed the decision.[57] Nevertheless, the opposition proved successful in attracting support from political leaders at both national and local levels.

At the time that the Lambda Legal Defense Fund litigated *Dale* it had already lined up an impressive list of amicus briefs, including submissions by the American Bar Association, the American Civil Liberties Union, the American Jewish Congress, and the American Psychological Association. The aftermath of the case, however, generated additional institutional support for gay rights. The Supreme Court's decision galvanized attention, but even more, opponents reached out through informal political networks to draw allies. The effect of the swelling support was to take an opposition message and make it broader and stronger—the Supreme Court had the law wrong. The Boy Scouts were not a private organization like a coffee klatch; they were a public accommodation, or at the very least a large service organization whose mission would not be compromised by admitting homosexuals. By framing the issue as one of discrimination, and in attracting the support of allies from the political world, opponents were also successful in expanding their networks to appeal to business and civic leaders. The American Medical Association issued a resolution recommending that youth groups end their bans on homosexuals, and at least fifty United Way campaigns have excluded the Boy Scouts because of its membership policy.[58] Four religious denominations have criticized the Boys Scouts' policy and the Court's decision,[59] and perhaps most impressively, opponents have convinced several corporations to stop funding the Boy Scouts. Among these businesses are such household names as American Airlines, Levi Strauss, Hewlett Packard, IBM, CVS Pharmacy, and Fleet Bank.[60]

This laundry list should not confuse anyone into believing that opponents of *Dale* have attracted majority support throughout American society. But it does suggest that what was at first a minority proposition—that the courts should not allow the Boy Scouts to exclude homosexuals—is hardly an extreme position. Because the cause of civil rights has a natural political constituency, and because homosexuals as a group have achieved social, political, and economic power, supporters of gay rights have been able to draw allies from the highest reaches of American society. In effect, opponents to the

Supreme Court's decision have used the decision to galvanize attention and support for their larger message—that discrimination against homosexuals should not be countenanced under the Constitution or by the courts.

- Elite opinion may lead popular opinion, but if mass opinion opposes the law, its legitimacy is sunk.

The involvement of elite groups in the opposition to *Dale* raises a question about whose opinions count in establishing legitimacy. Must the general public agree with (or at least fail to oppose) a judicial decision, or is legitimacy founded on the views of society's elites, including such opinion leaders as academicians, journalists, and government officials? Much has been written about the dichotomy between popular democracy and elite control of government. On one side is the "principal heavyweight [of the] pluralists,"[61] Robert Dahl, who argues that participatory democracy succeeds in anchoring control of government in the public, which then exerts influence over those who "rule" them.[62] Contesting him would be Benjamin Ginsberg, who worries that American democracy has become an oligarchy of sorts.[63] Although government may be responsive to public opinion, Ginsberg argues that popular opinion is really manufactured elite opinion, "spawned by a mixture of self-interest and idealism. Elites have the resources needed to successfully peddle these carefully tailored opinions to mass publics through the mass media, which are dominated by elites."[64]

In some sense it does not matter whether Dahl or Ginsberg is correct. Both acknowledge that public opinion matters; the debate between the two theorists is whether popular opinion is authentic or whether elites first construct and then disseminate a range of conventional wisdom that dominates public debate. In fact, there are some who would paint the relationship in reverse, saying that "elites attend to public preferences."[65] Regardless, most research on democratic representation shows that government institutions ultimately respond to changes in popular opinion.[66] Although the connection has weakened in the last fifteen years as divided government (or gridlock) has limited the ideological range of most legislative action, government policy consistently tracks popular opinion on issues salient to the public.[67] To the extent that it responds to outside opinion (and the data are murky), even the Supreme Court's decisions have been loosely linked to changes in popular attitudes.[68]

The upshot of this research is that legitimacy ultimately turns on the views of the mass public, however those perspectives are actually created. Elites may "drive" mass opinion, and, as masters of the institutions of government and commerce, elites can shape the meaning of judicial rulings by their decisions to implement court decrees. But elites are only able to blunt the legitimacy of judicial decisions with which they disagree, not completely invalidate them. This is illustrated by the public's reaction to *Dale*. So long as the general public continues to believe that homosexuals do not merit civil rights protection, the *Dale* decision will stand as accepted law permitting an organization that supposedly preaches good citizenship to exclude gays and lesbians.[69] If anything, this dynamic is the converse of the initial response to *Brown v. Board of Education*. Intellectuals and editorial boards may have favored the Supreme Court's first decree to eradicate segregation, but *Brown I* was arguably ineffectual in desegregating schools because its underlying tenets had not yet been accepted by the general public. Only after elite advocacy, presidential intervention, and additional social mobilization had altered public attitudes did the Court's second ruling in *Brown* take hold.[70] But therein lies an important point about the relationship between elite and mass opinion: public opinion is not static. Social advocacy and mobilization may ultimately modify the initial reaction to judicial decisions, a point that the opponents of *Dale* have likely taken to heart. As we will see later, legal mobilization outside of the courts may have as much power as the courts themselves in setting the meaning of legal norms.

THE LOCUS OF CHALLENGE

Where the courts' decisions are likely to come under greater scrutiny—and where unpopular rulings are likely to be challenged—are those cases that the public is aware of and feels strongly about. Predominant among these are "politico-moral issues," matters in which "moral disputes . . . spill over into the political arena."[71] According to Bradley Canon, "disputants approach [politico-moral] questions not in terms of political wisdom or experience, but in nonpolitical terms of absolute right and wrong."[72]

> One and perhaps both sides see the issue through moral eyes. In these eyes, the question is not what policy is rationally best for the commonweal, or even what policy will favor their own economic interests. Rather, the question is what does the Bible command, or what does natural law or abstract moral justice or some other standard require.[73]

As Canon explains, slavery and abortion are among the most critical politico-moral disputes in American jurisprudence, although desegregation, affirmative action, school prayer, child labor laws, and gay rights likely qualify.[74]

Critical opposition may also arise in other areas of law that both generate press coverage and personally touch people's lives. The courts' rulings on the Fourth and Fifth Amendments are often salient, drawing as they do on the public's fear of crime. To the extent these decisions are seen as expanding the "rights of criminals,"[75] they attract attention and generate opposition.

So too, First Amendment jurisprudence often involves politico-moral issues. Many of these disputes address the bases and bounds of democratic citizenship, and, being imbued with civic meaning, the cases invite the public's attention and sometimes wrath. Canon has already identified school prayer as a likely topic, but questions of free speech often generate controversy and opposition. Many of the fact patterns involve deliberately provocative statements, including protestors who seek to burn the American flag or "Fuck the Draft,"[76] and as much as American civics education may preach tolerance, it is still the rare human reaction to permit, if not affirmatively protect, messages and slogans that one despises. The fact that the press is specifically covered under the First Amendment also ensures that much of the case law gets publicized and is familiar (at least in passing) to some of the public.

It is possible for other issues, including economic matters, to galvanize the public's attention and stir opposition, but core questions of rights generate the most critical opposition. As Mary Anne Glendon chronicles in her book *Rights Talk,* Americans have a tendency to transform social controversies into a clash of rights, the result of which is "an absolutist formulation of rights at the expense of compromise."[77] By compromise Glendon means a resolution of the zero-sum debates between opposing combatants, but rights cases also threaten the legitimacy of legal rules set forth by the courts. To the extent the parties and observers see an issue through the frame of "exaggerated absoluteness,"[78] they are less likely to accept a decision with which they disagree.

Scholars of judicial impact have observed this phenomenon for years, concluding that judicial declarations of controversial rights often generate serious opposition to the courts' injunctions.[79] But impact analysis tends to contrast legal decisions that are followed with those that are not, leaving us without a vocabulary to explain what "the law" is when people reject case law, particularly decisions from the Supreme Court. In a sense, the findings from impact studies state an obvious truth—that when people reject judicial precedent they envision a different notion of law that they insert as the controlling legal or constitutional norm in the situation. Put another way, a legal norm exists, it's just not one decreed by the courts. Consider, again, the aftermath of *Brown I* in many parts of the country. The Supreme Court may have overruled *Plessy v. Ferguson* and ordered school desegregation, but one could hardly look at the actual response on the ground and believe that the constitutional norm handed down by the Court—that segregated schools were neither equal nor acceptable—had supplanted existing understandings and practices. Instead, many people went right on believing that segregation was perfectly acceptable.

To some this may sound like the most epistemological and abstract premise—that law or constitutional norms may exist in the absence of controlling authority. How can we believe that law exists, or that people understand the constitutional norm to follow, unless legislatures, courts, or executive agencies hand down rules, decisions, and regulations? From the earliest time law has been based on concrete and sometimes sacred texts. What I am proposing is law in the absence of formal law, constitutional norms apart from specific wording in the Constitution or controlling language in judicial decisions.

The idea is not as strange as it may sound. Commentator Jonathan Rauch has advanced the notion of "hidden law," which he calls "the norms, conventions, implicit bargains and folk wisdoms that organize social expectations, regulate everyday behavior, and manage interpersonal conflicts." For example, until recently "hidden law regulated assisted suicide," he says, "and it did so with an almost miraculous finesse. Doctors helped people to die, and they often did so without the express consent of anybody. The decision was made by patients and doctors and families in an irregular fashion, and crucially, everyone pretended that no decision had ever been made."[80] Admittedly, Rauch's concept of hidden law might be interpreted by others as simply social norms. But what makes hidden law different from social practices is that, like formal legal mechanisms, hidden law helps to establish rights between and against individuals. The stakes are often higher, too. These are not questions of etiquette—the social practice of covering one's nose while sneezing, for instance. Acts of etiquette may reflect social expectations, and some may even be enforced by informal mechanisms like shaming, but where etiquette sets the aspirations of social practices, hidden law establishes the minimum level of rights and liberties that people have against one another *apart from* those formally established by government. What Rauch aims to say is that, notwithstanding formal statutes that punished the taking of life, a hidden law existed in which relatives, doctors, and (hopefully) patients understood that a terminal patient's life could be ended if he were suffering. In effect, there was an informally understood and socially practiced right to die.

The ability of hidden law to construct rights and liberties calls to mind the U.S. Constitution, a formal document that is the highest law of the land and that establishes much of the legal relationship between citizen and government. Yet, just as formal law has a corollary in hidden law, the actual Constitution and its amendments must compete for legitimacy and control with an informal and popularly held view of constitutional rights and norms. I call this concept *mass constitutionalism,* which is contrasted with the formal manifestations of constitutional law, the Constitution and its amendments, as well as judicial decisions interpreting the document. Like hidden law, mass constitutionalism is a stable of popularly held beliefs about constitutional rights, a series of norms, understandings, and expectations about the meaning and reach of constitutional law that governs throughout civil society.

The notion that a powerful mass consciousness of constitutional rights exists apart from the Constitution finds support in the work of Patricia Ewick and Susan Silbey, who distinguish between legality, which is a "constellation of values, norms, concepts, [and] practices that circulate within in a culture,"[81] and formal law. According to Ewick and Silbey, legality is law uncoupled from legal institutions, encompassing "the meanings, sources of authority, and cultural practices that are commonly recognized as legal, regardless of who employs them or for what ends. In this way, people may invoke and enact legality in ways neither approved nor acknowledged by the law." By contrast, law refers specifically "to aspects of legality as it is employed by or attributed to formal institutions and their actors."[82]

The classic example from Ewick and Silbey is the person who puts a chair in the snow after shoveling out his car, a claim of exclusive use that is respected by others who refuse to challenge the chair by parking in the open spot. As the authors explain:

> The chair signals to the neighborhood a type of ownership. In doing so, it often elicits the same sorts of deference or respect accorded more conventional types of property (i.e., the neighbors park elsewhere). Similarly, the violation or transgression of this property may lead to conflicts and disputes more commonly associated with property as it is formally defined by the legal system (i.e., informal claims of trespass). Without naming the concepts of constructive or adverse possession, the person placing the chair in a clearing among mounds of snow implicitly invokes conventional justifications for property on the basis of investment and labor. . . . Yet property here is construed very differently than its doctrinal sense demands or would allow. Even without registered deeds and titles, stamps and seals, the law is both present and absent in organizing social interactions on [this street].[83]

Rauch would classify these practices as hidden law, reflecting the social expectations that "regulate everyday behavior and manage interpersonal conflicts."[84] Are they formal law? No, since none of the parties must invoke statutes or court decisions, nor do the participants require legal representatives (e.g., police officers, lawyers, judges) to establish the property expectations of those involved. Rather, drivers reach a common understanding of the shoveler's earned "legal" interests. These understandings are legal, in that they represent acceptance of the rights and privileges of individuals against each other.

How, then, do law and legality differ from the formal Constitution and mass constitutionalism? In some ways the latter pair is a subset of the former. That is, if law refers to formal depictions and enforcement of legal norms—statutes, court decisions, speeding tickets, and such—then "the Constitution" covers one aspect of formal law, the constitutional document and various decisions outlining its terms. Similarly, mass constitutionalism would include those cultural practices and meanings that involve subjects covered by the Constitution. Just as a driver might put a chair in the snow to stake his claim regardless of the law's sanction, a public official might post the Ten Commandments in government offices because people should "govern in the name of God."[85] "Without naming the concepts of" religious free exercise or the countervailing tensions of religious establishment found in the Bill of Rights, the person posting the Ten Commandments "implicitly invokes conventional justifications" for the influence of religion on government administration.[86] Put another way, if legality encompasses a constellation of legal norms, then mass constitutionalism might simply reflect cultural practices of constitutional rights and principles.

Ewick and Silbey see legality as an overarching concept with popular practices and formal adjudication each reflecting a society's norms and understandings. Although this notion has resonance for constitutional norms, the constitutional dimension represents a more bifurcated process where the formal document sometimes is said to be the controlling concept itself. Thus, mass constitutionalism is a distinct and reciprocal alternative to the formal Constitution. Where judicial decrees track social expectations and norms, the formal and mass constitutions are identical. When, however, a critical mass of the public objects to a formal decree, popular constitutionalism diverges from its formal brethren and holds sway. Far from reflecting the absence of law or constitutional principles, mass constitutionalism says that constitutional norms and understandings still exist—they're just different from those handed down by the courts. One may wait to see if the formal law adjusts to changed expectations and understandings of constitutional rights,[87] but if a critical mass of people or institutions refuses to accept and follow a constitutional holding, the mass constitution has prevailed over formal law, as a popular veto has blocked the formal Constitution from acceptance.

It is significant that I call the term mass and not popular constitutionalism. Kramer, who places authority for constitutional construction with the public, titles his work *Popular Constitutionalism*.[88] Although we agree on the locus of power, popular implies a "bottom-up social movement type of activity."[89] Yet, "as Michael Kammen, Stephen Daniels, Michael McCann and Bill Halton, and other scholars have urged, much of what is labeled 'popular' really should be labeled 'mass' to capture its elite, bureaucratic (top-down), etc. dimensions."[90] In many ways, this issue mirrors the Dahl-Ginsburg debate referenced earlier, for popular constitutional understandings may arise organically from the grass roots or be diffused from elites to an accepting public. Because both mechanisms are possible—and because, as will be shown later, elite institutions played a significant role in advancing hate speech regulation—I use the term mass constitutionalism.

What does it mean under this typography for a right to be constitutional—especially one that may exist in opposition to the courts' interpretations of the Constitution? On one level, constitutional rights are defined as those of the people against government. Rights, of course, exist in other avenues of life—the rights of children against their parents, the rights of tenants against landlords—but constitutional rights establish the relationship of citizens and their government. We know, for example, that citizens are free from the government's quartering of troops, that the government may not seize property without due process and just compensation, and that government programs may not differentiate between individuals without at least a rational basis. Each of these rights, firmly established in formal constitutional law, provides protection for, or advantages to, citizens vis-à-vis government. Thus, when people turn to the mass constitution—when, for example, they challenge court decisions—they are rejecting the lines that the formal Constitution has drawn between citizen and government. The criticisms of *Roe v. Wade* and the school busing decisions reflect demands to reconfigure those boundaries. Government must prohibit women from killing unborn babies, abortion opponents say. Government must allow parents to choose their children's school, desegregation's critics inveigh.

MASS CONSTITUTIONALISM AND THE FIRST AMENDMENT

The scope of constitutional rights may also be greater than the four corners of the Constitution's words, showering constitutional connotations and constructions on other relationships that are not technically those between citizen and government. The First Amendment is an excellent example, for people often act as if the formal doctrine covers—or ought to cover—more behavior than it actually does. Of course, the First Amendment applies only to government institutions,[91] but just as some individuals and institutions may adopt legal rules that are not required of them—witness companies that offer family leave even when they are exempt from the statute requiring it, or organizations that offer a smoke-free work place when ordinances only cover restaurants—civil society has extended the reach of the First Amendment by using it as the benchmark for private behavior. In this respect, the First Amendment may be different from other parts of American law. People treat the First Amendment as if the formal law extends outward to control private disputes over free speech. There are plenty of examples of this, where people use language from the First Amendment to describe or defend the behavior of individuals or private institutions. Stanley Fish views this dynamic pejoratively—deriding people who "just yell 'First Amendment rights'" to lionize expression that fails to involve the Constitution[92]—but the First Amendment is not just a refuge for scoundrels here. Chapter 5 describes the behavior of administrators at private colleges and universities, who report that they regularly measure their institutions' policies against the terms of the First Amendment. When Colorado College, a private college, was challenged for inviting a Palestinian activist to campus to commemorate the first anniversary of September 11, its spokesman seemed to suggest that the First Amendment required the appearance.[93] Because First Amendment jurisprudence occupies such a hallowed position in American culture, it is often extended beyond its jurisdictional limits to become a larger, accepted legal norm. "Political, social, cultural, ideological, economic and moral claims . . . that appear to have no special philosophical or historical affinity with the First Amendment, find themselves transmogrified into First Amendment arguments," says noted constitutional scholar Frederick Schauer.[94]

A critical observer might describe such private behavior as representing free speech norms, not constitutional standards. Again, because the scenarios do not pit citizen against government, the private standards are those of free speech, not the formal and legally enforceable ground of constitutional rights. Admittedly, this is a fine line, but the private construction and acceptance of these norms is as much about constitutional law as it is about generic understandings of open discourse, for in these situations people point to, or base their judgments for private activity on, a constitutional provision. These invocations, thus, are not just social norms. They are phrased in rights talk, they are made against institutions, and they find their reference in the Constitution.

The demand to speak one's mind is often phrased as a right—the right to do as one wishes vis-à-vis his fellow citizens. Regardless of whether the claim is directed against government, the speaker seeks to establish his relationship to society and cement the rights he holds against others. These are not simply the social conventions of polite conversation—don't talk back to your mother, say thank you for a compliment. Although both help to establish the bounds of social behavior, speech norms and speech rights are distinguished by the urgency, location, and phrasing of the demands. Speech rights seek to establish the privileges and entitlements that one is owed by the institutions of civil society. In the speech code controversy, for example, proponents seemed to seek protection from the speech of others. Their demands were not calls on government. Rather, actors turned to a prestigious and central institution of civil society—higher education—to make a claim against society as a whole. Racial intolerance had acquired a new life, and if government could not (or would not) respond to a perceived crisis of racist threats, then activists would turn elsewhere for protection.

The process almost resembles one of transference—in which activists make societal claims against nongovernmental institutions instead of the government itself. Nonetheless, the claims are very much rights-based—as people sketch out their place and privileges against others in society. In many cases these "private" demands for speech are founded on popular understandings of the First Amendment. The claims do not develop out of thin air; they flow from or are intricately connected to the First Amendment, which serves as a barometer for free speech across society. As Dennis Chong has found in his research on civil liberties, people often base normative speech judgments on their understandings of the formal, First Amendment rules involved. This was very much true in the debate over college speech restrictions, where, regardless of the public or private status of a school, both proponents and opponents grounded their arguments in the First Amendment.

The relationship between civil society's speech restrictions and the First Amendment's formal jurisprudence covers many topics. As Richard Abel has masterfully documented, there are numerous settings in which speech is restricted without the government's intervention. Internet service providers regulate chat rooms; newspaper editors and advertising executives control content; even "scholarly institutions constrain [the topics for] research."[95] Many of these restrictions turn on mass constructions of the First Amendment, such as when newspaper editors justify controversial stories on the "protections" of a First Amendment that does not compel their editorial judgments.[96] The very fact that people apply their interpretations of the Constitution when creating rules for informal or private discourse suggests that they are socially constructing the First Amendment. At the very least, they are applying the formal doctrine to situations and settings outside of its authority.

The result is a symbiotic relationship in which social construction of the First Amendment influences the document's practical and ultimate meaning, just as formal interpretations of constitutional law prime social applications and constructions. The supposed bright line between formal First Amendment jurisprudence and societal speech norms is not as clear as some commentators suggest, for as Chong reminds us, people may "have difficulty separating their understanding of what the law *is* from their opinion of what the law *should be*."[97] Formal First Amendment jurisprudence may treat public and private speech differently, but the actual practice of speech restrictions, and more importantly the public's tolerance for open discourse throughout civil society, depends in many cases on people's understanding and acceptance of formal First Amendment jurisprudence.

SOCIAL PRESSURES VS. FORMAL INTERVENTION

What I have described so far is a system of law and legal construction that centers both authority and meaning-making outside of formal institutions. My intention is not to disparage the courts or their powers, for the public generally defers to the judiciary's declaration of law. Even when a critical mass opposes a legal decree, the courts still catalyze the legal meaning-making function. Nonetheless, neither the Supreme Court nor the lower courts as a whole are able to control the meaning of constitutional norms, most notably those based on the First Amendment. The courts necessarily rely on societal consensus for public acceptance and legitimacy, but even more, the meaning of law, both private and public, is based on extra-judicial processes. As other scholars have said, "the central norms of the constitutional regime depend for their effectiveness on the attitudes of the political community."[98] "The great battles for free expression will be won not in courts but in committee rooms and protest meetings, by editorials and letters to Congress and through the courage of citizens everywhere."[99]

One reason extra-judicial processes have so much influence over legal meaning is that democratic societies are constantly balancing social pressures with judicial intervention to enforce behavioral norms. As Franklyn Haiman explains, "A free society will always draw the line between what it considers immoral and what it makes illegal as close as possible to the more serious, direct, immediate, and physical of the harms, and it will leave to the operations of social pressure, education and self-restraint the control of behaviors whose harms to others is less serious, less direct, less immediate, and less physical."[100]

Put another way, the most clear, recognized moral wrongs[101] will be codified into law and enforced through the judicial system, but social pressures will be left to handle those issues that, while objectionable to many, are not so universally recognized as wrong. Here a diagram may be helpful. In the figure below, the center circle represents codified law, covering conduct widely accepted as wrong. The middle ring reflects the informal or hidden law that Jonathan Rauch has described—those social expectations and understandings of morality that regulate behavior. While there is agreement that particular behavior is immoral or improper, these views are not codified into law; either the consensus is not sufficiently strong or there is a sense that informal mechanisms are effective at enforcing the social norm. The outer ring then represents moral views that have not yet achieved societal support but maintain a constituency that seeks their acceptance and eventual codification. The relative size of the spheres reflects the number of norms that may exist in each region, not the extent to which they are controlling or powerful. It is axiomatic that a greater number of moral perspectives exist in society than ever achieve a critical level of acceptance. Similarly, as Rauch convincingly argues, formal law need not codify each of the various understandings and expectations that order social behavior.

Spheres of Formal Law and Social Pressure

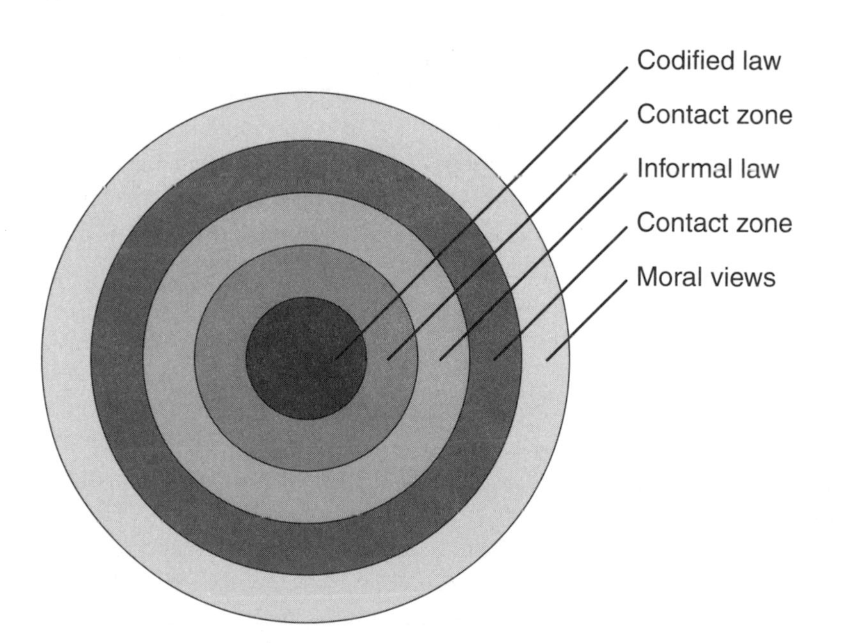

Under this typography, murder, rape, and business fraud would all fall in the center circle; there is little disagreement that each of these actions is grossly improper, and as such, we as a society prohibit them by codified law. By contrast, sexual fraud would probably fall in the middle circle. While many agree it is improper to induce another into bed on false pretenses, we do not have sufficient consensus that these acts should be legally actionable;[102] instead, we try to discourage these offenses by social pressure. The outer circle, then, includes such measures as complete gambling bans. Even if several groups believe that gambling is dangerous or immoral, there is far from societal agreement to eradicate gambling, whether informally by discouraging church bingo games or more formally by criminalizing the slots.[103] As the United States has learned from prohibition, some of the vices decried by both political and religious leaders actually find a sizeable constituency.

The same typography works if we think of the rings as representing aspects of constitutional law. Here the center ring is the formal constitution, the middle ring is mass constitutionalism, and the outer ring represents constitutional views that do not command a critical mass of support. So, for example, one might find *R.A.V. v. City of St. Paul,* in the center circle, the Supreme Court having declared that public bodies may not pick and choose among particular messages when banning hate speech. Nonetheless, as chapter 5 claims, there is now a critical mass of support in civil society to informally regulate hate speech, particularly those messages that target a recipient's race or ethnicity. For this reason, mass constitutionalism conflicts with the formal constitutional norm, representing a situation in which the practical, societal effect is to limit hate speech in everyday life even though formal constitutional law urges otherwise. The outer ring, then, would include proposals to regulate hate speech against bases other than race or gender, perhaps political affiliation. Although some would claim that *any* hate speech weakens the social fabric, the prevailing view eschews and enjoins those verbal attacks that target immutable characteristics, especially traits that historically have been the subject of abuse or discrimination.

What separates codified law from informal law, and what lies between informal law and moral views, is a realm I call the contact zone. This is where advocacy, mobilization, and diffusion take place in a free society, as various interests battle it out to enshrine their moral views into the public's consciousness and ultimately into formal law. The outer contact zone, that between moral views and informal law, reflects social diffusion more than organized mobilization. Psychologists might call the process one of contagion, whereby a behavior pattern, attitude, or emotion is spread from person to person or group to group through suggestion, propaganda, rumor, or imitation.[104] Sociologists, too, would root norm diffusion in network analysis, tracking how new ideas are replicated between social groups, eventually achieving "traction" in the public's consciousness.[105] Paul DiMaggio and Walter Powell, for example, examine isomorphic forces like mimicry that explain why people or organizations seek to follow or adopt the norms of others.[106] At the popular level, Malcolm Gladwell's book *The Tipping Point* offers an easily understood model in which information brokers, whom he describes as "mavens," interact with "connectors," those who are highly influential across communities, to spread ideas or behaviors. Context matters in Gladwell's theory—as it does in other models of norm diffusion—for an idea that may be irresistible at one time or place may be rejected under different circumstances.

Political scientists might tinker a bit with these theories to introduce the notion of advocacy into the model. As people seek to establish their moral views in informal law, they may organize to push their agenda. Before becoming embroiled in the public airing of his own gambling habit, former Education Secretary Bill Bennett was known for his crusade-of-sorts to bring virtue to political and social behavior. Apart from specific legislation or case law—which Bennett certainly advocates—he has also pushed for "moral clarity" in personal behavior and social norms, including such topics as patriotic zeal, the centrality of the nuclear family, and the decline of standards in education.[107] What he and others like him seek to do—regardless of their ideological perspective—is to convince others throughout civil society to accept their perspective on questions of morality and informal law or rights.

Presuming that an idea achieves a critical mass of social acceptance, its activists may seek to enshrine this view in the codified law. Doing so implicates the inner contact zone, a sphere recognizable as traditional political mobilization and legislative or judicial activism. Rather than just directing their efforts to society as a whole, activists take their case directly to the organs of government. Litigation is filed, lobbyists corner legislators, all in the interests of formally changing law. Together they advance a common theme—that a matter is so serious, and its perspective so widely accepted, that government must take action to prohibit certain behavior or legally recognize other interests.

Of course, some groups lobby before their perspectives have achieved acceptance in hidden law, and legislators and courts may respond to causes that are not broadly backed. But it is still unusual to expect government action on behalf of proposals that do not have a sufficient level of mainstream support, for codification generally turns on popular acceptance and organized mobilization. Drunk driving provides a good example, as Mothers Against Drunk Driving (MADD) fought it out in the contact zone to codify its views into law. Up until the founding of MADD, impaired driving was loosely enforced, as drunk drivers were often let off with a slap on the wrist. In essence, the judicial system was willing to relegate the oversight of drunk driving to social pressures. But MADD came on the scene arguing to legislators and judges that drunk driving was morally on par with homicide. Drunk driving ought to be so universally condemned, they said, that its practice deserved serious legal punishment.[108] Through MADD's hard work, most states have adopted this view and have strengthened their drunk driving laws.

Activists may target both attitude change and codified law simultaneously, but the more likely trend is for people to build a base of support before seeking policy change. In some cases it's almost an unconscious process, as people seek to build networks and create social acceptance for their views. Only after they reach a certain threshold of support do most activists go about testing their numbers and power by seeking to enshrine their views in the codified law. At this point they may be in for a rude awakening—that their numbers are nowhere near as great as they believe, and that by extension they must concentrate on changing popular attitudes before they seek legal reform. The gay rights movement is a good example here, where the seventeen years between *Bowers v. Hardwick* and *Lawrence v. Texas* may be explained by the movement's understanding that it was best to wait to achieve social acceptance for homosexuals before activists petitioned the U.S. Supreme Court to formally recognize gay privacy rights.

In some cases, groups are able to begin their quest for formal legal change from the sphere of moral views, jumping over the necessity of popular support to gain a toehold in statute or case law. Arguably, this occurred in the early civil rights movement, where activists achieved victory in *Brown v. Board of Education* before much of the country was prepared to accept the Supreme Court's decisions. Of course, the civil rights movement was hardly an unfamiliar idea in 1954—indeed, President Truman had already desegregated the armed forces[109]—but it would be a stretch to say that civil rights had achieved social acceptance at the time of *Brown*. So too, the women's movement serendipitously obtained legal protection from Congress under Title VII at a time when neither the general public nor most of Congress itself was committed to gender equality.[110]

These achievements notwithstanding, there is still a great deal of debate about whether social change is best achieved by vaulting popular opinion to seek the protection of the courts or other government agencies or waiting to generate greater popular support before petitioning government. Certainly, there is a long history of advocacy groups like the National Association for the Advancement of Colored People (NAACP) and the National Abortion Rights Action League (NARAL) appealing to receptive courts to win legal protection, but at the same time scholars like Rosenberg and Wendy Brown claim that activists would be more effective in the long run by focusing on legislative action and public opinion.[111] Regardless of who is correct, it is evident that activists choose both paths. Although infrequent, it is possible that activists may succeed in convincing legislators or judges to adopt a formal course of action before sufficient support develops in civil society. Moreover, as was argued earlier, the decisions rendered by traditional organs of government flow back to civil society where individuals and institutions may accept or reject these dictates. To the extent that activists can trade on the legitimacy of the Supreme Court and encourage other institutions to implement the Court's decisions, they may succeed in changing social norms and expectations by invoking the formal law. Normally, though, neither the legal nor political branches are likely to get out front of popular opinion. For the individuals or groups that seek to enshrine their views of morality or rights, the ultimate battleground is civil society.

EXTRA-JUDICIAL LEGAL MOBILIZATION

This depiction of legal or social change is one that would have been discounted by many scholars as recently as twenty-five years ago. Writing in 1983, Frances Zemans explained that "the political science perspective on the law has remained the same." Whether "the terminology is 'social change' or 'social control,'" the discipline presumes that legal change "is unidirectional, emanating from state actors and imposed upon the citizenry." Since that time both legal mobilization and social movement theory have evolved to explain bottom-up activism. As Zemans defines it, legal mobilization is "the process by which . . . desires or wants are transformed into demands as an assertion of rights."[112]

"[M]uch of the best known work [of legal mobilization] has focused attention primarily on mobilization of the law by individuals seeking resolution of mostly 'private' disputes," says noted mobilization scholar Michael McCann.[113] McCann and scholars like him have recently extended legal mobilization theory to group activities, trying to understand how individuals collectively come to envision their needs or wants as warranting legal or political rights. But even so, most of the research has looked at the workings of social movements, particularly those led by a central social movement organization,[114] focusing on traditional movement activities such as "legislative lobbying, informal negotiation, collective bargaining, or mass demonstration."[115] This is the inner contact zone of the model discussed earlier. Whether activists choose litigation or lobbying, the presumption is that actors will take their demands for legal change to government institutions. Even when movements eschew traditional political channels for popular protest, they may pressure law-making institutions into adopting their agendas.[116]

By contrast, a theory of mass constitutionalism envisions legal mobilization that takes place outside of traditional legal settings and often by decentered social movements. This view finds some initial support from Zemans, who acknowledges that "[d]efining legal mobilization as the act of invoking legal norms to regulate behavior is purposively broad enough to include the earliest stage of legal activity."[117] Adds McCann, "legal practices and rights discourses are not limited to formal state forums."[118] "Efforts to create and give meaning to norms, through a language of rights, often and importantly occur outside formal legal institutions such as courts . . . (and constitute) an activity engaged in by nonlawyers as well as by lawyers and judges."[119] Indeed, "legal mobilization is generated not [only] by the writing of new laws, but by changing social perceptions of the nature of a problem and the appropriateness of the intervention of state authority."[120]

The process of changing social perceptions falls squarely into the outer contact zone, in which individuals and groups advance their perspectives of rights, morality, and hidden law on the public at large. To the extent that activists seek rights, their demands have a legal cast, a connection that is firmly cemented when actors invoke or reference the Constitution. Yet the process is one of extra-judicial mobilization, for the "activism" addresses attitudes and behavior more than it does formal law. People are transforming their desires or wants into demands for rights, which they make on civil society as a whole. Activists may stage media events, publish books or manifestos, or otherwise target prestigious nongovernmental institutions to advance particular norms or rights.

I call such activism extra-judicial legal mobilization, or EJLM, the process by which people mobilize for legal change outside of the formal law. EJLM blends elements from both legal mobilization and political activism. Like traditional legal mobilization it recognizes that activists may mobilize law and seek to change it, while similar to political activism it addresses legal activity that takes place outside of the courts.

EJLM not only focuses attention on extra-judicial activities, but it also suggests a more informal mechanism for mobilization. This is not traditional social movement theory in which a central movement organization directs activities. There need not exist an NAACP or NARAL to coordinate activists. Rather, mobilization in EJLM is more of a "mind meld," reflecting contemporaneous, collective beliefs *and* action *or* advocacy to advance legal change. As John McCarthy and Mayer Zald explain, a movement may encompass "a set of opinions and beliefs in a population which represents preferences for changing some elements of the social structure and/or reward distribution of a society."[121]

Movements arise when people who see themselves as connected develop beliefs for social change and are willing to voice those views with an eye toward changing public attitudes. This is not to say that social movements fail to involve *action;* to the contrary, most social movements eventually take up protests or organized appeals. But an advantage of EJLM is that it focuses on the nascent movement, when people who dislike existing law or social structures begin to connect with others who share their views. The fact that these collective beliefs exist throughout society, and that proponents see themselves as somehow connected, means that the political or legal status quo is under potential threat. Over time activists may take their demands to the realm of formal law, but at first their path is to argue for their own legitimacy and seek respect and support for their views. Indeed, if political or legal processes remain closed to their interests, activists may satisfy themselves with changes in the hidden law.[122]

EXTRA-JUDICIAL LEGAL MOBILIZATION AND OPPOSITION TO COLLEGE HATE SPEECH CODES

The prospect of extra-judicial legal mobilization and its potential influence on informal law and mass constitutionalism suggest that the true force for social or legal change may come from within civil society as activists turn their sights on popular opinion and seek to win over or co-opt influential institutions. Mobilization like this—seeking to change attitudes and mass practices that construct legal norms—may do more to affect the actual meaning of legal rights than by litigating to win the courts' approval.

In many ways this prospect drove the speech code debate—at least the opponents' reactions suggested as much. Although some critics claim that they were concerned only with the practices of public colleges and universities, a closer examination of their advocacy reflects a greater concern with censorship and thought control across all of academe. In this respect, the codes' opponents seem to have understood the potential influence of hate speech regulation on mass constitutionalism. The threat was not limited to formal, First Amendment doctrine, although, to be sure, some critical race scholars hinted at such goals. Rather, the greater fear was that the codes might indoctrinate new generations of college graduates, convincing opinion leaders and perhaps the public at large that free speech must give way to punish hateful messages. Indeed, the critics' heated response seemed designed not so much to convince the courts to hold the line on the First Amendment but to urge the public to reject any encroachment on free speech.

To the opponents of free speech regulation, the drive for college hate speech policies would undoubtedly have resembled a movement—an extra-judicial movement that threatened the legal norms of free speech, if not formal constitutional law itself. First, by their very terms, many of the speech codes challenged constitutional doctrine. It is not just that the codes equated expression with a "speech act," claiming that verbal attacks represented "a mechanism of subordination reinforcing a historical vertical relationship,"[123] but many of the policies engaged in what the courts would have, and did, deride as viewpoint discrimination. At Michigan the speech code prohibited expression that "stigmatized" or "victimized" others on the basis of race. At Mt. Holyoke students could be disciplined for "jokes . . . related to an individual's personal background or attributes." At Wisconsin racially demeaning speech was forbidden. Whether at public or private schools, these policies refused to accept a constitutional rule that permitted intimidating and hateful speech.

Second, the codes were linked in the press to a group of prolific and articulate "outsider" scholars who themselves were pushing to reshape the constitutional balance between free speech and equality. Regardless of whether these academicians were the true authors of the policies, their scholarship seemed connected to the speech policies. The quartet of Mari Matsuda, Richard Delgado, Charles Lawrence, and Kimberle Crenshaw, for example, urged the courts to replace "neutral principles" in the law with "formal legal rules . . . to eliminate the effects of oppression, including affirmative action, reparations, desegregation, and the criminalization of racist and misogynist propaganda."[124] Matsuda, in particular, offered a three-part proposal to ban racist speech "of racial inferiority . . . directed against a historically oppressed group . . . [which] endorses or implements persecution, hatred or degradation of the group."[125]

That said, there are reasons to doubt whether outsiders actually led the speech code campaign (a point taken up in greater detail in the next chapter). None of these scholars were activists, at least not in the sense of traditional mobilization. They did not organize, lobby, or litigate. A Lexis search of the three most prominent critical race scholars—Matsuda, Delgado, and Lawrence—finds but six court cases (other than *Doe* and *UWM Post*) from 1986 to 1998 in which their names were cited.[126] In only one of these cases, *Doe v. Hartz,* do such scholars turn up as a litigant, attorney, or amicus curiae, and even then it is Matsuda joining a list of faculty arguing that the Violence Against Women Act is constitutional. Nor was it just Matsuda, Delgado, and Lawrence. The proponents of hate speech regulation did not organize politically, nor did they follow the example from sexual harassment law and litigate to limit racist speech. To the contrary, when the hate speech codes appeared in litigation or congressional hearings it was the work of their opponents, who tried to convince lawmakers that the codes were a dangerous experiment and that either the courts or Congress needed to step in to halt the spread of political correctness.

Why then would the codes' critics fight policies that might literally have been an academic exercise? Precisely because they realized the influence of academe over American social life and mass constitutionalism. Much of the antiwar protest in the 1960s originated on college campuses, and colleges and universities proved receptive venues for civil rights and women's rights activism. Academic research can grab the attention of opinion leaders, raising some issues to the national agenda. Moreover, the ideas introduced in collegiate settings can influence succeeding generations of American leaders who become acquainted with these perspectives and proposals while at college. In short, the codes' opponents had much to fear from campus activism and legal mobilization. If academe—a venue that zealously prizes open inquiry—could restrict offensive speech, then others who looked to the academy's lead might follow. What the opposition presciently understood was that this fight was for control of the public's understanding and acceptance of free speech norms. It was, one might say, the ultimate exercise in the social construction of law.

The Rise of Hate Speech Codes

For all the controversy about college hate speech codes, few people have been able to say how prevalent they really were, nor have many studies investigated the forces behind the speech codes. Milton Heumann, Thomas Church, and David Redlawsk have done a fine job of chronicling developments at a few schools, and John Arthur and Amy Shapiro provide a broad overview of controversial issues confronting American colleges.[1] At the same time, Dinesh D'Souza offers a screed against "Illiberal Education" in academe, and Alan Kors and Harvey Silverglate, of course, purport to have uncovered a "politically correct worldview" of censorship on college campuses.[2]

As should be obvious by now, I have serious concerns with the work of D'Souza and Kors and Silverglate, for they appear to base broad and polemical conclusions on limited and potentially biased data. This is not to say that their views must be wrong—although I suspect they are—rather that it is difficult to evaluate the credibility of their claims. D'Souza relies largely on the experiences of five schools to make his contentions, and Kors and Silverglate base their book on reports they have received from aggrieved students and their advocates. Even accepting that these reports are true, the two authors cannot estimate how prevalent the offenses were or if they have taken place at a wide swath of schools.

The research presented here starts from a different premise, utilizing a compilation of empirical methods to estimate the number of schools that adopted various hate speech policies and investigating the potential influences that spawned such measures. As the appendix details, the work includes quantitative analysis and qualitative and archival research. Some of the findings are based on interviews, but in each case the stories told are illustrative of larger patterns found in the research.

Together, the findings paint a richer and subtler understanding of the college hate speech codes, uncovering a diverse set of policies and detailing the divergent motives that led to their adoption. In the end, this chapter questions the perceived "tidal wave" of draconian speech policies, suggesting instead that both the number of policies and their prohibitions were more modest. It also disputes the traditional explanation of the speech policies as told by their opponents. Although the speech codes were primed by the civil rights and women's rights movements and connected to racial unrest on campus, their adoption owes more to college administrators acting on instrumental motives than to mobilized constituencies or identity politics.

PREVALENCE OF COLLEGE HATE SPEECH CODES

A good place to begin is estimating the number of schools that adopted hate speech codes. A 1991 ABC *Nightline* program put the number at 125, although a year earlier other publications calculated that 137 colleges had created such policies. Even if the true number lies somewhere in between, these reports place speech codes at less than 10 percent of American colleges and universities, hardly evidence of a full-throated political or legal movement.

The difficulty in assessing these estimates is that they come from anecdotal reports. By contrast, as table 3.1 shows, an empirical calculation provides a more expansive picture. Using a random, stratified sample of 100 four-year schools, the data suggest that nearly one-third of American colleges and universities adopted a hate speech code between 1987 and 1992.[3] (The appendix provides a full explanation of sampling mechanisms.) Of these, 1 percent of institutions adopted policies against fighting words, 15 percent banned generic verbal harassment, 14 percent prohibited verbal harassment against groups, and 4 percent punished offensive speech.

The empirical results tell us many things, the evaluation of which depends in some sense on one's perspective. On the one hand, the clear majority of schools failed to adopt a hate speech policy, a sign perhaps that the move to speech codes was not overwhelming. On the other hand, it is significant that a third of American colleges adopted some kind of speech policy. Nearly 500 schools initiated speech policies, and within four to five years of one another, a collective dynamic of sorts that warrants closer scrutiny.

Table 3.1. Estimated Number of Four-Year Schools with Hate Speech Policies, 1987–92 (range at 95 percent confidence level)

Type of Speech Policy	Estimated Number	Estimated Percent
No speech policy	897	65
Fighting words	14	1
Verbal harassment	207	15
Verbal harassment of groups	193	14
Offensive speech	55	4

Note: Due to rounding, percentages do not sum to 100.

Still, the results show that it is a misnomer to speak of a typical "hate speech code." Certainly, the term hate speech has been batted about in popular discussions, but not all speech codes are alike, nor did they each present the same constitutional concerns. The policies need to be examined on a continuum, seeking to evaluate each category of restriction against prevailing First Amendment norms. In this respect, it makes more sense to condense the speech policies into three or four groups for comparison. On one end of the spectrum would be those schools that did not adopt any speech policies. By definition, these schools did not trample free speech, for they took no action. The next two steps, fighting words and verbal harassment, just skirted constitutional concerns, taking refuge in two lines of cases that permit limited speech restrictions. According to *Chaplinsky v. New Hampshire,* public entities may prohibit words "which by their very utterance inflict injury or tend to incite an immediate breach of the peace."[4] Over time the courts have cut the definition of fighting words in half, forbidding only those words that "incite an immediate breach of the peace,"[5] but the prohibition presumably still exists. In addition, there exists a common law category of harassment, which itself is a narrow, subjective basis to restrict expression.[6]

The next most respective category of speech policy, verbal harassment of groups, would contradict current constitutional norms. In the 1992 case of *R.A.V. v. City of St. Paul,* the U.S. Supreme Court ruled that public bodies could not punish particular hateful messages while leaving others untouched. But at the time that the speech codes initially arose—between 1987 and 1992—the constitutionality of group harassment policies was uncertain. Indeed, the fact that the Supreme Court heard *R.A.V.* suggests that the law on this question was ambiguous, thus necessitating the Court's final determination.

There was no such uncertainty, however, for the final category of speech codes, those that prohibited offensive expression. Years earlier the courts had ruled offensive expression constitutionally protected, forbidding public bodies from censoring such speech. Whether judges believed that offensive expression had its own merit (by introducing controversial ideas into public debate) or simply felt that the term "offensive" was overbroad or vague, the law was clear on this subject: offensive expression could not be restricted.[7]

To claim, then, that college hate speech policies violated the Constitution and First Amendment is itself an overstatement. Only those schools that adopted offensive speech restrictions truly challenged existing constitutional standards as of 1987. Of course, *R.A.V.* redrew constitutional boundaries in 1992, the justices ruling that prohibitions on verbal harassment of groups must fall. But even so the two categories of prohibited speech codes encompassed just 18 percent of American colleges and universities. Nor is this the full picture, for private schools are free from the First Amendment and may choose to adopt any speech restrictions they choose.[8] If one exempts private institutions from the ranks of unconstitutional speech policies, the set of unlawful college codes narrows considerably. Under this analysis, only 1.5 percent of American colleges and universities adopted unconstitutional policies prohibiting offensive expression. Even adding public schools that proscribed verbal harassment of groups, just 9 percent of schools could be said to have transgressed the First Amendment.

Is it really possible that the hate speech controversy was fought over 9, or even 1 percent of American colleges and universities? Did the opposition truly arise to oppose those policies that formally breached the First Amendment? Fifteen years later, some of the leading opponents of the speech policies seem to claim so. In a November 2002 interview with the *Washington Post Magazine,* Thor Halvorssen of the Foundation for Individual Rights in Education (FIRE), said that his organization "doesn't oppose private college speech codes if the rule makers are honest about them." By this, Halvorssen means that private schools are free to create rules by which their members may voluntarily associate. At public schools, by contrast, restrictive speech policies "are manifestly unconstitutional."[9]

The trouble with Halvorssen's comment is that it ignores the tenor of the early speech code debate. The codes' opponents did not confine themselves to the "legal technicalities" of college hate speech policies. Casting their gaze across the whole of American academe, opponents challenged the codes because they feared a breakdown in free expression, because they saw a looming "thought control" championed by self-appointed academic censors. Might one find similar language in First Amendment cases protecting speech? Absolutely. In fact, many consider the First Amendment to be the last bulwark against censorship and the loss of free thought. Yet the First Amendment was technically inapplicable to several of the college speech codes. Why, then, would its name be spoken in the hate speech debate, why would advocates draw from its history of jurisprudence to oppose speech codes, whether at public or private schools? Because of the very relationship between the Constitution and mass constitutionalism. As advocates came to recognize, the speech codes threatened the First Amendment's persuasive reach, an influence found not only in the doctrine's technical application but also in its public comprehension and use.

WHY DID THE CODES DEVELOP? A CRITIC'S THEORY OF MOBILIZATION

By now the opponents' objections to college hate speech codes have been well chronicled. Fearing an end to open discourse and the imposition of political correctness, critics challenged the speech codes for attempting to alter the balance of First Amendment jurisprudence. Opponents perceived a whirlwind of political activism spreading across American campuses, as bands of progressive activists rose up at many campuses to instill new rules of intellectual and social engagement. Ultimately, the critics said, hate speech codes were designed to reshape popular acceptance of the relationship between free speech and social equality, with free expression forced to bend when hateful messages disenfranchised historical minorities. If activists could succeed in higher education—a socially influential institution—the thinking was that they might also persuade the courts to go along with the new balance. At the very least, the codes would influence successive waves of college students, who would graduate having been socialized to the new norms of speech regulation.

Although their objections are clear, it has been difficult at times to deduce the opponents' explanation for the rise of hate speech policies. George Will, for example, has blamed dispirited liberals for the speech codes, saying national political defeats led progressives back to the Ivory Tower where they crafted new, restrictive measures. Dinesh D'Souza has drawn on this vision, decrying a new orthodoxy that arose on college campuses, much of it tied to progressive thinkers who sought to establish their political agenda in academic thought. And, of course, Alan Kors and Harvey Silverglate believe that multiculturalism and postmodernism have led to "censorship, double standards, and a judicial system without due process"[10] on campus.

What ties these and other explanations together is the critics' use of mobilization and diffusion rhetoric. None of the codes' opponents, and almost none of the news stories about the codes, viewed the policies as coincidental or isolated measures limited to individual campuses. Rather, the commentaries read as if observers were watching a storm move across the nation, raining down speech policies as it passed over new campuses. This was no mere tempest, say opponents, for its aim was to reshape popular understandings of free speech. When the storm clouds cleared, critics feared that the squall would leave a mass of changed expectations in its wake.

The critics' depiction of the speech code campaign is an interesting and provocative thesis, but by itself it is missing several parts. Who were the movement's leaders? How did they organize or network with each other? What triggered their activism? Of course, commentators were not looking to build a theory of social activism, rather to counter the rise of speech restrictions. But is it possible to construct a more detailed model that reflects their charge of campus activism?

Such a model must begin with the critics' notion of an organized campaign, campus activism merging both legal and political mobilization. On one level, critics posited political motives and goals for the speech code campaign. According to George Will and others, the codes owed their inception to progressive activists, dispirited liberals who aimed to accomplish on campus what they could not in national civil rights policy. But on a different level, the model was one of legal mobilization. Activists were not simply looking to change policies or political alliances, critics charged, they had their sights set on American legal norms, indeed the most sacrosanct area—free speech and the First Amendment. If the process had to begin on college campuses, so be it, but the ultimate goal was to change the legal tradition under which discriminatory expression went unchecked.

The picture that emerges from the critics' postulates is a theory of legal mobilization carried out in non-judicial settings, or extra-judicial legal mobilization. This is the model presented in chapter 2 and apparently adopted by the speech codes' opponents. According to critics, activists mobilized to redress discriminatory behavior, they employed legal arguments, and they sought to change legal doctrines. But rather than petitioning the courts, the progressives took their campaign to a non-judicial venue, one that was still open to their interests and where the results they achieved might have real influence on the legal, political, and social worlds around them.

Yet who were these activists? Critics say the organizers were liberals, but can we be more specific about the claim? Might the activists have been liberal, white college administrators, officials who took it upon themselves to adopt policies that protected minorities? Not if one accepts social movement theory, for most movements are led by individuals who aim to benefit directly from the movement.[11] Here that group would likely include African Americans, who have often been prevalent targets of hate speech. To be sure, other racial, ethnic, sexual, and religious minorities have been victimized by bigotry over the years, but none can hold a candle to African Americans, who have faced both hate speech and systemic discrimination. Many of the speech codes were crafted to provide special protection against racist speech, and African Americans had only recently won their formal civil rights. If blacks were concerned about backsliding during the Reagan-Bush years, or if they sought to address the "soft racism" of discriminatory speech, then hate speech codes may have been a useful tool.

It is unlikely, however that African Americans could have enacted speech codes on their own. Comprising a small percentage of academe, blacks would have needed to mobilize allies or "conscience constituents"[12] to advance hate speech rules. Sympathetic supporters might have included other racial and ethnic minorities, women, gays and lesbians, and younger, politically liberal faculty.[13] Certainly, hate speech codes were not limited exclusively to black victims, and other racial minorities might have seen an auxiliary benefit in such policies. So too, feminists might have considered the codes a capstone to sexual harassment rules, confirming that discriminatory expression could be punished. Even gays and lesbians might have joined the cause. Although few speech codes included sexual orientation as a covered category, the gay community nonetheless might have backed the speech code movement as a step toward greater protection for themselves.

Minority activists might have found additional support from liberal, white faculty and administrators, many of whom had reached political consciousness in the 1960s and 1970s and who, by the mid-1980s, were taking positions of power on college faculties and within college administrations. To the extent that liberal whites sought to eradicate racist actions as well as verbal attacks, they would have been natural allies to speech code activists.

One of the tenets of collective behavior is that people do not organize for movement action without connections between the various actors. Theorists describe this in different ways. John Kingdon, for example, has examined the creation of government policy, positing that proponents must see themselves as bonded in a common pursuit.[14] Others emphasize the importance of existing social networks between supporters, claiming that mobilization is easier to initiate if a movement's leaders already have activist experience and/or if its members are already familiar with or connected to one another.[15]

In the case of speech codes, this link may have been provided by the anti-apartheid and divestment movement, which came shortly before hate speech codes arrived on the national scene. Although many of the students behind divestment had graduated by the time of hate speech codes, the links they established may have spurred their successors. At the very least, the divestment movement raised the subject of racial justice on college campuses. It also empowered progressive students and faculty, showing them the collective power they might wield by working together.

Still, if this narrative can posit movement actors and their network of connections, what would have moved them to action? Why would activists have advanced speech restrictions on college campuses, and why in the late 1980s? George Will offers a potential explanation, arguing that activists shared ideological interests, which they believed were under attack at the time. Ideology, however, means something different here than the usual political nomenclature. Although observers have criticized the speech codes as reflecting left-wing liberalism, their charge was not simply that the proponents supported progressive causes or politicians; it was, more, that the activists subscribed to a number of "relativist" political philosophies,[16] including deconstructionism, postmodernism, feminism, critical legal studies, and critical race studies. Divergent as they are, each of these philosophies claims that the world must be evaluated through a lens other than a white male norm. The philosophies are also associated with identity politics—the notion that people will organize based on their shared immutable characteristics.

It is important to distinguish identity politics from what is commonly called "collective rights consciousness—the recognition that problems previously thought to be personal are instead collective and the rising sense of entitlement to relief from those problems."[17] Identity politics is a subset of collective rights consciousness. Mancur Olson, one of the leading theorists of collective action, locates the roots of such rights consciousness in the social dislocation created by industrialization and urbanization during the nineteenth and early twentieth centuries,[18] but a more recent notion ties such consciousness to the rise of legal rights in the late twentieth century and its effect in creating legal expectations.[19]

Regardless of who is right about the rise of rights consciousness, its importance here is in its effects—how it "can help to forge a common identity of experienced victimization and aspiration among diversely marginalized citizens in ways that enhance the prospects of collective organization."[20] Or, put more simply, whether racial, ethnic, or sexual minorities would come to see themselves as linked by their immutable characteristics to rally for policies, measures, or rights that would advance their collective interests. Certainly, political events of the mid-1980s would have given minorities cause to see themselves as connected. As chronicled earlier, both the Reagan administration and the federal courts had shown themselves unreceptive to affirmative action and civil rights legislation; the economic gap between whites and blacks was widening; and national attitudes on racial tolerance had worsened. It is understandable, then, that those who had benefited most personally from civil rights policies would be on edge at the prospect of backsliding. Considering that formal political and legal processes were increasingly closed to progressive interests, it is also conceivable that activists might have retreated to campus, an environment traditionally more receptive to liberal interests, and in this case civil rights and affirmative action.

Nevertheless, as social theorists remind us, the "relationship between being treated badly and taking [political or] legal action is problematic."[21] Even if progressives were disappointed with national political trends, why would they mobilize for campus activism? Why, in particular, would they push for speech restrictions? A potential answer lies in the reports of racial violence that was said to be sweeping the nation's colleges. From the U Mass brawl to attacks at Michigan, Penn State, and the Citadel, these incidents might have unnerved minority students and faculty—not to mention their liberal allies—who may well have organized to protest against the emergence of racist threats.

It is one thing, however, to hold rallies or protests, and another thing entirely to propose measures that restrict speech. Both the civil rights and women's rights movements had focused on racist and sexist actions, not derogatory speech that reflected such prejudice, although by the mid-1980s sexual harassment law had begun to suggest that discriminatory speech was a problem and could be restricted. Indeed, with discriminatory actions already prohibited by the law, activists may have believed that a new, more deliberate approach was required to eradicate discrimination in both thought and deed. Certainly, the critical race theorists advocated as much. Arguing that "neutral principles" of First Amendment jurisprudence served only to "entrench existing power," scholars such as Mari Matsuda, Richard Delgado, and Charles Lawrence called for "legal tools that have a progressive effect"—measures "best implemented through formal rules, formal procedures, and formal concepts of rights . . ." to rebalance the pendulum between unrestrained expression and true racial equality.[22]

Even if the critical race theorists were not the primary activists behind the speech codes, opponents saw their handwriting in the policies. No longer was this some intra-academic initiative to regulate student behavior; the controversy had larger implications on American society and the legal system. If liberal theorists could influence a new wave of college graduates, then successive cohorts of educated elites would sally forth into the halls of influence and power believing that free speech must give way to hate speech restrictions. Even if traditionalists could hold the line in court—preserving the historic preference for relatively unhindered expression—the social practice of free speech might nonetheless change.

A GOOD STORY, BUT DOES IT HOLD UP?

The critics of college hate speech policies offer an intriguing story for the development of these policies, and, while few of the critics were social movement theorists, it is possible to construct a cogent model of progressive mobilization behind the hate speech codes. But does this hypothesis truly explain the development of speech policies? Were the hate speech codes really the work of mobilized activists, those motivated by identity politics? Were the policies actually intended to reshape free speech norms, pushed as they were by adherents of critical race theory? Or, conversely, have the critics confused correlation with causation, the perceived connection between identity politics and critical race theory a mere coincidence? Did other forces or people create the hate speech policies?

There are many ways to investigate the rise of college hate speech codes. The most popular so far has been the case study, tracking the development of antihate policies at individual schools. The approaches include the empirically sound—for example, Milton Heumann, Thomas Church, and David Redlawsk's edited narrative of the experiences at Michigan, Brown, Wisconsin, Dartmouth, and Duke.[23] But all too often anecdotal or superficial reporting has been the norm. Much of the analysis has been left to newspaper or magazine reporters, who, while usually well intentioned, do not have the time to fully investigate the story, let alone to compare one school against another. And, of course, there are polemics like Kors and Silverglate's tome, that, while compiling many different reports, are unable to assess the relative prevalence or power of particular experiences.

The question of hate speech regulation and the resulting controversy over free speech and academic freedom are too important to be left to agenda-driven research or news reports that scratch the surface. In 1994, Vanderbilt University's First Amendment Center sponsored a study of speech policies at public universities, concluding that over 350 schools regulated some form of speech. Yet as helpful as this research was, it represents a single snapshot of hate speech policies, and then only at public schools. Nor were researchers able to estimate the likely sources behind speech codes.

To examine these questions, I undertook research using both quantitative and qualitative methods. With no agenda other than a thorough and empirical assessment of the forces behind hate speech codes, I drew a random, stratified sample of 100 four-year colleges and universities, testing nearly 50 potential, explanatory variables against the rise of hate speech policies. I began with the period 1987–92, reflecting the initial rise of speech codes through the Supreme Court's decision in *R.A.V. v. City of St. Paul,* a case interpreted by many as the death knell of hate speech regulation. The book's appendix describes the details of this methodology for those so interested, but in brief I tested the speech policies in two different ways. First, the speech codes were matched in bivariate relationships with 47 independent variables reflective of the critics' hypothesis as well as several other alternative or complementary theories. Among the variables tested were:

- The percentages of African Americans, Latinos, Asians, and women in a school's student body, faculty, staff, and administration.
- The presence of a minority studies or women's studies program, a law school, or a gay/lesbian organization on campus.
- A school's prestige and selectivity.
- Past anti-apartheid protest on campus.
- Racial or ethnic incidents on campus.
- Conservative activism or support on campus.
- A school's public/private status, its size, religious affiliation, and in-state, part-time, and graduate enrollments.
- The influence of alumni or state legislators.
- The political climate of a school's surrounding community or state.

Where an independent variable proved statistically significant in the bivariate tests, I checked its influence in a series of regressions using both Ordinary Least Squares and Logit. In the latter case I divided the dependent variable into dichotomous pairs of no code/any code and two varying pairs of constitutional codes/unconstitutional codes.[24]

QUANTITATIVE FINDINGS

The bivariate results provide support for *some* of the mobilization model. As table 3.2 shows, 9 of the 47 independent variables tested in bivariate relationships with the speech codes were statistically significant at the .05 level, connecting the speech codes to schools that were prestigious and selective, had experienced anti-apartheid protest, maintained black or minority studies departments, sponsored gay/lesbian organizations, enrolled graduate students and full-time undergraduates, and employed few female faculty. Apart from the curious, negative connection to the percentage of female faculty,[25] these results are consistent with the critics' theory of the speech codes. Hate

Table 3.2. Statistically Significant Relationships between College Hate Speech Codes and Independent Variables*

Variable	Bivariate Relationships (Direction of Relationship)	Univariate Regressions (Direction of Relationship If Any)
Anti-apartheid protest	Positive	Positive
Black studies department	Positive	—
Full-time students	Positive	—
Gay/Lesbian group	Positive	—
Graduate students	Positive	—
Minority studies department	Positive	—
School prestige	Positive	Positive
School selectivity	Positive	—
Women faculty	Negative	—

*Significant at the .05 level. More detailed data are available in the appendix.

speech policies were most prevalent at prestigious, activist institutions, particularly those that offered departmental or organizational affiliations for racial, ethnic, and sexual minorities.

Univariate regression, however, narrowed the potential explanations even further, for only two independent variables were consistently related to the hate speech codes in these tests. As table 3.2 demonstrates, a school's prestige and its experience with anti-apartheid protest each positively predicted the development of hate speech codes. That is, prestigious schools and institutions that had seen divestment protest were more likely than other schools to have created hate speech codes. Other variables were associated with some categories of speech codes. For example, the most restrictive hate speech policies, those prohibiting offensive expression, were also linked to black or minority studies departments, conservative student newspapers, and graduate enrollment. But in examining hate speech codes as a whole, only two factors were consistently connected to the codes—a school's prestige and prior anti-apartheid activism.

These results may give the critics solace, for the findings continue to support some of their hypotheses. There is a distinguished line of research that links a college's prestige to the liberalness of its faculty (and presumably its student body, too).[26] The higher a school's academic prestige, the more likely that its campus culture will be liberal. Accepting this presumption for the moment, the regression results thus put hate speech codes at activist, liberal schools. Like the opponents have long claimed, hate speech regulation may well have been the product of progressive, politicized academicians. At the very least, speech codes were linked to highly visible institutions, those that are known not only for their fine academic reputations but also potentially for past anti-apartheid protest. It is no wonder, then, that the codes at these schools would garner public attention.

Still, the quantitative data have several limitations. As the appendix explains, many of the independent variables are collinear with each other, making it impossible to conduct multivariate regression without extensive factor analysis. But even if the regressions were conducted, the variables already uncovered in table 3.2 fail to identify the likely activists behind the codes. Were these measures pushed by African American faculty or students, by feminists, or by gays and lesbians? The data do not say. There are no positive, statistically significant links between the speech codes and racial minorities, women's activists, or gay or lesbian organizations on campus. The only potential connections are to prior anti-apartheid activism or minority studies programs, but even here the hypothesis must be that a small core of adherents pushed the codes regardless of allied support across campus. Nor, for that matter, do the data suggest that racial or ethnic incidents spurred proponents into action.

The quantitative data, thus, present mixed conclusions. On one hand they lend some credence to the critics' charge of liberal activism. Certainly, there are connections to a school's prestige and liberalness, not to mention its experience with past progressive protest. But to call the speech codes a movement—or to ascribe their rise to mobilization—is premature at best, for there simply are few connections to the groups one would expect in a mobilized effort.

One thing is certain, though. No matter the basis of their adoption, the speech codes failed to respect the traditional constitutional distinction between public and private speech restrictions. According to the quantitative data, private colleges were no more likely than public institutions to adopt hate speech codes, just as public universities were no more likely than private institutions to limit their policies to milder terms. Might this be a powerful clue? Were schools allied to advance new speech norms? Were the lawyers kept out of the process, refused the chance to amend new policies and avoid a collision with the First Amendment? Or were the codes never intended to be enforced, thus rendering their terms almost irrelevant? The possibilities are as many as they are tantalizing.

NARROWING THE SUSPECTS—QUALITATIVE RESEARCH

If this tale were a Sherlock Holmes mystery, the inspector would have gathered a list of potential suspects by now but still lack the likely means. To fill in the details of the speech code story—and most of all, to unmask the actors who pushed for these policies—the account now turns to qualitative research, including both archival research and interviews with faculty, staff, and administrators at several schools within the random sample of 100 colleges and universities. It is important to note that qualitative research is not the same as anecdotal reporting, although at times it can be difficult to distinguish the two. Here, I have selected eight schools for additional study, balancing schools that adopted speech codes with those that did not, as well as comparing schools that shared several of the independent variables associated with the speech codes and those that did not.

Like the quantitative data, much of the research method is described in the book's appendix, although a brief overview may help the reader to assess the results. In each case I combined archival research with direct interviews. I began by utilizing Lexis/Nexis and other online search tools to investigate news coverage of the speech codes at each of the eight schools. Recognizing that certain schools were more likely to receive extensive coverage in major publications than others, I was careful to sample from regional and local media as well. I was also fortunate to receive access to the archives of the National Institute Against Prejudice and Violence, which subscribed to three clipping services in the 1980s and 1990s and had a plethora of news stories about the speech codes at both noted and less known schools. In addition, I ventured to campuses for secondary research, reviewing copies of past campus newspapers, local coverage of campus events, as well as archived deliberations from campus committees, the faculty senate, and relevant administrative offices. Having steeped myself in the chronology of events (and in several cases uncovering memoranda that revealed internal deliberations), I then turned to a series of interviews with faculty, staff, and administrators who were involved in, or familiar with, their campus's consideration of hate speech policies. In this way, the qualitative research should provide a comprehensive account of what happened on these campuses.

One of the natural questions about this research is how definitively the results can be applied to other campuses, or, put another way, can the results I found be generalized? Like any case study, I cannot guarantee that the experiences at these eight schools are similar to other institutions, but they are exceedingly instructive in both amplifying the quantitative data and explaining the rise of college hate speech codes. Moreover, the schools chronicled here were not chosen with any ideological goal in mind. They were selected as representative of the larger sample of 100 colleges and universities, which itself is a random portrait of America's institutions of higher learning.

Some of the eight schools I studied have been chronicled in the national media, and readers may be aware of certain events that occurred at these campuses. Still, I must present the institutions with pseudonyms. Throughout the interviews I offered participants confidentiality, refusing to name them in the finished product or in additional interviews with other participants if they wished. To fulfill this deal I must use monikers for both the individuals and schools involved, forestalling the risk that a quote might be traced back to its source. My goal, of course, is not to be obtuse but rather to respect the promise I made to interviewees. Even with these pseudonyms, the qualitative research tells a compelling story.

SYMBOLIC INSTRUMENTALISM

Like the quantitative data, the qualitative research places hate speech codes at prestigious, progressive institutions with an activist past. But where some might see the speech policies as the work of mobilized liberal activists, the qualitative data suggest that speech codes were advanced by college administrators, top-level officials at that, who were largely acting on utilitarian or instrumental motives. In a few cases students pushed for hate speech policies, but for the most part administrators were motivated by their desire to diffuse racial unrest on campus, to mollify alumni or improve press coverage, or to maintain pace with what they saw as the "mainstream" of American higher education administration. Certainly, some administrators were sincere supporters of the hate speech policies and believed in the aims of speech regulation, but these officials were concentrated more heavily at the bottom of college administrations—and then, most predominantly in student services offices. The higher the level of policy adoption, the more likely that administrators acted on utilitarian motives. Indeed, one might even go so far as to say that the policies were intended as symbolic, perhaps even cynical, measures at some schools, adopted so that officials could say they had taken action against racial intolerance while comfortably assured that the policies would rarely be invoked.

This picture of policy adoption does not ignore the link to prestigious, activist, and liberal campuses, for it is true that hate speech policies were more likely at schools like Michigan, Stanford, Brown, and Wisconsin. But as emblematic as these schools have become in the hate speech controversy, the critics may actually have the story backward. It is not so much that progressive students or faculty mobilized to push ideologically driven speech policies, but that the speech codes were a defensive reaction to likely protests over racial harassment and violence. Whether or not racial incidents were on the rise, they had generated increased attention in the national media, and campus administrators feared heightened news coverage and campus protests if their schools were fingered as harboring a "race problem." It is hardly a stretch to imagine students protesting racial incidents more readily at UCLA than at Hampton-Sydney College. Furthermore, familiar schools like UCLA risked greater news coverage—with all its musings over national trends—if administrators were seen as not "getting out front" on this issue. Hate speech codes thus became a defensive shield of sorts at liberal, activist schools where students and faculty might mobilize over racial intolerance.

What is especially interesting about this dynamic—and one not picked up in the quantitative research—is that the motivating incidents were not always contemporaneous to policy adoption or even occurring at the same school where speech codes were adopted. At some schools the mere threat of racial violence moved administrators; at others the lesson from a neighboring institution was example enough; at still another group, incidents set policy into motion that took over a year to reach finality. No matter the exact details at each school, this is one area where the traditional story of the speech codes has some resonance: but for the increased coverage of racial incidents on campus, the hate speech codes might never have been adopted.

That said, the likely model here is not one of mobilization but of policy diffusion. Campus politics and potential mass action may have been priming influences, but the officials who acted were riding a wave of national policy adoption in the late 1980s and early 1990s. For a time hate speech measures became a trend in higher education administration, earning a badge of respectability when such schools as Michigan and Stanford adopted them. For other administrators with national ambitions, these examples became the standard. Networked through their professional organizations, officials read about the policies and learned how other schools were handling incidents of intolerance. Indeed, the process was an academic version of "keeping up with the Joneses," or as sociologists might say, a case of institutional isomorphism.[27] If hate speech policies were appropriate for the most prestigious schools in America—if they were being written about in *Academe, Lingua Franca,* and the *Chronicle of Higher Education*—then they were worthy of consideration by other schools too.

Regardless of their exact motives, college administrators were ultimately responsible for the creation of hate speech policies. At some schools presidents or chancellors directed the process; at other institutions leaders stayed behind the scenes but still controlled the strings; at only a few places did officials leave policy adoption to mid-level administrators, most often the student services staff. In some cases, state legislators, regents, and their attorneys played a role in the process. Together, these experiences challenge the traditional explanation of hate speech codes, for the college policies have more in common with theories of organizational behavior and policy development than they do legal or political mobilization. Perhaps administrators made ill-considered decisions, maybe the policies themselves drew improper lines, but with few exceptions the speech codes were not created with the intention of changing First Amendment norms or challenging the courts. College officials had other more instrumental or institutional goals in mind.

In order to keep the reader's attention and not belabor various points, the book tells the experience of five institutions from the eight visited for archival and qualitative research. The reader can rest assured that no story is left untold from the remaining three schools, for many experiences are shared among the set of eight institutions. The five that are presented here offer the clearest, most vivid examples of the motives behind the hate speech codes, reflecting policies that were created to forestall further controversy, to follow the lead of other schools, and in a few instances, to sincerely advance the terms of the policies. They also show how top campus officials were able to control, and in one case halt, the development of hate speech codes.

Millennium University

Millennium University is a large state school ultimately answerable to a systemwide chancellor. A prestigious school with an excellent reputation, Millennium is often known for the political involvement of its faculty and students. Nearly a quarter of the school's enrollment is graduate students, who come from across the country; the vast majority of undergraduates, though, reside in-state. Almost half of the student body is female, with racial minorities comprising about a third of student enrollment.

The story of MU's speech code is one of two-track activities, for the school attempted to adopt its own hate speech policy in response to student complaints against racial harassment. Indeed, the initial measure would seem to confirm the critics' suspicions, as top administrators proposed an expansive policy that would satisfy the demands of minority protestors for greater protection against racial harassment. This policy, however, was later overturned by a rule covering the entire state school system, a much more limited speech code drafted by the system's general counsel.

Like several schools, MU was rocked by racial incidents in the late 1980s.

In 1987 a black female student reported that others had vandalized her property and scribbled racist epithets across her door. In another incident minority students were heckled and taunted by fraternity members as they walked home one evening. These incidents drew the attention of the Black Students Association. BSA members were outraged at the incidents and pressed MU president Geoffrey Senger and student affairs officers to take action against the perceived rise in campus racism. Most notably, they called for an explicit policy prohibiting racial harassment—especially racial taunts.

Their cries drew the attention of MU's student conduct office, where one administrator acknowledges that the combination of racist incidents and student protest spurred him into action. "We were on a moral crusade," he says, trying to attack what he and others saw as an increase in racism at Millennium. In response to BSA, this administrator says he "pulled out the University's sexual harassment policy" and tinkered with it to create a policy against "verbally abusive language, including racial, religious or ethnic slurs or other derogatory remarks."

In many ways the process was a one-man operation. While this administrator consulted with other student affairs officers and higher-level administrators at MU, the policy was born not from committee deliberations or widespread organizing but from one administrator responding to problematic incidents and student protests. Nonetheless, it is clear that the policy found a friendly ear in President Senger, who approved the creation of a Grievance Board to "help in investigation and recommending action" against those who committed racial harassment.

It is hard to say how active Senger and other MU administrators intended the Grievance Board to be. There is one report of the new policy being enforced in 1989 against a student who "yell[ed] abusive racial and sexual epithets at fellow students causing them pain and humiliation," but the research reveals no other cases. Still, Senger was a strong supporter of the policy, seeing the opportunity to test the courts' approach to racial harassment. In an August 1989 letter to system chancellor Sherwood Tucker, Senger said existing policy:

> does not sufficiently allow us to prevent such intimidation. . . . Although the press accounts of racial harassment at [MU] have been exaggerated, some incidents have occurred which demand immediate and effective attention. . . . Although our regulations may test the limits of First Amendment analysis, I believe it is in the best interests of the campus to assume a strong posture in this regard and risk the consequences of judicial intervention. In *Bakke* [other schools] were willing to test the limits of traditional equal protection analysis in the interests of ethnic and cultural diversity. I believe the issue before us furthers the same agenda.

Before Millennium's policy could be made permanent, it had to be approved by the chancellor's office, and by extension, the system's general counsel. President Senger submitted the policy to central administration at the beginning of 1989, but as early as December of 1988 the general counsel had noted that the Millennium policy "may have problems with vagueness." Debate between Senger and the university's central office continued through the spring and summer of 1989; the university's president and general counsel stuck to a cautious path, while Senger urged a more ambitious approach.

Senger, however, was eventually overruled by Tucker and the general counsel, the latter of whom was fully cognizant of existing constitutional law and drafted the system's final hate speech policy to cover little or no new legal ground. That Tucker opposed Senger's approach does not mean that he failed to support a racial harassment policy, rather that he sought a more muted approach. Tucker had no intention of "risking the consequences of judicial intervention" with an expansive hate speech policy, but he also recognized that "there was a climate [of racial intolerance] developing, and one could sense that it was getting worse. I regarded it as a matter that the [university system] should deal with and not ignore," said Tucker.

If Tucker could not ignore the changing racial climate, it was in part because he faced pressure from the Millennium State Legislature, and in particular Representative Dan Myers, to issue a policy against racial harassment. Myers chaired the House committee on Millennium's appropriations, a position that by definition gave him Tucker's ear. Myers represented a sister campus of Millennium and in the process of constituent service had become aware of "racial tensions" in the university system. Expanding his inquiry, Myers concluded that the situation was "tense, hostile and explosive." As he reported at the time, " I believe the racial tensions which have plagued the [system] are no longer simply individual campus issues, but rather problems which warrant immediate statewide attention." To wit, Myers asked Chancellor Tucker to compile a report documenting racial or ethnic incidents that had occurred across the university system over the past three years.

According to Myers's directive, the university system was supposed to count any campus incident in which a person "*felt* denied or excluded because of his or her race, ethnicity, religion or sexual preference regardless of whether the individual had actually filed a complaint with system officials" (emphasis added). This was a very broad definition, leading university officials to fear that the data would show "the number of incidents with racial overtones which occurred on the campuses in the last three years [has been] quite high." Indeed, the eventual report did just this, but interestingly, few of the incidents were so egregious that they would have triggered the system's eventual hate speech policy.

At the same time that the university's central office was compiling statistics for Myers, interest was growing across the system for a speech code. The *Chronicle of Higher Education* had just published a piece advising colleges to "develop strong procedures to deal with incidents of racial harassment," and the story triggered a flow of memos from the various campuses to the system's central office asking that senior staff "consider revising universitywide regulations to include either a general prohibition against harassment or a specific policy prohibiting racial harassment." The interest drew both from the growing national attention to racial harassment and speech codes—particularly at peer institutions—and from the sense of some student conduct and judicial affairs staff that racial incidents on campus required a new administrative response.

If interest was growing throughout the system, Representative Myers eventually tipped the scales in favor of a speech policy. In 1988, he convened a legislative hearing to consider Tucker's report. Alarmed at what appeared to be a "lack of administrative response to racially motivated behavior on campus," Myers introduced and succeeded in passing legislation requiring the system to "develop and implement programs and policies to identify and correct behaviors, practices, or policies that result in differential treatment of students." As defined in the resolution, differential treatment could be regarded as a form of harassment.

The university was quick to respond. In late 1988, Tucker's office called a systemwide "Harassment Policies Workshop" to "bring campus judicial and other student affairs officers together with the [General] Counsel to discuss how judicial policies can best address the problem of harassment yet be consistent with the law and sound educational practices." In the opening speech, participants heard from a close aide to Chancellor Tucker who cautioned, "Let me say at the outset that we are not here today to discover the reasons why our campuses have been experiencing so much racial confrontation in recent years. We'll leave that discussion to another time. We are here because of our serious obligation to address these manifestations of antisocial behavior in a manner that is in keeping with sound educational practice and consistent with the law."

The last phrase—"consistent with the law"—was a very telling remark, for while Tucker may have been persuaded by his fellow administrators and the state legislature to take action, he was careful to create a policy that broke little constitutional ground. In fact, the task of drafting the rule was specifically assigned to the General Counsel's Office, a clear break from traditional procedure. Normally, student behavior rules would be drafted by the student affairs staff at the central office, but in this case the responsibility was transferred to the system's lawyers.

What emerged was a brilliant job of legal craftsmanship—a policy that seemed on its face to pronounce a new standard of racial civility on the system's campuses but that in reality was consistent with existing law. The final rule adopted by Chancellor Tucker prohibits "fighting words" by students. Fighting words, however, are defined as:

> those personally abusive epithets which, when directly addressed to any ordinary person are, in the context used and as a matter of common knowledge, inherently likely to provoke a violent reaction whether or not they actually do so. Such words include, but are not limited to, those terms widely recognized to be derogatory references to race, ethnicity, religion, sex, sexual orientation, disability, and other personal characteristics.
>
> [Fighting words are actionable under the policy only] when the circumstances of their utterance create a hostile and intimidating environment which the student uttering them should reasonably know will interfere with the victim's ability to pursue effectively his or her education.

What makes the legal draftsmanship so deft is that the policy singles out particular hate speech, for example racially abusive epithets, only as part of a larger category of fighting words. The rule thus allows the system to express its displeasure with certain kinds of speech without threatening the policy's constitutionality by limiting its reach to particular viewpoints. For that matter the policy is bounded by the definition of fighting words, which had shrunk from *Chaplinsky*'s initial test to cover only those words that are "inherently likely to provoke a violent reaction." Contrary to Senger's initial call, this was a policy that broke no new constitutional ground.

The policy's wording was anything but happenstance, its development presided over carefully by Tucker and the General Counsel's Office. Their goal was a policy that sat well within existing law. According to the general counsel, his office carefully scrutinized the District Court's decision in *Doe v. University of Michigan.* "We eliminated the terms 'stigmatize and victimize' from [our] policy. We believe that our 'fighting words' approach should weather a challenge better than the Michigan policy."

Two years later following the decision in *UWM Post v. Board of Regents,* the General Counsel's Office was asked its opinion about the continued constitutionality of the system's speech policy. In response, an attorney said:

> The opinion does not suggest a need to change our policy. The court's relatively narrow reading of the fighting words doctrine does suggest that we should continue to exercise great caution in bringing charges. The court's opinion may help

> to deter lawsuits challenging our policy and should on balance be helpful should such a challenge be filed. I encourage each of you to continue to discuss the matter with me or the General Counsel before bringing charges under the policy.

Still later, the General Counsel's Office weighed the system's speech code against the Supreme Court's 1992 decision in *R.A.V. v. City of St. Paul,* concluding that the policy "passes muster under the Minnesota case and does not need to be changed" because the rule "prohibits *all* fighting words under circumstances where they constitute harassment. No distinction between various kinds of fighting words is made. Therefore, no such issue is raised under the doctrine announced by Justice Scalia in *R.A.V.*"

Tucker's adoption of a systemwide speech policy meant that the earlier proposal at MU was dead. Millennium administrators attempted to negotiate with the central office, exchanging drafts of implementing language, but in the end administrators acknowledge that the "true rule" on the books is the systemwide policy adopted in 1989. All other language is exhortative but unenforceable. Today students at MU are held to the fighting words policy, with the Millennium campus also expressing its strong condemnation of racial harassment. In a veiled slap at system administrators, the MU student handbook says:

> Although [Millennium University] deplores all forms of racial harassment, it is precluded by law and [system] policy from imposing discipline for a wide range of behaviors that may be considered offensive. Accordingly, it relies largely on clearly stated values, education, and conciliation to create an environment that is free from harassment.

The development of a speech code at MU reflected little involvement by students or faculty. Even more, their reaction after the policy's enactment evidenced little support for speech regulation. Four bills were introduced in the Millennium Student Council following the systemwide rule; although one favored the speech policy, two were opposed, and one proposed to put the rule to a student referendum. None of these, however, passed, the issue eventually petering out for lack of student interest. As the Council's president explained, the speech policy "doesn't really address the issue of racial conflict. . . . [It's] a political move designed to mollify minority students and provide the [chancellor] with an excuse for not facing up to the real issues that trouble and divide the university community."

The faculty were even more adamantly opposed to the speech rule. A faculty committee on academic freedom urged Chancellor Tucker to amend or revise his policy, claiming that the fighting words formula was "vague and, if enforced, [would] interfere with freedom of expression." Committee members also voiced "grave concern . . . that a policy so central to the mission of the university as well as to academic freedom was not brought to" the faculty senate and student council "for input before its issuance." Speaking for many participants, one professor speculated that the policy was a response to "political pressure from the Legislature to do something," and that there was a "politics of race" emerging at MU. Tucker, however, refused to budge, saying the policy was strictly a matter of student conduct and therefore outside the province of the faculty. He admitted to consulting the system's presidents before issuing the speech policy, whom he characterized as sharply divided on the issue. In the end, Tucker said, the decision was his.

Plains University

Like Millennium University, the hate speech policy at Plains University was developed by high-level administrators, drafted by university attorneys, and endorsed and advanced by the institution's president. So too, officials were responding to outside political influence, in this case the state's regents. But where Millennium legislator Dan Myers saw racial tensions throughout the MU system, Plains's regents were responding to incidents at other institutions across the country. Even those faculty who later entered the debate at Plains had an eye on developments at other eminent schools that they sought to emulate.

Plains is a large public university with a good, if perhaps underrated reputation. Pulling mainly from its region, 90 percent of Plains's students are undergraduates, less than 10 percent of whom are minorities. Plains is also among the most liberal and activist schools within its state, and as a result has become accustomed to controversial local headlines when ideological groups collide on or near campus. Two years before the adoption of Plains's hate speech code, representatives of the Ku Klux Klan participated in a forum on campus, drawing over 2,500 protestors. The KKK's appearance led Plains president George Jaffe to propose a Minority Issues Task Force to "review the actions that campus organizations are taking on minority issues," including recruitment and retention of minority faculty, staff, and students. A year later, anti-Semitic graffiti was scrawled across campus, leading Plains administrators to convene a panel discussion on ethnoviolence with representatives of black, gay, Jewish, and Hispanic student groups.

These developments aside, the Plains speech policy actually originated with the state Regents for Higher Education, an appointed body based in the state capitol. In early 1989 the board of regents adopted a statement on racial and sexual harassment as part of its policy on affirmative action and equal opportunity. The policy said in pertinent part:

> The Board of Regents is particularly concerned about the continuing societal problems of racial harassment and sexual harassment. It is the policy of the Board that such conduct cannot and will not be tolerated at the institutions under its governance and control. Each institution shall develop and maintain specific policies which seek to: (i) identify prohibited conduct in these areas; (ii) educate campus constituencies with regard to these negative behaviors; (iii) eliminate such behaviors; and (iv) set forth the manner in which such behaviors or conduct are to be addressed.

It is difficult to determine the Regents' motives behind this policy. The minutes of their meetings are scant in details, noting only that the policy had been endorsed by officials at the various state colleges and drafted by the Regent's general counsel. The memories of many of the participants have faded over time, although a key staff member recalls that the Regents were responding to a "general and rising tenor" of racial intolerance at the state's schools. Others believe the Regents were reacting to developments at other well-known universities. If the Universities of Michigan and Wisconsin believed racial harassment policies were a good idea, this thinking goes, then the Regents would want to "keep up with the Joneses." Still others say that the policy was really addressed to discriminatory actions, not hate speech, for the policy does not mention "speech," preferring to use the more ambiguous term "conduct." Nevertheless, an attorney for Plains, one of the individuals who helped to write the campus policy, says she and others generally believed that the Regents' directive was intended to reach speech and improve the campus climate at Plains and its sister institutions.

Several observers contend that the Regents' action was a political exercise, a symbolic measure to eradicate prejudiced thinking on campus. The preamble of the final Plains policy—a statement by President Jaffe—might seem to support this view:

> Clearly there can be no place in the university for bigotry, intolerance, racial or sexual discrimination, anti-Semitism, and the like. These are the products of closed minds. As a university we must allow expression of sometimes uncomfortable or controversial ideas and discoveries. But we have no obligation to provide a forum for the worn-out tokens of fear, ignorance and prejudice. They insult our

> intelligence; they assault our dignity; they are contrary to the nature of a university; they cannot be tolerated here.

Following the Regents' pronouncement, the task fell to each of the state universities to draft their own implementing rules. At Plains, the Regents' statement was sent initially to the Affirmative Action Office, but as officials began to realize that the policy had serious legal implications, the responsibility for drafting was transferred to the General Counsel's Office and ultimately to a single attorney. That the policy was drafted by a lawyer says much for the policy's intentions. While the policy opens with a broad statement by President Jaffe, the primary drafter herself acknowledges that she tried to "say as much as possible" without challenging existing law. By that, she means she tried to cover as much discriminatory expression as possible under the policy without overstepping the constitutional boundaries set down in *Doe v. Michigan.*

The drafting attorney reports no protests, calls, or organized clamoring for a hate speech policy at the time she began work on the Plains policy. Rather, the process was very much a top-down operation: the Regents required a policy; President Jaffe wanted to state the university's clear opposition to discrimination and intolerance; and the General Counsel's Office tried to keep the policy within existing legal bounds. Under state law Jaffe had authority to issue administrative policy such as the hate speech rule, which he did in 1990. According to the terms of the policy, Plains prohibited: (1) Behavior or conduct addressed directly to an individual(s) and that threatens violence or property damage, or incites imminent lawless action, and that is made with the specific intent to harass or intimidate the victim because of race, religion, ethnicity or national origin; or (2) "Fighting words," such as racial and ethnic epithets, slurs, and insults, directed at an individual(s) with intent to inflict harm or injury or that would reasonably tend to incite an immediate breach of the peace, or (3) Slander, libel or obscene speech that advocates racial, ethnic, or religious discrimination, hatred or persecution.

The policy at Plains, much like the rule adopted at MU, reflects the careful legal draftsmanship that went into its development. While on its face the policy may seem to take great strides in singling out racial and ethnic hatred for punishment, the policy actually breaks little constitutional ground. Hateful actions and violent threats have historically gone unprotected by the First Amendment, and fighting words too may be prohibited. Interestingly, the Plains policy ties its definition of fighting words to the second half of the *Chaplinsky* test (words "that would reasonably tend to incite an immediate breach of the peace") while also seeming to incorporate part of the now discredited first half of the test (words that "inflict harm or injury"). *Chaplinsky,* however, looked to whether the speech itself was harmful, not whether the speaker intended it to be so, as the Plains policy requires. In this case, the Plains speech code seems more like a small extension of assault law[28] than a fundamental challenge to constitutional jurisprudence.

If the Plains policy steps over the constitutional line it is in the third paragraph, where the rule prohibits particular obscene messages. In Plains's defense, the constitutionality of this language was in flux at the time of its adoption, for the third section is directly analogous to the facts in *R.A.V.* There the St. Paul, Minnesota, city council took an area of speech that was already unprotected—fighting words—and picked out particular fighting words whose messages were so egregious as to justify restriction. At Plains, the policy selected two areas of speech that lack First Amendment protection—defamation and obscenity—and sought to punish particular racist, ethnic, and religious messages within those areas.

As a practical matter, obscenity was hardly a serious problem at Plains University, nor were defamation cases often prosecuted on campus. When colleges and universities face problems from racism and the like, the greater number of cases come from simple verbal attacks, not those that specifically employ sexual or scatological depictions (obscenity) or seek to tarnish another's reputation (defamation). The purpose of section three, then, was to permit the university to express its serious opposition to specific hateful messages (racism) while limiting the provisions to areas of speech that had historically been unprotected.

Of course, the Supreme Court's decision in *R.A.V.* changed the constitutional playing field, forbidding laws or rules that engaged in viewpoint discrimination even if the restrictions governed an area of speech like fighting words or obscenity that had been previously unprotected. As a result, regulations like the St. Paul statute—and the third section of the Plains speech policy—are now unconstitutional. A later chapter addresses the university's response to *R.A.V.*, but at the time that Plains adopted this policy, neither the lawyers nor President Jaffe sought to court a constitutional challenge. Just the opposite, they were trying to express the university's symbolic opposition to racism while sticking to what they thought was an established area of the law. That they have been proven wrong (with *R.A.V.* arguably overturning the policy) does not change their initial motivation.

Shortly after President Jaffe received a draft from the General Counsel's Office, the Plains campus was rocked by a racial incident. Although the incident did not precipitate the university's new hate speech policy, it may well have convinced President Jaffe to speed up its adoption. The climactic event took place in the first months of 1990 when a black woman was accosted by a drunk, white fraternity member, who proceeded to hurl racist slurs at her as she attempted to deliver a pizza to the frat house. What otherwise might have been considered an isolated bad act by an inebriated student became a rallying cry for black students on campus, many of whom said the incident was indicative of the racist treatment they received at Plains. Within a week of the incident the Black Students Association had led a protest outside the perpetrator's fraternity and organized a rally of over three hundred students to demand university action on a number of concerns. Protestors submitted twenty-one "concerns" to administrators, seeking among other things a multicultural resource center and increased minority recruitment. Still, even in a list that asked, "Why is there a need to sell both Coca-Cola products and Pepsi products, in knowing Coca-Cola is invested in South [Africa]?" not one of the demands called for a speech code.

The response from President Jaffe to the incident was swift. Before the students had even rallied, he sent a memorandum to minority students' organizations, the student senate, and campus fraternities announcing five directives he had issued. Among these were a review of the fraternity in question, a program for greater cultural sensitivity at fraternities, a possible expansion of the Ombudsman's Office "to work with problems of racial and cultural harassment and intimidation," a "review of the Code of Student Rights and Responsibilities about its adequacy in dealing with issues of discrimination," and the creation of an advisory board for campus minority groups to consult in the minority affairs office.

One month later President Jaffe adopted the university's speech policy on racial and ethnic harassment. Again, the policy and incident are not absolutely linked, for the speech code had been in the works for nearly an entire academic year before the racial incident. But its promulgation so soon after the controversy seemed to put the issue of racial harassment into play at the university. Rising racial tensions motivated students and faculty to consider additional mechanisms to combat intolerance, and the adoption of speech restrictions seemed to spark the interest of faculty and some administrators who up until then had been silent on the question of hate speech codes. However, there was an interesting divide in the response of students and faculty and administrators. By and large, students pushed for what they saw as "concrete actions," including better minority recruitment and additional funding for minority services. By contrast, it was faculty and staff who tinkered with what even they acknowledged to be symbolic measures.

Most of the subsequent activity was led by the University Senate, comprised of faculty, administrators and a few student representatives, and its Campus Relations Subcommittee (CRS). While neither body had shown much interest in speech regulation prior to the university's new policy, they began to take heed once other eminent schools adopted hate speech codes. In the year before Jaffe announced the speech policy, University Senate charged the Subcommittee to:

> Identify and make recommendations concerning any actions that might be taken within the university community that would reduce the increasing incidence of racist, sexist, anti-Semitic, homophobic and xenophobic behavior on campus and in student living areas, both on and off campus.

This charge might seem like an open license to consider speech restrictions, but its end-of-the-year report shows just how inactive the Subcommittee had been. Reporting back to University Senate, CRS said it "was not able to think of ways of reducing or increasing the increasing incidence of racist, sexist, anti-Semitic, homophobic and xenophobic behavior on campus and in student living areas that have not repeatedly been suggested in the past." Nor did the Subcommittee have a strong reaction to the new hate speech policy after it was enacted. CRS members reported that they had "examined the President's statement about racial harassment which was included in the *Policy on Racial Harassment* . . . [and have] no suggestions for changes in the statement."

Within a year, however, hate speech had become a more pressing topic at other campuses across the country, and the American Association of University Professors had issued a Preliminary Report on Freedom of Expression and Campus Harassment Codes.[29] In response, the University Senate gave CRS a more ambitious charge: "Preliminary to the development of a policy statement to be presented to the University Senate, review the AAUP Preliminary Report . . . and forward comments to" the Senate. Senators also assigned the Subcommittee new members with a personal interest in the topic. Among these were one of the few openly lesbian faculty members, an African American law professor, the Director of Affirmative Action, and the newly appointed Director of Minority Affairs. As the CRS chair recorded the deliberations from their initial meeting:

> We all talked about a sense of powerlessness in being on this committee, having such vast ambitions for social change, but few resources and little, if any authority. After leaving the meeting, I got to thinking that, after all, *ideas* are very powerful and I feel that is really what our mandate is, to brainstorm and come up with ideas that might help alleviate the problems with which we are concerned. As faculty at an institution of higher education, ideas are indeed our province. So, let's

> tackle our tasks with optimism and enthusiasm, or at least hope and self-confidence.

In a sense, it is odd that University Senate would ask CRS to help draft a statement on harassment codes, as Plains had just adopted an administrative rule on the subject a year and a half before. Their reason has as much to do with academic politics and the gap between faculty and high-level administrators as it does with the desire of a school like Plains to keep up with what it saw as a national trend. If *Academe,* the journal of college faculty, was suggesting that schools needed to reconsider the balance between freedom of speech and hateful attacks, then Senators believed the matter deserved faculty attention and could not be relegated to a group of administrators who might be motivated by internal politics or expediency.

If anything, CRS members felt more strongly about this than did the University Senators. Although the Senate had asked CRS to forward comments on the appropriateness of campus harassment policies, the Subcommittee essentially drafted its own addition to the university's academic policy manual. Noting that Plains should respect and uphold the "principles of free inquiry and open discourse that are at the center of the academic enterprise," the proposal nonetheless sought to limit:

> speech that is addressed directly to individuals and meant only to threaten violence, property damage or imminent lawless action and that has "no essential part of an exposition of ideas and [is] of such slight social value as a step to truth that any benefit that may be derived from [it] is clearly outweighed by the social interest in order and morality."

The CRS chair says the proposal "was intended as a philosophical statement," drawn in part from a report authored by the dean of Michigan Law School,[30] but it is difficult to see how the CRS "statement" was not also a proposal for a more restrictive speech code. Apart from the fact that they were entering a field already occupied by the university's racial harassment policy, the Subcommittee's members were seeking to advance a wholly new understanding of speech regulation under the guise of a philosophical statement.

At first the CRS statement passed through the Senate's Executive Committee, but since "the issue [had] been widely discussed on campuses throughout the country," the Senate's chair asked that the issue be discussed within the full University Senate. The proposal was thus scheduled for a University Senate meeting, where it faced stiff and organized opposition. A leader of the local ACLU chapter presented a researched memorandum explaining why the proposal would be unconstitutional, and he was joined by several faculty who believed that the CRS proposal was too sweeping and threatened existing constitutional norms. In early 1992, University Senate defeated the CRS statement.

Less than two weeks later the CRS chair was quoted in the student paper announcing that the Subcommittee intended to rewrite the resolution and submit it again. "People jumped to conclusions. They thought we were going to legislate behavior, when all we meant to do was to encourage people to be sensitive," she claimed. The chair gathered the Subcommittee, and together they attempted to draft a new policy statement. The end of the academic year, however, intervened, and by the next fall the Subcommittee's chair had been replaced by a leading civil libertarian on campus. Still, the group saw value in an exhortative statement, and in the spring of 1993, CRS sent the University a new proposal, urging that:

> We in the university community should remind ourselves periodically about our individual responsibilities to help maintain civil discourse. Speech which subjects persons to insults and demeaning epithets because of their gender, race, religion, sexual orientation, or other affiliations or status disrespects the dignity and equality of these persons and can be harmful to them and their participation in university activities and in our society. Each of us has an important responsibility to engage others in discussion about the disrespect and harm that such speech causes whenever we perceive other persons consciously and deliberately to have employed offensive behaviors or insulting speech. It is also important to express concern about unintentional or thoughtless use of speech or actions that may be perceived as disrespectful or harmful to others. It is especially important for those in the community who are role models or carry other kinds of authority to engage in critical discussion of this kind, which of course must have a civil nature in itself, and not limit a speaker's rights or autonomy.

After tinkering a bit over semantics, the Senate's Executive Committee approved the suggested statement, but a month later CRS's proposal failed for good. There are no minutes that explain this decision, but according to a CRS member, University Senators were simply "tired of the issue." Having lost a second time in the University Senate, CRS abandoned its efforts to draft a philosophy statement or policy regarding hate speech. To this date the issue has not been raised again within the faculty or other university bodies. The harassment policy adopted by President Jaffe remains the university's only statement on hate speech.

That speech restrictions seemed to fall off the radar screen so quickly at Plains is an interesting question. Why would people who had pushed some form of a proposal for two years simply give up their activism? The answer, I think, is twofold. On one level, the move to establish additional speech restrictions was never that popular on campus. Certainly, students did not get behind the initiative, with several even openly critical of the proposal in the campus paper. Nor was the push ever led by more than three to six committed members of the Campus Relations Subcommittee. Indeed, while their activism shows the ability of a few key people to put an issue on the university agenda, it also reflects how issues that bubble up at universities (and perhaps within other organizations as well) can settle back down if they do not have sufficient support across the institution.

The Plains experience also reflects the power of priming within academic policy-making. I doubt that CRS or any other campus body at Plains would have unilaterally raised the question of hate speech rules had they not already been primed by both campus and national events to consider the topic. The coupling of Jaffe's proclamation with racial protests highlighted the problem of racial harassment on campus, and the ongoing debate about hate speech at other universities convinced some faculty and administrators that the topic deserved attention at Plains. The CRS chair and her colleagues may have had a political or social agenda in mind when offering their initial hate speech proposal, but they would not have had the stage without the priming influences already at play.

The differences in priming may also explain why faculty and administrators were the advocates of additional speech restrictions while students were generally neutral or opposed. Certainly, all three groups were primed by Jaffe's proclamation and the racial tensions on campus, but students would not have been as readily aware of events at other campuses. As a whole, students do not read the *Chronicle of Higher Education, Academe,* or *Lingua Franca,* and they would have had little interest in following or even adopting administrative measures enacted elsewhere. Seeing only what they perceived as a rise in racism on campus, students pressed for concrete actions such as minority recruitment and scholarships to address what they saw as the underlying problems. Faculty, administrators, and some staff, however, saw the issue as a philosophical statement of the university's priorities and protections. Primed by their peers' debate at other institutions, they too took up the question of hate speech at Plains.

Middleberg College

In August 1989, Middleberg College adopted a "Statement on Human Rights." A quaint, private liberal arts institution tucked into a bucolic hamlet, Middleberg might seem one of the last schools in need of a formal policy. Middleberg's enrollment is strictly undergraduate, a large majority of whom are women, and administrators say that much of campus operations is accomplished more "by consensus than legalistic rules." Nonetheless, Middleberg's president adopted policy prohibiting sexual harassment as well as "[h]arassment based on race, national or ethnic origin, religion, age, and/or disability." Under this latter section harassment included "unwelcome slurs, jokes, graphic or written materials as well as all other verbal or physical actions related to an individual's personal background or attributes." By contrast, sexual harassment was defined as "a range of unwelcome behavior [of] a sexual nature having the purpose or effect of interfering with an individual's work performance or creating an intimidating, hostile or offensive working or academic environment."

Given the many bases protected under the policy, one might think that it evolved as a response to racial tensions, much as was the case at MU. Although the eventual rule would gain speed as a result of notorious incidents at nearby schools, the policy-making process was actually jump-started by Middleberg's female students, who pushed for a policy against sexual harassment. Up until the mid-1980s, allegations of sexual harassment were handled informally at Middleberg. A student might complain to a dean about improper advances, upon which a male faculty member would be dispatched to urge the offender to "fly right." But students of the 1980s did not feel that administrators were taking their charges seriously, or that the college was recognizing their unease. In informal discussions, faculty-student conferences, and in women's studies classes, students began to talk more openly about their experiences with sexual harassment. Their efforts were fueled in the 1985–86 academic year when a notorious case of sexual harassment came to light. During a student party a professor propositioned a student and tried to kiss her, and when she refused he threatened her grade. In the past this incident would have been handled informally, but students and faculty went to the academic dean to complain, who himself referred the matter directly to the college's president. According to those involved, the professor was immediately put on leave, an unprecedented measure at Middleberg.

The college's quick and powerful response moved other women to come forward and talk about their experiences of sexual harassment. "Students Against Sexual Harassment" (SASH) was founded, and in the 1986–87 academic year students began to push faculty and administrators to do more to protect against sexual harassment. The Middleberg student government became involved, as did the African American and Hispanic students' associations. Under pressure from students and a collection of sympathetic faculty,

Middleberg president Elaine Goodie appointed a small group of faculty and staff to evaluate the extent of sexual harassment on campus. The group undertook a formal survey and reported back to Goodie that sexual harassment was a fairly serious problem at Middleberg. In turn, Goodie appointed a task force to advise her on how to improve conditions.

At about this time racial tensions exploded at a neighboring university, as black and Hispanic students brawled after a tense basketball game. Over at Middleberg a town meeting was called to talk about the incident and the worsening climate at the university campus. Since students from Middleberg regularly visited the university, they were concerned for their safety. It is interesting, though, that much of the town meeting concerned students' physical safety rather than the more general questions of racial inclusion at the university or at Middleberg itself. Nonetheless, President Goodie felt compelled to create a new task force to consider issues of racial inclusion at Middleberg. According to Goodie there was no single incident or event that led to the task force, nor does she believe that the town meeting had any sustained effect other than "sharpen[ing] rhetoric" on issues of racial equality. But with racial incidents rising on the national agenda and a sexual harassment task force already under way, Goodie seems to have considered a new task force on racial inclusion to be a necessary prophylactic. She charged the task force to examine the issue of racial inclusion at Middleberg and "recommend things appropriate to deal with the question."

Both task forces worked independently of each other, and yet each reached the same recommendation: that the College hire an ombudsperson to deal with issues of harassment. At this point neither task force was thinking of punitive, "legalistic," measures. Instead they proposed a model in which victims of harassment could approach the ombudsperson to mediate a matter, take a case to a formal adjudication, or simply explore options. As one member said, "we thought soft educational strategies and mediation were better than [a] strict adversarial process."

The idea of an ombudsperson had been percolating around Middleberg for years, but when both task forces recommended the same thing, the idea gained steam. Still, the task forces did not carry the same influence. As faculty and administrators agree, sexual harassment was the driving force behind the hiring of an ombudsperson and the creation of policy. That there was also a separate task force on racial harassment gave the process an added push, but even members of the racial task force acknowledge that their work did not achieve the same influence or sense of urgency as did proposals from the sexual harassment task force.

If there is a central link throughout the process from student demands to eventual policy it is President Goodie. On one hand this is a process that began with traditional bottom-up activism. Students awoke to shared concerns and protested to faculty and administrators for a better response by the college. But students could not orchestrate the development of policy, nor were they involved in many of the discussions. For that matter, they were relatively uninterested in a hate speech policy, focused as they were on cases of sexual advance. Students may have placed the issue of harassment on the agenda and pressured the college for a new response, but it was President Goodie who oversaw—and perhaps even preordained—the college's eventual policy. It was she who immediately suspended the English professor who harassed and threatened the student at the party. Respected as a strategic thinker, she had to know that a change in traditional college procedure would affect student (and even faculty) expectations. She appointed the group of fact finders to investigate incidents of sexual harassment, and she responded with a task force to recommend policy. She even appointed the task force members, careful as one self-described "campus radical" said, to ensure that moderates became the prime spokespeople for institutional change. Most importantly, she created the task force on racial inclusion when neither students nor faculty were pressuring the college for new policy.

Having initiated two task forces, Goodie was hardly in a position to ignore their conclusions when both bodies reached the same recommendation—hire an ombudsperson. In 1987–88 Middleberg hired its first ombudsperson, a woman who came from a school where formal rules dominated. By contrast, Middleberg is a small, residential community where "people act on person-to-person discussions rather than by formal rules." For example, when a poster from the lesbian students association was defaced, a "clamor [went] up [on campus] about vandalism and homophobic hatred." Students had meetings in residence halls, sometimes moderated by student services staff, while others brought their concerns directly to faculty considered friendly to the cause. Sometimes these discussions confronted the perpetrator, but more often they set out a community norm that particular behavior was wrong. As a former dean explains, "the issue gets raised," and the proper norm is set out, "but no policy is invoked." Community standards are often set by informal networks at Middleberg.

By contrast, the college's first ombudsperson began to call for a formal harassment policy shortly after she arrived at Middleberg. Complaining that she could not enforce standards of behavior unless they were codified, the ombudsperson eventually convinced President Goodie that a harassment policy was necessary. Goodie met weekly with the ombudsperson to shape such a policy, molding proposals "into the language and method that worked" at

Middleberg College. Goodie also established a formal committee to advise her on drafts of the policy. It was an interesting process. According to those involved, the "process was porous," including task force members as well as students and faculty representing African American, Latino, Asian, and gay groups, among others. Many of these discussions were outside of formal channels, requiring "a great deal of negotiations." Nevertheless, the original drafts emanated from Goodie. She expanded the text to include racial, ethnic, and religious harassment, much as the policy reads today.

Goodie's intentions remain a bit of a mystery, for she failed to speak publicly about the need to protect against harassment other than sexual advances. The expansion of the policy was more by incrementalism than bold fiat. If sexual harassment deserved a policy response, and if racial tensions were rising at other schools, then it made sense for Middleberg to broaden the policy proposal. There was no defining racial incident on campus, nor was the policy ever seen or promoted as a racial harassment measure or a hate speech code.

Goodie recommended that faculty senate consider the harassment policy even though she could have adopted it as an administrative regulation herself. Again this strategy reflects the culture of Middleberg where consensus is valued over contentiousness, but it may also represent a calculation by Goodie that the policy would encounter less opposition if it were seen as coming from the faculty rather than imposed on the college from above. Those who participated in deliberations over the policy remember the Senate meeting as being charged, although there is disagreement about the level of contentiousness. One women's studies professor derided a group of "young men" among the faculty who claimed that the policy's rhetoric was too harsh. Others say the opponents were an unorganized group with different interests, "some admirable, some political, some truculent." Surprisingly, though, the policy did not generate near the controversy that faced curriculum changes, which the college took up at about the same time. As a former administrator says, the latter initiative was "painfully political," dividing the faculty and opening up the college to external charges of political correctness.

Yet one could make the same charge against the college's harassment policy. Like those who wanted to diversify college curricula, the Middleberg speech policy was rooted in notions that social policy must respond to and take account of the previously disadvantaged. As a former top administrator explains the policy, its goal was to:

> change the terms of social interaction . . . to reformulate the hierarchy to honor participation of all members [of the College. . . . This process requires] a change of

> heart, a change in the capacity to see the effect of habitual behavior on another. [It] requires reflection, a willingness to be corrected by self and colleagues.

That the policy did not generate such organized opposition reflects ultimately the degree to which it was seen as covering sexual harassment. To be sure, the policy includes expansive language about verbal harassment on other bases, but the process itself had begun with questions of sexual harassment, and much of the discussion in the faculty senate concerned the pervasiveness of sexual harassment and the need for the college to take a strong stand against this behavior. Concerns about free speech and academic freedom were raised in faculty discussions, but the policy was never seen as focused on hate speech or verbal attacks. Indeed, one of the prime participants in the process says she is "surprised" that the policy would be labeled a hate speech policy. Her reaction is particularly confusing when she reports that the college worked closely with its outside counsel in drafting the policy. While the specific legal advice is not available, most recall that the college's attorneys thought the policy was "too far reaching." No one suggested that the policy was unconstitutional or illegal—if only because Middleberg is private—but the attorneys cautiously suggested that the college simply track Title VII's language in prohibiting sexual harassment. Goodie and those close to her rejected this advance and enacted a policy that, while not initially seen as such, had the potential to severely limit offensive and hateful speech.

Mt. Michaels College

In some ways, the genesis of the Mt. Michaels College hate speech policy resembles that of the Middleberg speech code, for student demands jumpstarted the policy-making process at both schools. The schools also share several characteristics. Each is a private, liberal arts institution, small and exclusively undergraduate. At the time, nearly half of the Mt. Michaels student body was female, with approximately 7 percent encompassing racial and ethnic minorities. But if students could grab the attention of Mt. Michaels administrators, the number of activists was small—involving two or three students—making a claim of organized mobilization difficult to sustain. In truth, the Mt. Michaels's experience fits somewhere between that of MU and Middleberg. While perhaps prompted by students, Mt. Michaels's policy reflects the decision of a high-level administrator, the dean of students, to issue a new rule. Her motives were undoubtedly less utilitarian than those at Millennium University, but even so the Mt. Michaels policy is best understood as an administrative decree to preserve campus peace and protect racial minorities.

Mt. Michaels's speech policy was adopted in the 1986–87 academic year. Like many such policies, the rule is not called a hate speech code, instead carrying the title "Harassment, Sexual Harassment and Assault Policy." Nonetheless, the policy includes a section prohibiting "harassment," which it defines as:

> verbal or physical conduct that (1) threatens, insults, demeans or abuses a person (2) because of his or her race, color, religion, ethnic origin, sexual and affectional orientation or associations, or mental or physical disabilities, and (3) unreasonably interferes with the person's work or academic performance and/or creates an intimidating, hostile or offensive working, educational, or social environment.

The policy is considered a separate statement to the college's Student Conduct Code and may be enforced by either the Student Grievance Board or student services staff. At the time the speech rule was written the Grievance Board was comprised of seven students and three faculty members and chaired by a student. Complaints about student infractions would come to the Dean of Students Office, which would refer to the Board those cases it considered sufficiently serious. All others would be dismissed or handled with minor punishment. But as one administrator acknowledges, the Grievance Board could "not [be] trusted to make good decisions." According to campus legend, the Board was little more than "a vehicle for the fraternities," which dominated much of Mt. Michaels's extracurricular and social life. In some sense, then, the hate speech rule was an attempt by administrators to claim jurisdiction over behavior they considered especially serious but the Board had not. For the first time, student services staff felt empowered to take disciplinary action against harassment cases that previously would have gone to the Board.

While stories of the Grievance Board's ineffectiveness are many, it is not entirely clear that Mt. Michaels had experienced that many cases of racial or sexual harassment up to the mid-1980s. It is important to note that Mt. Michaels had historically been a predominantly white-male institution, and even by the 1980s the school did not have a long history of gender or racial integration. The mid-1980s, however, found Mt. Michaels rocked by serious and terribly divisive protests on campus about the college's South African investments. As happened at many colleges at the time, a divestment movement arose on campus, with students protesting and lobbying trustees to divest the college's holdings. The trustees, however, held firm, which "some students saw as racist, or at least as a signal of institutional racism." Campus members remember this time as horribly "painful" and "vicious" with much "finger pointing." In some sense it reflected a period of clashing cultures, with more liberal and racially diverse students battling "the old guard" of the fraternities. At one of the divestment protests, members of a fraternity staged a lewd and inflammatory stunt, which angered many and only exacerbated tensions.

One of the consequences of these tensions was that minority students began to talk to student services staff about racial harassment they experienced on campus. Independently, the student life office had hired a consultant to survey students' worries about the "campus climate," the report from which confirmed a concern among racial minorities and to a lesser extent women. It is unclear whether the divestment protests had sparked a heightened wave of racial incidents or whether the protests themselves empowered students to come forward and talk about the problems they were facing. In either event, administrators were taken aback by how prevalent these incidents appeared to be. Staff and administrators had heard earlier stories of harassment third hand, but in confronting new reports one assistant dean remembers thinking that "this is viciousness. . . . [What a] painful place" Mt. Michaels had become. Administrators were committed to maintaining the college's minority enrollment, and yet the campus appeared to be increasingly uninviting for minority students.

In the midst of these discussions a proposal was put forward to protect minority students from harassment, which the dean of students seemed to adopt almost immediately. As one participant remembers it, "a couple of students of color were working with the dean of students to get better support [from the college]." They asked for protection from harassment, "and the Dean said, 'we can do that.'" Initially the dean appeared inclined simply to take the college's existing sexual harassment policy and substitute race for gender, but the proposal was later expanded by student services staff to its present form. The proposal was then adopted carte blanche by President Phillip Rubin's office.

When questioned about how quickly the policy seemed to go through the college's administration, a key participant appeared incredulous about the query. "Why wouldn't you say 'we won't tolerate harassment of students, of students of color?'" she demanded. The policy was "the right thing to do" and had to be advanced to curb the level of "viciousness" that had infected campus from the divestment controversy. Nonetheless, it is surprising, as one administrator said, "that a dean would sit down with a student and hammer this out." In fact, it is remarkable on two levels: one, that the dean would be so immediately responsive to the student's request, and two, that the college president would adopt the policy without much fanfare *or* reaction. Respondents recall that legal counsel was consulted on the policy, but they also remember it being "fast-tracked" and implemented with little controversy.

A similar phenomenon explains both the policy's speedy enactment and the modest reaction on campus. Mt. Michaels administrators felt under siege. The college was still experimenting somewhat with coeducation, involving regular battles with the vestiges of the previous all-male culture, the fraternities. Officials were concerned about maintaining minority enrollment at a time when such numbers were beginning to drop nationally, but even more they feared the repercussions from a college-wide fight over an issue (divestment) that had obvious racial overtones. Even after all my research I find it difficult to say whether administrators genuinely shared the concerns of minority students or whether they worried more about the potential news stories that would paint Mt. Michaels as inhospitable to minorities. Of course, these are not mutually exclusive motives, although I do see a divide between student services staff, who seemed truly pained by the reported experience of minority students, and President Rubin, who sought to appease alumni and manage the college's image. Either way, it is easy to understand why administrators would push a policy that minority students had said would improve their experience at St. Michaels.

For the purely utilitarian administrator, the Mt. Michaels harassment policy proved a success. Officials were able to express their support for minority students by enacting the code, while simultaneously avoiding criticism or opposition from others. As one person explains, "there were enough big political issues at the time" to overshadow the policy's adoption. Apart from the heated charges over divestment, a group of students had occupied the administration building and were suspended, in turn triggering a drawn-out lawsuit. "People were willing to do anything to have some peace," says an administrator describing the mood of the college at the time. Students, faculty, and staff reacted less to the code's specific provisions than to the larger idea that the policy was addressed to the vitriolic campus atmosphere. If the policy had been adopted at a different time when its provisions were the primary issue "without other baggage," the proposal might have drawn more scrutiny.

That scrutiny might have come from campus liberals, who, while supporting civil rights, might have raised free speech objections to the policy if they had given it more careful attention. But what about campus conservatives—those who might have opposed the policy for advancing a larger PC agenda? The answers here are less definite. On one level conservatives might have been appeased at the time, since Mt. Michaels's trustees had just declined to divest the college's holdings. Or, more likely, they may simply have missed the policy's adoption. This was a measure that was created and pushed forward largely by administrators. Only a few students were aware of, and involved in, its creation. There were no campuswide meetings to discuss its terms, nor was the measure sent to Academic Senate for consideration. Much of the machinations went on behind the scenes. Its timing is also instructive. As one administrator explains, the policy was adopted almost "two years before the PC craze" garnered national attention. Without PC's salience, campus conservatives might simply have let the policy slide as, at best, a sop to campus minorities.

Emilia College

Certainly, not every prestigious, liberal school with an activist past created hate speech codes. Some faced little racial turmoil on or near campus, others were indifferent to national trends in collegiate administration, and still more were led by presidents or other top officials who actively resisted hate speech regulations. Benno Schmidt at Yale was perhaps the most visible college president to speak out against hate speech policies, but other schools eschewed speech regulation at the behest of their leaders. Nowhere was this truer than at Emilia College, a private, liberal arts school with an international profile and student body. Emilia had a long history of progressive student activism, which, when coupled with a series of racial incidents on campus, might very well have led to the creation of a hate speech policy. But the strong stand of Emilia's president, its dean of the faculty and top faculty leaders, told a different tale. Although the college adopted a sexual harassment policy, its faculty and trustees simultaneously enacted a statement protecting freedom of speech and expression.

The story begins in January of 1986, the second year of President Christine Ertel's tenure at Emilia College, when she opened a college convocation by reflecting on the civil rights movement. A progressive herself, Ertel urged students to continue the struggle by learning "to live together with . . . people of many cultures and races." That Ertel would "press for diversity," as the student paper described her speech, presaged her ultimate strategy to address racial tensions at Emilia, though her tone was also in keeping with the general tenor of the campus during the 1985–86 academic year. In anticipation of a meeting of the board of trustees, the faculty senate had recommended that the college divest itself of all investments in South Africa; the board, however, limited divestment to those companies that had refused to sign the Sullivan Principles.[31] Students staged a sit-in, expressing disappointment with the board's "go slow" approach, but for the most part the end of the academic year went without incident.

The same, however, was not true for the following academic year when, in the fall of 1986, unknown perpetrators spray-painted racist statements across campus. Concerned that these incidents were connected to racist violence at neighboring schools, President Ertel quickly called an all-college meeting to "discuss 'racial tension,'" and soon after established a "Presidential Commission [on] racial and cultural awareness to evaluate us, define the extent of our problem, and make recommendations for our action." Renamed the Committee on Community Policy, its members conducted extensive research and issued a report on the racial and ethnic climate at Emilia. This report would later form the basis of the Emilia Plan for Diversity.

By establishing the Committee on Community Policy, President Ertel had raised students' expectations for a more diverse and accepting campus climate. Yet, while Ertel supported the new committee and hired a local consulting firm to evaluate "multicultural and human relations issues" at Emilia, she failed to cultivate students or advise them to be patient while the process played out. Their patience, thus, evaporated in the next academic year when unknown perpetrators spray-painted additional racist graffiti across campus and sent several students racist and homophobic notes. The Dean of Students Office took the lead in investigating these incidents, but by then a "Concerned Group of Students" had organized to protest "instances of racism" at Emilia as well "as an unpleasant picture of institutionalized racism inherent in the structure of the institution." As the Group complained in a press release: "We realize that change takes time. However, we expect [Emilia] to have *initiated* the long-term proposals" that have been before President Ertel for several years. Fed up, the Group demanded that within ten days the college release "a plan for redressing racism at every level of the institution" and "complete a policy on civil rights." Students staged a press conference and organized a march on campus in front of visiting parents.

Ertel almost met their deadline, releasing a draft civil rights policy within two weeks. It is difficult to know if Ertel was motivated by the students' protests or whether such measures were already in the works, but her efforts were effective in silencing the student protestors. Said one of the leaders of Concerned Students, the proposed policy is "a big step. It's not perfect, but it's a damn good start." Nevertheless, the policy statement was fairly generic, committing Emilia College to "make positive efforts to overcome the effects of societal patterns of exclusion or underrepresentation of minority group members in the College community" without saying what those efforts would entail. The board of trustees would dilute the policy further, eventually promising to "enhance the opportunities available to all."

The ultimate surprise would come in the summer of 1988 when President Ertel established a task force to create a "specific design" to address racism on campus. In doing so, Ertel announced that Emilia was determined to "confront incidents of racial intolerance, discrimination, and prejudice." If anything, she sold the college short. Where other schools gave lip service to diversity or created bland, generic policies as political cover, Emilia undertook a much bolder stroke to address what President Ertel saw as the root cause of racial intolerance—a homogenous academic community. Observers at the time saw Ertel as either heroically idealistic or hopelessly naive, but her vision reached fruition in the Emilia Plan for Diversity, which was released to the college community that fall. Among its thirty-nine provisions, the plan called for the "definition, implementation and enforcement of a civil rights policy" and the adoption of "an aggressive affirmative action policy." Perhaps most ambitiously, the Plan aimed to "increase the minority population at" Emilia, setting a benchmark for a faculty and student body that were to reach 20 percent minority by 2004. To this end, the Plan appropriated almost $400,000 for the various tasks.

In the events that followed, Emilia College created a harassment policy, but unlike those schools that banned hate speech, Emilia took deliberate steps to avoid the restriction of expression. Some of the reason may be that the college chose to face the problem of campus racism head-on—by appropriating money to create "a more inclusive and culturally diverse campus community"—rather than simply adopting a speech code that might or might not be enforced. But Ertel herself was a strong proponent of open dialogue (witness the many college meetings and forums she called on racism and diversity), and she was surrounded by an academic dean and faculty leaders who feared any measures that would suppress speech on campus, especially that of faculty in the classroom. Again, Ertel took the initiative, appointing a Task Force on Institutional Diversity to assess the success of the Emilia Plan while also creating an Ad Hoc Committee on Academic Freedom "to draft a statement of academic freedom for the College, and to review the interim grievance procedures in light of that statement."

The Academic Freedom Committee began its work in the fall of 1989, "reviewing materials from other campuses and a variety of legal and judicial opinions" to seek guidance on the appropriate balance between free expression and provisions against harassment. The Committee says it consulted "with all constituencies in the College" and scheduled two open meetings prior to the release of its proposed "Statement on Academic Freedom and Freedom of Expression" late that fall. At the time Emilia had a generic antiharassment measure on the books, under which the college refused to "tolerate unlawful harassment based on race, color, creed, disability, national/ethnic origin, age, religion, sex, sexual orientation, or disabled Vietnam-era veteran status." The policy acknowledged that speech could constitute harassment, but even here the implication was that verbal harassment was limited to sexual advances.

In its proposed statement the Academic Freedom Committee took up this point, arguing that speech, even objectionable views, deserved protection at Emilia. As the statement said, "Freedom of speech and expression is of paramount value in an academic community . . . [which Emilia] College must preserve and protect. . . . It must do so even when the ideas and values expressed are believed to be inimical to a conception of humane society." The policy tracked existing constitutional law well, acknowledging that "freedom of speech and expression cannot be absolute." For example, "speech that is libelous, slanderous, [or] incites to riot" is not protected at Emilia.

Interestingly, the policy premised protection on academic freedom—meaning that "speech directed at persons with clear intent to cause substantial injury" theoretically could be punished. Indeed, this is the very basis under which many other schools have justified their hate speech policies. But at Emilia the emphasis was different. Not only was there no policy that affirmatively singled out hate speech for prohibition, but faculty leaders were actively on guard against any measures or enforcement pattern restricting speech. In February of 1992 the board of trustees adopted a formal Statement of Academic Freedom and Freedom of Expression, and to date there has been no move to enact additional policies dealing with hate speech. Instead, the college has directed its energies to the ambitious goals in the Emilia Plan, trying to diversify both the student body and the faculty. Although Emilia did not ultimately meet the timetable originally envisioned, the legacy of President Ertel lives on: the college has put its efforts into affirmative measures to improve the campus climate rather than relying on "reactive" policies to discourage hate speech.

AN INTEGRATED UNDERSTANDING OF HATE SPEECH CODES

Even while resisting speech restrictions, the experience at Emilia College confirms the tale told at other schools chronicled here: The consideration or adoption of hate speech policies was not the work of mobilized constituencies with a leftist agenda. Certainly, the codes were linked to liberal and activist campuses, but unlike the anecdotal explanation propounded by the codes' critics, the policies were not advanced by mobilized minority groups or liberal ideologues. Instead, the codes owe their development to high-level administrators operating under institutional or instrumental motives.

Interestingly, the codes were connected to racial incidents or tensions on campus, a factor not picked up in the quantitative analysis. The qualitative investigation now explains why—administrators were not necessarily responding to incidents immediately preceding the policies, or even to events on their own campuses. Officials were spurred by a simmering undercurrent of racial tensions across the nation and saw their role as preserving order and maintaining their schools' good names. There are several ways of looking at this. In some cases, administrators genuinely believed that hate speech policies would improve the campus climate and make their schools more welcoming to minorities. The experience at Mt. Michaels suggests as much, where student services staff were concerned about the "viciousness" directed against minority groups. So too, MU officials initially reacted to a series of racial incidents. In both cases administrators acknowledge they felt compelled to "do something" to improve the climate for minorities on campus, and it is instructive that administrators at both schools were quick to accept and propose a hate speech policy. Even at Emilia College, President Ertel initiated the Emilia Plan (albeit without a speech rule) because she sought to improve the campus climate.

This is a plausible, and indeed even laudable, interpretation of the move to hate speech codes, but the better explanation is that administrators responded with policies to protect and even enhance the reputation of their schools and themselves. Put another way, they proposed administrative policy as a form of proactive crisis management. Officials feared that racial tensions would give way to serious incidents, which in turn would draw considerable and unfavorable attention to their schools. They certainly had an early warning. At Plains, the Klan's visit received wide play within campus, local and regional media, and the perceived increase in racial tensions throughout the Millennium system even drew in state legislators. At other schools racial unrest spawned substantial, negative coverage. The 1986 brawl at the University of Massachusetts–Amherst reached the *Boston Globe* and the *New York Times,* and racial unrest at the University of Michigan generated no fewer than fifteen stories in the *Chicago Tribune* over the course of a month. Alumni, lawmakers, opinion leaders, potential applicants, peers, and even members of the campus community read these stories. At the very least the reports were embarrassing to an institution and its leaders, who often appeared in the stories as unable to gain control of their schools. At worst they painted schools as harboring racists, campuses where attitudes were so bigoted that few decent people would want to attend.

Under these circumstances a campus executive would naturally seek to reduce tensions on campus, simultaneously taking a school out of the news while reassuring the public and campus constituencies that the school was committed to racial tolerance. This was the case at the University of Michigan, where interim president Robben Fleming put the university's speech policy on a fast-track to enactment. There were also elements of this strategy at MU and Plains, although in both cases administrators were responding as much to the concerns of state leaders. At MU, Chancellor Tucker was faced with a state senator who publicized racial incidents from across the university system. Whether or not these incidents had reached a crisis point, Tucker undoubtedly felt he had to do something to appease legislators, if only to stop the potentially bad publicity about the university. Tucker may well have initiated administrative policy on his own to address racial harassment, but the fact that he had a pack of legislators sniffing around the state campuses meant that he had to take action quickly. A harassment policy, thus, served three important aims: It demonstrated the University's commitment to address racial intolerance, it appeased legislative investigators, and in doing so it took the story of campus racism off the front pages.

At Plains the crisis was not so immediate, as the board of trustees decreed a racial harassment policy two years before the notorious campus incident. But even here they were taking a prophylactic measure to guard against what they had seen arise at other schools. Indeed, in some ways the Plains's policy reflected a kind of academic "keeping up with the Joneses." Having watched racist incidents embroil institutions elsewhere, and aware that elite schools like Michigan, Brown, and Pennsylvania were drafting novel hate speech rules, the trustees called on Plains to adopt new antiharassment policies. Nor was this national preoccupation limited to administrators. Even after President Jaffe had adopted the university's hate speech rule, the university senate responded to articles in *Academe* and the *Chronicle of Higher Education* and asked its Campus Relations Subcommittee to consider additional approaches to hate speech regulation.

This explanation will undoubtedly strike some readers as too cynical, as if I am charging university administrators with adopting showy, expansive policies simply to cover their backs. That criticism has two elements: one, that administrators intended the speech codes to do no more than deflect attention from their schools, and two, that university leaders would not have acted but for potentially bad publicity. I do not doubt that administrators had concerns other than their schools' reputations, and indeed this explanation may complement other motives. While I am not familiar with the former leaders of MU or Plains, I am acquainted with Robben Fleming, who presided over Michigan's speech policy. Fleming had served as the university's president from 1967 to 1979 and returned on an interim basis in the mid-1980s. I have no doubt that he thought Michigan's speech policy would improve racial conditions on campus, not just reduce press coverage.[32] So too, Jaffe had been quite vocal in speaking out against racism and intolerance at Plains. Nevertheless as chapter 5 details, most of the speech codes were enforced so rarely that they effectively became symbolic measures. Given these circumstances, it is appropriate to ask whether administrators were serious in adopting the speech codes or whether they had different motives.

At the same time, it is not simply the case that administrators acted to stave off controversy. The very fact that racial tensions would move them reflects some serious (and positive) changes in American social and political life. It seems inconceivable that fifty years ago college administrators would have been concerned about campus conditions for blacks or that the media would be poised to cover stories of racial harassment at college. In a sense the success of the civil rights movement (and perhaps even the women's rights movement) influenced administrators, convincing them and others that improved race relations were an important societal goal. For that matter, it is important to recall that the speech codes were linked to prestigious, progressive, and activist institutions. Even if administrators feared their schools would attract press coverage over racial intolerance—the contradiction between liberal reputations and racial tensions too tempting for reporters—it is difficult to imagine officials taking action unless they believed that minorities had a right to better treatment on campus or they feared recriminations from minority academicians who would demand those rights.

RESTRICTING SPEECH

If administrators had instrumental objectives, why would they consider, let alone adopt, policies that proscribed speech and expression? It is one thing to propose a rule against racist actions, another thing entirely to establish codes that seemed to challenge existing free speech doctrine. The answers here are far from clear, but as an initial matter some schools did not see themselves as drafting a "speech code." A top administrator at Middleberg, for example, expressed shock that anyone would label the harassment policy a "hate speech code." Certainly many of the college policies addressed expression, but officials may have intended the measures as "civility restraints,"[33] setting parameters for the *manner* in which ideas can be conveyed, rather than limiting the *substance* of a speaker's underlying message. For example, Middleberg's President Goodie claims she was less interested in "propos[ing] 'rules' of behavior" than in helping the College "find the ambient center" of respectful coexistence. Slurs and epithets would be unacceptable, but scholars could still engage in a serious debate about genetic gender roles. MU, too, sought to restrict fighting words rather than tackling the essential content of offensive messages.

With due respect to the intentions of Middleberg administrators, the college's original policy—and those at several other schools—was concerned with more than just the manner of expression. Even modeled as civility restraints, the speech rules at best skirted the line between viewpoint discrimination and time, place, and manner restrictions. If an administrator truly were interested in improving community dialogue, it seems likely that she would have chosen a statement of philosophy—which can be advanced through persuasion—instead of a disciplinary rule that threatened punishment. She might also have followed the approach at Emilia College and adopted affirmative measures over reactive policies.

So, were college administrators trying to pull the wool over the public's eyes? Were they secretly aligned with Millennium's Geoffrey Senger, seeking to "test the limits of" First Amendment boundaries by advancing new speech norms? In all likelihood, no. Administrators were certainly open to new approaches to counteract an unexpected and potentially ominous rise in racial intolerance, but few intended to enforce the policies systematically. For that matter, they relied on lawyers and other administrators to draft the policies, not critical race scholars or other activists who sought a "non-neutral, value-laden approach" to racist hate speech.[34] Of course, there are the odd examples—Michigan, where Professor Sally Anne Patton was involved in the drafting, Wisconsin, where Richard Delgado led the charge, and Stanford, where Professor Thomas Grey was the chief architect—but with the exception of Delgado, none of these academicians was a true disciple of critical race theory, nor in most cases were faculty involved in drafting such policy.

If critical race theory or any of the related "relativist" philosophies had an effect on the development of college hate speech codes, the influence was subtler, persuading administrators to consider a wider range of policy options than they previously would have entertained. Critical race theory had become an accepted school of thought, perhaps more so at liberal and activist institutions, and if nothing else it offered a new approach to address a wave of racial turbulence that many thought had been eliminated by the civil rights movement. If administrators truly felt at wits end in handling racial harassment and verbal attacks, then hate speech restrictions were the newest alternative. What's more, speech codes may have seemed akin to the new line of sexual harassment litigation in which activists had convinced the courts to penalize offensive speech that created a hostile or intimidating work environment.[35] If sexist speech could be punished, some administrators may have reasoned, then racial and ethnic hate speech could be regulated, too. Finally, the notion of hate speech prohibitions was in line with the emerging push for multicultural curricula on many campuses. Just as some faculty and students sought new classes that incorporated comparative perspectives—especially those that valued traditions other than a "Western, heterosexual, white-male norm"—administrators also may have been drawn to conduct codes that ostensibly enforced civility and respect for difference.

It is one thing to say that administrators were primed by the philosophical and pedagogical debates swirling around them and another thing entirely to claim that policy adoption was led or controlled by ideological activists. No one can deny that Richard Delgado helped to craft the University of Wisconsin's speech code or that other faculty (although not necessarily critical race scholars) were involved in some of the earlier hate speech measures at Michigan and Stanford. But the proliferation of similarly minded speech codes had less to do with the influence of ideology than with the prestige of the first institutions to adopt speech policies. Administrators at schools from Millennium to Plains to Middleberg looked to the example of their prestigious brethren, but more importantly public leaders did as well. The Plains Board of Regents was familiar with the situation at Michigan and Wisconsin, and state legislators near Millennium kept a keen eye on such top schools "back East." With court cases yet to come contesting such speech codes, momentum began to build to follow the path of these academic trendsetters.

Finally, it is worth considering whether administrators ever expected to enforce the speech rules they enacted. This point is examined more closely in chapter 5, but it offers a compelling, if again potentially cynical, explanation for the codes' content. If the codes were intended primarily for their symbolic effect, administrators could consider and enact expansive policies with little repercussion. Few, if any, students (or staff or faculty) would ever be charged under the rules, and schools might thus escape a court challenge while raising the flag of racial tolerance across campus. To be sure, a declaratory judgment would still be ripe (a fact that did in both Michigan's and Stanford's speech policies), but administrators could afford to take the risk of advancing expansive policies on the hope that they would either reduce racist attacks or provide cover against charges of inaction or racial insensitivity.

The Courts Act

The adoption of college hate speech codes attracted considerable attention and with it significant opposition. Not surprisingly, several of the policies were challenged in court. Beginning in 1989 and lasting until 1995, six courts, including the U.S. Supreme Court, were asked to consider measures that punished hate speech, whether committed at a university or within a municipality.[1] Each of these courts overturned hate speech policies, finding the rules vague, overbroad, or an "impermissible content regulation."[2]

Interestingly, at about this same time the courts were expanding the doctrine of sexual harassment law, enlarging the claim to address a hostile work environment, even when the alleged violation was based primarily on speech. This perceived disjuncture—between the expansion of hostile environment harassment and the judicial nullification of hate speech regulation—has been addressed to an extent in the legal literature, particularly by those who seek to narrow the scope of sexual harassment law to action and not speech.[3] Yet most of the discussion has focused on jurisprudential grounds, a defense of the courts that seems more riddled on closer inspection. As this chapter argues, the courts' disjointed treatment of analogous claims may have less to do with legal doctrine than with political, social, and cultural pressures that face judges. Recognizing that extra-judicial forces shape legal decisions need not threaten the legitimacy of those rulings; rather, this fact provides a broader understanding of the basis and power of law, showing that even codified law may be socially constructed.

The chapter is laid out in four sections, presenting first then second the court cases concerning college hate speech codes and sexual harassment law. A third section considers the traditional theories advanced for the differing lines of precedent, concluding that the distinctions are not as clear as the courts have claimed. A fourth part, then, offers several alternative explanations for the courts' decisions, the theories all aligned on a common point: the pressures involved in judicial decision-making serve to construct constitutional law—and most particularly free speech—by its social utility.

HATE SPEECH DECISIONS

In 1989 the University of Michigan became the first in a series of schools to see its speech code overturned when, in *Doe v. University of Michigan,* U.S. District Judge Avern Cohn ruled that the university could not:

> establish an anti-discrimination policy which had the effect of prohibiting certain speech because it disagreed with ideas or messages sought to be conveyed. . . . Looking at the plain language of the Policy, it was simply impossible to discern any limitation on its scope or any conceptual distinction between protected and unprotected conduct. . . . [T]he terms "stigmatize" and "victimize" are not self-defining [and are thus ambiguous]. These words can only be understood with reference to some exogenous value system. What one individual might find victimizing or stigmatizing, another individual might not.[4]

Two years later Judge Robert Warren adopted much of this reasoning in *UWM Post v. University of Wisconsin,* holding that the University of Wisconsin's speech code was also unconstitutional. Although the judge was more forgiving in determining that much of the code was unambiguous, he still ruled that Wisconsin's code was overly broad. Said the court, the "UW Rule has over-breadth difficulties because it is a content-based rule which regulates a substantial amount of protected speech. . . . Content-based prohibitions such as that in the UW Rule, however well intended, simply cannot survive the screening which our Constitution demands."[5]

The Michigan and Wisconsin decisions may well have stood as a model for the two later courts that considered the speech codes of Central Michigan University and Stanford University. In *Dambrot v. Central Michigan University,* a federal district judge overturned a campus rule that prohibited any "verbal . . . behavior that subjects an individual to an intimidating, hostile or offensive educational . . . environment by demeaning or slurring individuals . . . because of their racial or ethnic affiliation."[6] Borrowing from *Doe v. Michigan,* the *Dambrot* court found that CMU's policy was over broad, vague, and an impermissible viewpoint restriction. This decision was upheld on appeal by the U.S. Court of Appeals for the Sixth Circuit.[7]

Similarly, in *Corry v. Stanford University* a Santa Clara Circuit Court threw out Stanford's speech code on the grounds that the University "prohibited certain expressions based on the underlying message."[8] Although Stanford's code appeared initially to be different—professing to prohibit "fighting words"[9]—the court's decision followed the analysis of *Doe* and *CMU.* Because the speech code proscribed only those fighting words "based on sex, race, color, and the like," the court held it to be an "impermissible content-based regulation" prohibited by the First Amendment.[10]

It is important to note that these cases addressed hate speech codes that prohibited verbal harassment of minorities and offensive speech. Theoretically, one might also have expected challenges to generic verbal harassment policies, since, as some scholars claim, prohibitions against any kind of verbal harassment necessarily threaten the speaker's First Amendment rights.[11] However, what primarily concerned litigants—and undoubtedly troubled the courts—were those policies that sought to proscribe particular viewpoints and/or were overly broad.

In the midst of these cases the United States Supreme Court took up the question of hate speech prohibitions in *R.A.V. v. City of St. Paul, Minnesota.*[12] Although the case involved St. Paul's Bias-Motivated Crime Ordinance, *R.A.V.* had a clear connection to the collegiate speech codes. In its decision the Court ruled it unconstitutional to punish particular kinds of hateful messages as being worse than others. Even when these restrictions covered a class of expression that was already unprotected (i.e., fighting words), public bodies could not choose to proscribe particular epithets—for example, racist—while leaving others, perhaps anti-Catholic, untouched. As the Court said, public bodies could not impose "special prohibitions on those speakers who express views on the disfavored subjects of 'race, color, creed, religion or gender.'"[13]

Some may argue that these cases apply in limited circumstances and thus that the courts have not truly restricted college hate speech codes. As a matter of strict constitutional doctrine, of course, the cases are applicable only to public bodies (and, under the Leonard Law, to private schools in California as well), and there may remain questions about *R.A.V.*'s clarity. I suppose there will even be those who claim that each of the lower court decisions applies only to its judicial district and that *R.A.V.,* because it involved a municipal ordinance and not collegiate policies, has no relevance to the hate speech codes. These constructions, however, are overly narrow. Taking the arguments in reverse, it is a matter of basic jurisprudence that the courts look to other jurisdictions when hearing issues of first impression. *Corry* and *Dambrot* relied in part on the reasoning in *UWM Post,* and the Wisconsin decision borrowed from the reasoning in *Doe.* Moreover, any ruling of the U.S. Supreme Court, especially on an issue that appears integrally related to later cases, has precedential if not persuasive authority.

Relying on the legal restrictions of stare decisis is itself too narrow, for the power of judicial decisions is also explained by the manner in which they are communicated to interested audiences.[14] In these cases the courts were not only speaking in a single voice, but their message was read and understood as such outside of the courtroom. *R.A.V.,* in particular, was immediately recognized as applying to the speech codes. Said Justice Harry Blackmun in dissent, "I fear that the Court has been distracted from its proper mission by the temptation to decide the issue over 'politically correct' speech and 'cultural diversity,' neither of which is presented here."[15]

Blackmun was hardly alone in suggesting that *R.A.V.* was directed against campus hate speech codes. The first commentators on the case offered a similar analysis. As the *St. Louis Post-Dispatch* reported, political correctness "never appeared in Justice Antonin Scalia's decision on Monday striking down a hate-speech law from St. Paul . . . [b]ut legal scholars said Tuesday that Scalia's opinion was clearly aimed at the proliferating state laws, municipal ordinances and campus codes aimed at racist, sexist and anti-Semitic speech." Added Steven Shapiro of the ACLU: "This decision was clearly written in the larger political context in which the conservative wing of the court is concerned about the political correctness movement."[16]

As he had done through much of the PC debate, Charles Krauthammer jumped in to offer his own analysis. Explaining the decision, he said:

> The St. Paul opinion represents yet another battle in [Justice] Scalia's continuing campaign against group rights. [When it comes to offering] members of preferred groups . . . special protection from verbal or symbolic injury, Scalia has long tried to deter the state from making these kinds of hierarchical distinctions among the citizenry. [Justice Blackmun charges] Scalia with using this case to attack "politically correct speech." Scalia's opinion will, no doubt, chill the current ardor on campus for politically correct speech codes. . . . Scalia has indeed taken aim at political correctness. He is to be commended for it.[17]

Understandably, one might question the impartiality of Krauthammer or the ACLU, since each had an interest in extending the Court's message beyond the four corners of *R.A.V.* Krauthammer had been crusading against PC for up to a year by the time of *R.A.V.,* and the ACLU had also represented the plaintiff in *Doe* and wanted to confirm that collegiate speech codes were dead. Nevertheless, scholars and observers on all sides of the spectrum saw the *R.A.V.* decision as rooted in concerns about political correctness and what some saw as a growing movement to restrict speech on college campuses. Appearing on the *MacNeil/Lehrer NewsHour,* Professors Charles Fried and Laurence Tribe of Harvard Law School (two ideological opposites) both agreed that the *R.A.V.* decision was "going to have an effect on campuses which have passed these so-called 'politically correct restrictions.'" Said Fried, "[I]t seems to me that Scalia was putting his finger" on Stanford, "Michigan and Wisconsin, and a number of other places [where] certain kinds of speech are banned because they upset people who belong to certain categories."[18]

It is not at all surprising that the Court would premise its hate speech decision on concerns about political correctness. The lawyer who represented the plaintiff in *R.A.V.* brags that he hung his argument on "the connection between [St. Paul's] ordinance and the attempts to frame 'politically correct' speech codes on college campuses."[19] But he had a more than receptive court. Since the decision, individual justices have given hints of their disdain for political correctness and speech codes. In speeches at major universities, both Chief Justice William Rehnquist and Justice Clarence Thomas have decried such influences. Addressing a commencement ceremony at George Mason University, Rehnquist alluded "to disputes on numerous college campuses over 'politically correct speech.'" Declared the chief justice, "On occasion, one senses that [for] some universities today . . . there is an orthodoxy or sort of party line from which one departs at one's peril."[20] So too, Justice Thomas has "complained that 'a new brand of stereotypes and ad hominem assaults are surfacing across the nation's college campuses, in the national media, in Hollywood and among the . . . cultural elite' aimed at 'those who dare to disagree with the latest ideological fad.'"[21]

It is Justice Scalia, though, who reserves the greatest enmity for what he sees as politically correct speech restrictions. As Krauthammer noted, the *R.A.V.* decision may have been part of Scalia's ongoing battle to chill the nation's ardor for political correctness.[22] Certainly, his dissents since then have hardly masked his disdain for PC. In a 1994 case holding that gender may not be a basis for jury selection, a "sarcastic Antonin Scalia . . . ridiculed the Court's majority for its political correctness. 'Unisex is unquestionably in fashion,'" he declared.[23] Scalia's behavior did not escape other journalists. The *Washington Times,* among others, noted the mockery with which Scalia accused "the majority of politically correct 'anti-male-chauvinist oratory' and flawed reasoning."[24] It is hardly a leap to imagine that his opinion of political correctness would have influenced his decision on the related issue of collegiate hate speech.

The courts' hate speech decisions were enthusiastically received by the many opponents of college speech codes. Following *Corry,* headlines in the *Arizona Republic* declared "Campus Speech Codes R. I. P.," and its editors delighted that "the First Amendment has been reinstated on America's college campuses."[25] The *Rocky Mountain News* announced that hate speech codes were now "dead letters—unenforced law." Nat Hentoff, too, hailed the end of a doctrine that had suffered from "fundamental weaknesses."[26]

HATE SPEECH IN A DIFFERENT NAME

Interestingly, while the courts have overturned college speech codes, they continue to openly regulate another form of hate speech—sexual harassment—with no apparent concern about the contradictions this presents. Under Title VII of the Civil Rights Acts, and with the regulatory support of the Equal Employment Opportunity Commission (EEOC), U.S. courts readily and frequently penalize those who verbally harass others on the basis of their sex.

It has been over twenty years now since the federal courts first considered sexual harassment cases. Over that time the lower courts have legitimized the claim, with the Supreme Court deciding in 1986 that an action for sexual harassment is not only available under Title VII of the Civil Rights Acts but that the claim extends also to the creation of a hostile or intimidating work environment (HWE).[27] It is important to remember that the claim of sexual harassment is a creation of the common law. At no point has Congress passed legislation expressly prohibiting sexual harassment. Over time the EEOC has issued regulations defining and prohibiting sexual harassment, but the courts first created this doctrine by reading a claim of sexual harassment into the law of sex discrimination.

At any point the courts might have retreated, and, in fact, there were ample legal bases to refuse to create the tort. Judges might have declined to establish new law when there was not direct statutory support.[28] They might have concluded that the terms of the claim, including such requisites as "unwelcome," "hostile," or "intimidating," were too ambiguous to survive judicial scrutiny.[29] They might have dismissed the underlying theory of sexual harassment on the grounds that it would "chill" relations in the workplace by making co-workers walk on eggshells. Or, more to the point, they might have refused to extend the claim to verbal harassment. Certainly, there were constitutional grounds to limit sexual harassment claims to discriminatory actions and not speech, the courts having ruled historically that the First Amendment protects expression but not acts. If, as the *Doe* and *UWM Post* courts ruled, racist jokes and insults must go unpunished, then presumably sexist expressions ought to have remained unfettered too.

The reality has proven just the opposite, for there is now a long line of cases in which the courts have punished sexist expression, including jokes, offensive comments, and "gender-baiting." In *Katz v. Dole,* for example, the Fourth Circuit extended the notion of hostile work environment to prohibit "offensive sexually related epithets," including those "widely recognized as not only improper but as intensely degrading, deriving their power to wound not only from their meaning but also from the 'disgust and violence they express phonetically.'"[30] The *Katz* court was being a bit decorous in its description of actionable language, but it was talking about cases like *McNabb v. Cub Foods,* in which women "confront their tormenter in front of their manager with, 'You have called me a fucking bitch,' [only to be answered,] 'No, I didn't. I called you a fucking cunt.'"[31]

Many of these cases veer close to the fighting words doctrine, with the courts punishing sexist epithets that presumably might start a fight, but increasingly the claim seems targeted at the larger category of offensive, sexist expression. The lead comes from the Supreme Court, which has refused to overturn a case of sexual harassment based largely on "sexual innuendos." In *Harris v. Forklift Systems, Inc.,* the company president "often insulted [the employee] because of her gender . . . [telling her] on several occasions, in the presence of other employees, 'You're a woman, what do you know,' and 'We need a man as the rental manager'; at least once, he told her she was 'a dumb ass woman.'"[32]

Some courts have gone so far as requiring that employers "take prompt action to prevent . . . bigots from expressing their opinions in a way that abuses or offends their co-workers," in order to "inform[] people that the expression of racist or sexist attitudes in public is unacceptable."[33] Others have banned such inquiries as "did you get any over the weekend?"[34] As one commentator has noted, "many courts have permitted [sexual] harassment actions to proceed based in part upon offensive speech that was not directed toward the plaintiff."[35] Others have "permitted [sexual] harassment actions based in part upon speech that was not even witnessed by the plaintiff."[36] In fact, it was not until 1991 that a court ruled on a First Amendment defense to HWE. In *Robinson v. Jacksonville Shipyards,* the court balanced the "governmental interest in cleansing the workplace of impediments to the equality of women" against the free speech interest in "sexually demeaning remarks and jokes," as well as "pictures of nude and partially nude women in sexually suggestive poses."[37]

Not surprisingly given the terms of this test, the court found the First Amendment defense lacking. Yet Robinson is far from an anomaly. As others have amply chronicled, the courts are quite willing to uphold claims of verbal harassment in the workplace.[38]

The same is true for sexual harassment policies created for college campuses. According to a 1994 study, 300 of 384 public schools surveyed had a sexual harassment policy.[39] Almost all of the policies were modeled on the EEOC's regulations, and many took an expansive view of harassment. The University of Iowa's policy, for example, covered "verbal conduct," including comments, statements, jokes, questions, anecdotes, and remarks. Even a policy statement from the American Council on Education suggested that sexual harassment could include "inappropriate put-downs of individual persons."[40] Yet with a few exceptions—most notably *Cohen v. San Bernardino Valley College* and *Silva v. New Hampshire*[41]—the courts have largely refused to restrict or overturn the application of university sexual harassment codes to cases of verbal harassment.[42] "This is true even when a sexual harassment charge stems from classroom speech or office speech."[43] The situation is more pronounced at the primary and secondary level, where the Supreme Court has now ruled that schoolchildren can sue for student-on-student harassment.[44]

EXPLAINING THE JUDICIAL DISPARITY—TRADITIONAL THEORIES

How is it that the courts have treated measures with similar terms differently? If college hate speech codes are largely modeled on HWE, and if sexual harassment law now prohibits offensive speech as well as actions, why is it that the courts have invalidated college codes as unconstitutional abridgements of free speech while continuing to support the enforcement of Title VII's reach? Four conventional theories seek to explain much of the courts' behavior, explanations that ground the decisions in traditional legal precedent. That said, there remains a lingering sense that other factors may have driven this doctrinal schism—a view that the courts may have responded as much to extralegal forces as to precedent.

Overstepping the Terms of the Policies

Accepting for the moment that the hate speech codes share similar terms with HWE, the simplest theory for disparate outcomes is that colleges exceeded the reach of their policies in enforcing them. This is not the same as saying that the terms of the codes were unconstitutional, rather that administrators applied their policies so expansively that they included conduct that would have failed to meet Title VII's definition of harassment. As the court rightly noted in *Doe,* the University of Michigan issued an Interpretive Guide that was so "integrally related" to its speech code that it became "an authoritative interpretation of the [code] and provided examples of sanctionable conduct."[45] According to the Guide, students might have been found liable under the hate rule for any of the following misdeeds:

- Inviting "everyone on [your] floor [to a party] except one person because [you] think she might be a lesbian."
- Excluding "someone from a study group because that person is of a different race, sex, or ethnic origin than you are."
- Laughing "at a joke about someone in your class who stutters."[46]

Administrators did not issue an interpretive guide at the University of Wisconsin, but they also took an expansive interpretation of their speech code. As the court explained in *UWM Post,* students were prosecuted under the Wisconsin rule for the following altercations:

- At the University of Wisconsin–Oshkosh a female student referred "to a black female student as a 'fat-ass nigger' during an argument."
- At the University of Wisconsin–Oshkosh, a student angrily told an Asian American student that, "It's people like you — that's the reason this country is screwed up," and "you don't belong here."
- At the University of Wisconsin–River Falls, a male student yelled at a female student in public, saying, "you've got nice tits."[47]

Undoubtedly, each of these instances is offensive, and the students involved should be ashamed of their conduct. But not a single one of these instances would qualify as harassment under the standards of Title VII. As the courts make clear, behavior must be "severe" and/or "pervasive" to reach the threshold of harassment, a standard that is evaluated both objectively as a "reasonable person" would and subjectively according to the actual victim.[48] "Mere utterance of an ethnic or racial epithet which engenders offensive feelings in an employee does not sufficiently affect the conditions of employment to violate Title VII."[49] So too in the collegiate context, it seems unlikely that a single epithet would so alter the conditions of academic life that it creates a hostile or abusive educational environment.

For this reason, much of the *Doe* and *UWM Post* holdings make sense, but additional dicta call into question the dichotomy between hate speech and HWE cases. In *Doe* Judge Cohn examined the wording, application, and "legislative history" of Michigan's rule before finding that administrators had interpreted the code too broadly. At this point he could have ended the case with a judgment against the university. Nevertheless, he pressed on to consider whether the rule was also unconstitutionally vague. This is hardly unusual, for courts often look to multiple bases for their decisions, but his treatment of the "vagueness question" is peculiar. The judge found "the plain language of the Policy" to be impermissibly vague since "it was simply impossible to discern any limitation" on the terms "stigmatize" or "victimize." Both of these words, said the court, "are general and elude precise definition."[50]

Yet a similar argument could be made for the terms "severe" or "pervasive" under Title VII. Like stigmatize or victimize, "these words can only be understood with reference to some exogenous value system. What one individual might find [severe] or [pervasive] another individual might not."[51] The Supreme Court itself has acknowledged that a hostile environment "is not, and by its nature cannot be, a mathematically precise test,"[52] with even Justice Scalia accepting such terms as "abusive" and "hostile" despite their lack of precision.[53]

The Supreme Court's flexibility has filtered its way down to the lower courts, where many have been willing to read in a definition to the severe and pervasive tests; some have gone so far as to create a separate reasonableness test to measure pervasiveness. A good example is *Rubin v. Ikenberry,* where a federal court upheld the University of Illinois' sexual harassment policy even though its terms were at least as vague as the speech code in *Doe*.[54]

Nor is Title VII the only area of the law in which the Supreme Court tolerates ambiguity. The Court has upheld bans on "loud and raucous" noises despite their subjective nature.[55] And, of course, the standards for obscenity law are vague, it being difficult to define precisely whether a work is "patently offensive" or appeals to the "prurient interest."[56] In each of these areas the courts are willing to overlook ambiguous terms or even fill in the details of vague standards. Indeed, the Third Circuit has even approved a secondary school's racial harassment policy when it was based on such nebulous terms as "racially divisive."[57] Given such deference, it is difficult to understand why the *Doe* court was so reluctant to define "stigmatize" or "victimize."

Speech vs. Action

Others might explain the courts' varied decisions by the speech/act distinction, claiming that sexual harassment involves action but that hate speech concerns expression. It is well settled in U.S. constitutional law that the First

Amendment attaches to "expression," a term that is generally considered to mean speech. Certainly, some actions can be expressive, including the burning of the flag, a draft card, or the donning of offensive apparel,[58] but for the most part the courts tend to distinguish between speech, which is expressive and thus protected, and actions, which are neither. There are few bases to restrict protected speech.[59]

By their terms many of the college codes addressed "verbal or physical behavior," a sign that they were not targeted exclusively at expression. Nonetheless, their enforcement pattern suggests a threat to speech. In *Doe,* the plaintiff feared prosecution for stating his views of sex differences; in *UWM Post,* students had hurled insults at one another; in *Dambrot* a college coach used a racial epithet; and in *Corry* students had satirized racial differences. Granted, some of these expressions were hardly worthy of constitutional protection—reflecting fighting words or obscene epithets—but other cases show institutions clamping down on speech that was "merely" offensive. Even if such sentiments are unpopular or even grotesque, the courts have been reluctant to allow public bodies to restrict offensive opinions.

In HWE cases, by contrast, the courts often "try to finesse difficult First Amendment analysis by characterizing disagreeable expression as 'conduct,'" or actions, and not speech.[60] In the case of *Robinson v. Jacksonville Shipyards,*[61] for example, a federal court ruled that pornographic pictures "were not in fact expression but rather 'discriminatory conduct' . . . even though the fact remains that displaying pornographic pictures is expression."[62] Even the U.S. Supreme Court has bought in to the fiction that HWE addresses actions and not expression. In *R.A.V.* the justices overturned a municipal ordinance because it imposed "special prohibitions on those speakers who express views on the disfavored subjects of 'race, color, creed, religion, or gender.'"[63] Under this reasoning one might have expected the Court to overturn HWE, for the claim also limits expression "on the disfavored subject of gender." Yet the Court crafted a special exception for sexual harassment, saying such claims really reflect a situation where "a particular content-based subcategory of a proscribable class of speech can be swept up incidentally within the reach of a statute directed at conduct rather than speech."[64]

The problem with this exception is that it is an illusion, both as to the facts of sexual harassment and to the law of free speech. Sexual harassment often *is* expression, a reality that requires the courts to weigh the grounds for limiting such speech. This dilemma cannot be brushed aside with illusions that the First Amendment allows some de minimis level of content restriction. Even the four concurring justices in *R.A.V.* recognize this point, noting that "[u]nder the broad principle the Court uses to decide the present case, hostile work environment claims based on sexual harassment should fail First Amendment review."[65] Since the Court could not accept that result, the concurrence suggests, the majority crafted an exception to cover sexual harassment claims.

The Court has been widely criticized for its decision in *R.A.V.,* both for refusing to overturn the claim of verbal sexual harassment on First Amendment grounds and for failing to offer the lower courts clear guidance to adjudicate sexual harassment claims when the offending conduct is verbal.[66] In the next term after *R.A.V.* the justices declined "to mention the First Amendment objections to Title VII's harassment law" even though that case, *Harris v. Forklift,* was based largely on misogynist speech.[67] Without clear direction from the High Court, other "courts have consistently interpreted [Title VII to include] 'verbal expression.' Relying on the EEOC's definition of hostile-environment harassment, courts, both state and federal, have found employers liable for . . . 'obscene propositions,' sexual vulgarity . . . racial jokes, slurs, and other statements deemed derogatory to minorities . . . ."[68] Indeed, expression "is often a substantial, if not the primary, basis" that courts use to impose liability. The examples run from such cases as *EEOC v. Hacienda Hotel,* where the perpetrator compared the victim to a "dog" and "whore," suggesting that women "get pregnant because they like to suck men's dicks,"[69] to *Jenson v. Eveleth Taconite Co.,* in which a federal court formally recognized that pornographic pictures and "sexually-focused" expression "constitute acts of sexual harassment."[70] As one commentator has said, courts may be "offended by the implicit or explicit message of the expression—for example, that women should be sexual playthings for men, that women (or blacks) do not belong in the workplace—or that they should hold an inferior position in our society."[71]

Admittedly, much of the expression at issue in sexual harassment involves epithets, the kind of speech that might qualify as fighting words under First Amendment case law. But just as the Supreme Court has refused to allow St. Paul, Minnesota, to pick and choose in pushing hateful messages, it seems contradictory that the Court would single out just one type of epithet under Title VII—sexual. Indeed, when the conduct involves more general but offensive sexist expression, the courts seem to accept restrictions they do not permit for other kinds of speech. Again, the point is not that sexist speech is valuable and must be tolerated, rather that the courts have been inconsistent in outlawing college hate codes as violations of free speech while permitting claims of sexist expression to proceed under HWE. There may be other grounds for distinguishing the two prohibitions, but the disparity cannot be justified on account that one involves speech and the other action. Sexual harassment involves speech too.

Employment vs. Educational Settings

When defending its hate speech policy, the University of Wisconsin analogized its rule to Title VII, saying the court should find it constitutional because the policy's "prohibition of discriminatory speech which creates a hostile environment has parallels in the employment setting."[72] Federal District Judge Robert Warren disagreed, concluding that "Title VII addresses employment, not educational settings."[73] As an initial matter, the judge is correct in describing Title VII's reach. There can be little doubt that the legislation addresses employment settings. Section 2000e-2 is entitled "unlawful employment practices," and the Supreme Court made clear in *Meritor* that sexual harassment covers "acts of employees for which employers under Title VII are to be held responsible."[74] Judge Warren is also right that Title VII fails to mention academic life, whether in classrooms, residence halls, or extracurricular activities. Statutorily, there is little to suggest that collegiate speech codes would be included in Title VII.

But in some sense Judge Warren misses the point. The question is not whether speech codes are authorized by an employment statute; rather, the issue is whether college speech codes should be found constitutional given that the provision upon which they are based is constitutional. Put another way, if employers may restrict the speech of their employees in order to prevent a hostile work environment, why can't universities regulate the conduct of their members to avert a hostile academic environment?

Judge Warren did not answer this question, but the conventional explanation tells us that speech restrictions are acceptable in the workplace because, unlike college campuses, "the First Amendment has no application" there.[75] According to commentators, the First Amendment protects "public discourse"—those "communicative processes necessary for the formation of public opinion."[76] By their very nature, universities are concerned with public discourse, but as the same commentators maintain, "speech in the workplace does not generally constitute public discourse."[77] "Within the workplace . . . an image of dialogue among autonomous self-governing citizens would be patently out of place."[78]

That said, public employees have the right to speak on issues of public concern.[79] Private employees too have some speech rights, at least to the extent that the First Amendment is implicated when their employers seek to enforce Title VII's mandates against expression.[80] Admittedly, these rights are limited in the employment context, but the countervailing pressures are no different from those essential to collegiate life. Just as public bodies can restrict an employee's speech when it impinges "efficient operations,"[81] so too educators may regulate the content of classroom debate. The student who wants to discuss hermeneutics in physical chemistry or who writes a paper on gene therapy for Spanish class can expect a poor grade at best, for he is speaking out of turn and interfering with the instructor's pedagogy. If anything, the equality interests of Title VII are greater in the educational arena, where students seek essential skills to compete in the economic marketplace. If "the government's interest in workplace equality stands alone as a justification for punishing some verbal harassment,"[82] then "similar speech restrictions should be accepted in any sphere in which we could discern a strong commitment to equality, such as education."[83]

For this reason the courts have begun to knock down the wall separating harassment in employment and harassment in education. By 1994, 78 percent of public universities surveyed had adopted sexual harassment rules for their campuses, many of these policies conflating harassment in "work or learning environments."[84] Yet, the courts have largely refused to entertain challenges to university sexual harassment policies.[85] The cases include *McClellan v. Board of Regents of Tennessee,* in which the Supreme Court of Tennessee ruled "[t]here is no meaningful difference . . . between sexual harassment in the workplace and sexual harassment in the academic setting";[86] *Parks v. Wilson,* where a District Court explained that the "policies underlying [Title VII] support with equal force imposition of the same standard in the school setting"[87] as well as federal courts in Illinois and Ohio[88] which permitted students to bring sexual harassment charges under university policies premised on Title VII.

The courts have also approved a private right of action under Title IX to apply sexual harassment standards to academe. Title IX, of course, is federal legislation "designed to protect individuals from sex discrimination by denying federal financial aid to those educational institutions that bear responsibility for sexually discriminatory practices."[89] Title IX provides that:

> No person in the United States shall, on the basis of sex, be excluded from participation in, be denied the benefits of, or be subjected to discrimination under any education program or activity receiving Federal financial assistance.[90]

At no point does Title IX speak of sexual harassment, nor does it reference terms from Title VII or any other employment-related legislation or regulation. Yet, the "courts have regularly applied Title VII principles" when "reviewing sexual discrimination claims by teachers and other employees of educational institutions under Title IX."[91] "Courts have also relied upon Title VII . . . in recognizing that Title IX prohibits the existence of a hostile environment due to a teacher's sexual harassment of a student." In 1999 the U.S. Supreme Court affirmed this trend, holding that a private cause of action could stand under Title IX when "student-on-student . . . harassment was so severe, pervasive, and objectively offensive that it effectively barred the victim's access to an educational opportunity or benefit."[92] To be sure, the Court affixed responsibility differently than under Title VII, premising liability on deliberate indifference to known acts of harassment, but in other respects the Court's analysis mirrored Title VII's protection against harassment in employment.

That case, *Davis v. Monroe County Board of Education,* involved a primary school setting where the greater need for discipline may outweigh other interests in public discourse,[93] but Title IX has also been used to apply the HWE standard to sexual harassment at the university level.[94] These cases include such disputes as *Rubin v. Ikenberry,* where a professor regularly engaged in outrageous "sexual commentary, inquiries and jokes during class."[95] If, as the *UWM Post* court maintains, Title VII is limited to employment matters and Title IX restricted to academe, then cases like *Rubin* should have been rejected. But if anything, the courts have erred in the other direction. As the Supreme Court acknowledged in *Franklin v. Gwinnett County Public Schools,*[96] "a student should have the same protection in school that an employee has in the workplace. . . . Indeed, where there are distinctions between the school environment and the workplace, they 'serve only to emphasize the need for zealous protection against sex discrimination in the schools.'"[97]

Academic Freedom

If the courts are to justify different treatment for college hate speech policies and HWE rules, the distinction must turn less on the needs for equality or discipline in each venue than on the heightened importance of academic speech. Academic freedom and scholarly expression occupy a hallowed position in American culture and law.[98] From *Sweezy v. New Hampshire* to *Keyishian v. Board of Regents* and *Widmar v. Vincent,* the courts have considered the classroom to be "peculiarly the 'marketplace of ideas'"[99] and have given special consideration to academic dialogue. As the Supreme Court has said, "[s]cholarship cannot flourish in an atmosphere of suspicion and distrust. . . . Teachers and students must always remain free to inquire, to study and to evaluate, to gain new maturity and understanding; otherwise our civilization will stagnate and die."[100]

Perhaps the best example of a court's deference to classroom speech is *Cohen v. San Bernardino Valley College,*[101] where the Ninth Circuit Court of Appeals refused to enforce a college's sexual harassment policy against an English professor. In that case, the College of San Bernardino had adopted a sexual harassment policy modeled almost identically on Title VII's standards.[102] Shortly after its adoption, a female student charged her professor with violating the new policy for his "statements and conduct" in class. The professor taught a required remedial English course, and according to the District Court, used a "controversial teaching style," which included a "repeated focus on topics of a sexual nature" and regular "use of profanity and vulgarities." In the spring semester of 1992:

> He began class discussion on the issue of pornography and played the "devil's advocate" by asserting controversial viewpoints. During a classroom discussion on the subject, [the professor] stated in class that he wrote for *Hustler* and *Playboy,* and he read some articles out loud in class. . . . According to [the student, the professor] then told her that if she met him in a bar he would help her get a better grade. She also claimed that [he] would look down her shirt, as well as the shirts of other female students, and that he told her she was overreacting because she was a woman.[103]

Were a similar fact pattern to occur in the workplace, a court would likely uphold a claim of sexual harassment. Indeed, *Cohen* is not that different from *Morgan v. Hertz,* where a supervisor questioned employees about their sexual practices,[104] or *EEOC v. Horizons Hotel Corp.,* where a co-worker unleashed a "stream of comments about [the plaintiff's] body and propositioned her for sex.[105] In the instant case, however, the Ninth Circuit ruled that the professor's behavior "did not fall within the core region of sexual harassment as defined by the [College's] Policy. Instead, officials of the College, on an entirely ad hoc basis, applied the Policy's nebulous outer reaches to punish teaching methods that [the professor] had used for many years. . . . [The professor] was simply without any notice that the Policy would be applied in such a way as to punish his longstanding teaching style."[106]

It is difficult to see how the court could reach this decision unless it concluded that special "protection [should] be given a public college's professor's classroom speech."[107] Among other things, its conclusion that the faculty member had to be warned of the Policy's reach would be preposterous if applied in the workplace. In such case, a group of men who had previously hassled their female co-workers could not be held responsible under a sexual harassment rule unless they were first personally warned. This is simply not the case, as employees are held responsible for informing themselves of new personnel policies and conforming their behavior to any new standards.[108]

Cohen is one of the few cases in which a court has refused to apply a sexual harassment policy to the classroom setting,[109] but its deference may be reflected in the *Doe, UWM Post, CMU,* and *Stanford* courts' decisions to overturn university speech codes. One sees strands of this perspective in Judge Warren's statement that the UW Rule "limits the diversity of ideas among students and thereby prevents the 'robust exchange of ideas' which intellectually diverse campuses provide."[110] Universities occupy a hallowed position in American culture. We enshrine scholarly life, as politicians, journalists, and other opinion leaders prize the intellectual inquiry carried on there. It is not inconceivable that the courts would join this chorus by applying a heightened First Amendment standard to campus speech rules.

This approach, however, overstates the importance of campus speech while ignoring the fact that one of the most basic elements of university life—grading—routinely limits expression. Initially, we must remember that academic freedom is not an unfettered First Amendment right.[111] To the contrary, colleges may regulate expression of students where it materially disrupts class work or other university activities or unduly interferes with the rights of others.[112] In fact, as Cass Sunstein notes, "colleges and universities are often in the business of controlling speech, and their controls are hardly ever thought to raise free speech problems."[113] When faculty grade one answer as "right" and another as "wrong," the First Amendment is untrampled, as it is when a professor cuts off a student in class for going "far afield from the basic approach of the course."[114]

This point is born out by two cases on classroom speech. In *Bishop v. University of Alabama* and *Rubin v. Ikenberry* the courts made clear that academic speech is not immune from sanction. Both courts willingly deferred to a university's attempt to restrict coercive and harassing speech during classroom discussion. The Eleventh Circuit was perhaps the more adamant of the two, ruling that "educators do not offend the First Amendment by exercising editorial control over the style and content of student (or professor) speech in school-sponsored expressive activities so long as their actions are reasonably related to legitimate pedagogical concerns."[115]

There are those observers who would decry the *Bishop* and *Rubin* decisions, seeing them as clear cases of viewpoint discrimination.[116] But if they are viewpoint discrimination, they are no different from HWE, which has historically punished individuals for specific speech—that which discriminates against women.[117] The question is why so many observers, and several courts, instinctively flinch when similar prohibitions are applied to the college campus. Undoubtedly, some are worried about censorship or creeping restrictions on provocative thought. To be sure, there is precedent to fear censorship on campus. Apart from the McCarthy era, there have been cases in which university officials censored or expelled students because they deviated from "proper" values or beliefs.[118] And, of course, the fear of chilling speech is real, especially in an environment that relies upon open dialogue.

Still, it is possible to forbid harassment in the classroom without touching other speech that is endemic to the educational mission. That is exactly what the *Bishop* and *Rubin* decisions accomplished. The courts may think otherwise, but they have required such calculations for years. Just as employers must distinguish between harmless expressions of opinion and those that actively discriminate under Title VII,[119] the hate speech codes required schools to intervene against those who interfered with the educational rights of others.

ALTERNATIVE EXPLANATIONS

In many respects any of these conventional explanations could explain the courts' different treatment of hate speech codes and HWE. Still, there is a lingering sense that the distinctions are not as clear as the courts have claimed. Both the college codes and HWE address expression, each using terms that are potentially open to attack. If words like "stigmatize" or "victimize" are vague, then so is HWE's use of "severe" or "pervasive." For that matter, the walls between employment and academic settings are eroding as antidiscrimination measures from the former increasingly are utilized in the latter. If any of these traditional explanations are to stand, it must be either that judges object to the specific application of the codes or that the courts have expanded academic freedom to become an independent First Amendment right.

From a different perspective, though, the courts' decisions may have less to do with legal precedent and doctrine than with the power of extralegal factors to affect judicial decisions. Whether influenced by the persistence of organized litigants, responding to the political connotations of the issues, or acting on their own to address cultural or social concerns, judges may have been doing more than simply "applying the law" in upholding sexual harassment claims and rejecting collegiate hate speech codes.

The suggestion here is akin to the political model of judging, an approach that views the courts as political institutions and judges as political actors.[120] The political model contrasts with the traditional view of adjudication, which posits "a detached and dispassionate judge arriving at objective conclusions through the application of neutral rules."[121] The political and traditional models are actually more complementary than opposites, for few would suggest that judges are unmoved by precedent or that they respond directly to public opinion. But judges do not sit on high completely removed from societal influences. Courts are political institutions, and judges operate in a political environment. Among other things, judges may reflect the ideologies of the politicians who appoint them; they may bring certain biases to the cases; they may broker voting coalitions among their brethren; or they may be attuned to the effects of their decisions and the public's acceptance of their legitimacy.

This depiction not only better explains what courts do, but in the case of sexual harassment law and hate speech codes it may describe the courts' divergent treatment more accurately. This is not to say that legal precedent was irrelevant to the courts that considered hate speech and harassment cases, rather that there are alternative or complementary forces that may have shaped their decisions. Here there are three such potential motives, focusing on the organizational structure of litigants, their framing of the issues involved, and the courts' (and America's) general unease with sexual behavior in the public sphere.

Power of Advocates

In his book, *Hate Speech: The History of an American Controversy,* Samuel Walker argues that American law is shaped by the strength and resolve of interest groups who are willing to repeatedly advance their positions in court. The courts, after all, cannot choose which issues to hear, and the decisions that follow depend in some part on the willingness of various litigants to raise them. To the extent that an idea has "a vigorous and effective advocate," it stands a better chance of ultimately prevailing than if its litigants are only tepidly supportive. As Walker says:

> Freedom of speech for unpopular ideas did not become a living reality until the middle of the twentieth century. Although that protection was ultimately the result of a series of Supreme Court decisions, we must ask what caused the Court to change. The American Civil Liberties Union was a critical advocate for free speech for the unpopular. The ACLU was the lone champion of free speech through the 1920s and early 1930s and filed briefs in all the major cases through which the Court fashioned the body of modern First Amendment law. The perspective here shifts our focus away from the Court, now seen more as a reactive agent, and toward the advocates who brought the cases and arguments before it.[122]

Walker's theory is consistent with several other findings in public law. Over the past thirty years, "judicial scholars have found that litigant status does provide one explanation for the variation found in [the Supreme Court's] decisions to grant writs of certiorari. . . . Additionally, a number of studies have found litigant status to be significantly related to outcomes on the merits in the lower courts. . . . Many of these studies draw on the theoretical premise . . . that 'repeat players' are more likely than 'one shot' players to be successful in the courts."[123]

This analysis may help to explain the divergence between sexual harassment law and collegiate hate codes. Sexual harassment litigation has a long history of organized feminist support, the claim having developed in tandem with the women's movement. As women began to "see their situations as political and institutional rather than as personal, idiosyncratic dilemmas," they spurned "the biological and social assumptions of sexual harassment."[124] With support from the National Organization for Women (NOW) and the Women's Legal Defense Fund (WLDF), litigants came forward to challenge sexual advances on the job and the hostile environments in which they worked. Success only brought more success. Early victories gave others the confidence and motivation to file formal sexual harassment claims against their own co-workers or supervisors.[125]

These litigants also found an ally in the EEOC. Under current employment law, an individual may first register a complaint with the EEOC, which investigates the merits of the charge. If it finds a likely violation of Title VII, the EEOC has the right to prosecute the case in court, where it becomes a valuable organizational ally. The Commission has the experience and resources to effectively litigate such matters, and its status may well carry certain weight in the courts. As many studies have demonstrated, federal agencies have "overwhelming success" when appearing before the federal courts, winning over two-thirds of the cases in which they participate.[126]

The power of such organizational support—whether from legal advocacy groups like WLDF or from governmental agencies like the EEOC—should not be underestimated in measuring the courts' recognition of sexual harassment claims. Given that sexual harassment was once "so routinely considered normal,"[127] it has taken repeated, organized litigation to convince courts of the seriousness of sexual harassment and the need for judicial action. By contrast, the hate speech codes had no organized core of supporters. Backed primarily as instrumental measures by college administrators, the codes lacked passionate and committed support. If anything, the speech policies faced powerful opposition in the courts.

At each of the universities where codes were challenged (Michigan, Wisconsin, Stanford, and Central Michigan) the legal defense team was a joint venture between university presidents, deans, law professors, and both general and outside counsels. Yet their defenses seem to have been half-hearted. Although each school answered for its code at the trial level, only one university, Central Michigan, appealed the initial adverse ruling.[128] Michigan revised its code, and Wisconsin considered a new one, but neither school chose to defend its policy at the appellate level. Stanford's strategy is perhaps the most perplexing, since it was turned down by a state trial court, a decision that hardly carries significant weight on a constitutional issue. If Stanford's administrators felt strongly about their policy, or for that matter if Michigan or Wisconsin had been solidly attached to their hate speech codes, they almost assuredly would have appealed the trial courts' decisions. That only one school took this tack casts significant doubt on their commitment to the codes.

What's more, the universities were in the difficult position of playing defense against an organized opposition. Contrary to the experience of sexual harassment litigants, the universities were not joined by any legal advocacy groups, nor did the EEOC enter the litigation on their behalf. Rather, the universities found themselves pitted against an unbending wall of attorneys affiliated with the American Civil Liberties Union and the Individual Rights Foundation.[129] Given the ACLU's history as "a vigorous and effective advocate,"[130] it is not surprising that it and the amici would have prevailed over universities who were "one shot players" in half-heartedly defending their own speech policies.

Framing of the Issues

It is understood in political science that the public and policy-makers respond as much to the manner in which an issue is presented or framed as they do its actual merit. In the 1992 election, for example, Democrats and Republicans were able to influence public attitudes on government spending by focusing either on "broad, general appeals" or "specific forms of programmatic outlays." When Republicans framed the issue generally—"government spending must be cut"—public opinion seemed to swing against further expenditures, but when Democrats highlighted particular programs—"it is important to fund medical care for the elderly"—voters tended to favor the spending.[131] A similar phenomenon may play out in the courts, where judges are often persuaded by arguments or legal framing that appeal to their backgrounds, ideology, and values.[132]

In the case of college hate speech policies, opponents successfully framed the codes as a free speech issue. To be sure, the policies did regulate speech, but one might also have viewed them as antidiscrimination measures, as unusual but necessary responses to a new plague of collegiate racism. The national media had already reported that "Campus Racial Tensions—and Violence—Appear on [the] Rise."[133] Why, then, wouldn't observers—and the courts—view college antidiscrimination policies through the prism of civil rights and equal opportunity?

The answer to this question is complex, taking account of the broad (and potentially excessive) enforcement patterns of the hate speech policies, the lack of organized and vocal support for the speech codes, and the very fact that the policies regulated speech. But credit must also go to the codes' opponents, who framed the policies as extensions of political correctness. PC was a hot topic in the late 1980s and early 1990s, and the litigants who challenged hate speech regulations attempted to disparage the rules as political correctness run amuck. In *R.A.V.,* the petitioner equated St. Paul's ordinance with "attempts to frame 'politically correct' speech codes on college campuses."[134] So too, the plaintiffs in *Doe, UWM Post,* and *Corry* all suggested that the respective universities were subverting free and fair inquiry for campus rules that privileged certain views and groups.

It is difficult to say whether the trial judges in these cases responded to the opponents' design, but at least in *R.A.V.* the Supreme Court seems to have thrown out hate speech regulations for fear of political correctness. The clearest evidence comes from Justice Blackmun, who in a concurrence summed up his concerns with the majority's reasoning:

> [There] is the possibility that this case . . . will be regarded as an aberration—a case where the Court manipulated doctrine to strike down an ordinance whose premise it opposed, namely that racial threats and verbal assaults are of greater harm than other fighting words. *I fear that the Court has been distracted from its proper mission by the temptation to decide the issue over "politically correct speech" and "cultural diversity," neither of which is presented here.* If this is the meaning of today's opinion, it is perhaps even more regrettable.[135]

Several others have suggested that the *R.A.V.* decision was directed against PC. From newspaper reports to editorial commentary to academic analyses,[136] many observers agreed that the "decision was clearly written in the larger political context in which the conservative wing of the court is concerned about the political correctness movement."[137]

In this respect one cannot ignore the fact that the judges behind the hate speech cases are white and attended college at a very different time from the period in which the speech codes were adopted. Most of the judges graduated college in the 1940s or 1950s, a period in which few minorities attended college, let alone felt free to fight harassment against them on campus (or elsewhere). Thirty years later, nearly 17 percent of college students were nonwhite,[138] and minority students felt empowered to organize for their own interests. Affirmative action had succeeded in allowing more minority students to go to college, but it also created conflicts between affluent white students who came from homogenous schools and communities, and the more diverse classmates they found on many college campuses.[139] That schools crafted speech codes in response to ethnoviolence might have been lost on a judiciary that came of age in a different time. This is not to say that older judges cannot grow with the times or consider other perspectives. Indeed, Avern Cohn, the judge in *Doe,* has become a fan of the scholarship of Mari Matsuda, a leader in critical race studies.[140] Nonetheless, one has to consider whether the *Doe, UWM Post, CMU,* and *Corry* courts were setting legal rules for an educational environment that no longer existed.

Restricting Sexuality

If hate speech policies have been framed as PC prohibitions on academic debate, Title VII and HWE have also been painted as legitimate restrictions on crass sexual overtures. Hence, rather than considering the expressive interests at issue in each measure, the courts may have privileged HWE over hate speech codes in order to eliminate sexual conduct in the workplace.

The idea that Title VII would some day proscribe sex in the workplace would likely have come as a shock to many of the legislators who almost accidentally gave birth to the measure. Congressional opponents only agreed to add "sex" as a protected basis under the law "to highlight the absurdity of the [legislation] as a whole and contribute to its defeat."[141] They calculated incorrectly, and with the law's passage the courts have extended Title VII to include sexual harassment as a form of sex discrimination. Even here, though, many of the fact patterns seem to turn on questions of sex not gender. According to two leading commentators, "the predicate acts underlying a sexual harassment claim [must] be sexual in nature."[142] Whether based on conduct or expression, the primary basis for sexual harassment claims is sex.[143] Indeed, in an article provocatively titled "Whores, Fags, Dumb-Ass Women, Surly Blacks, and Competent Heterosexual White Men," Ruth Colker contends that "women who are presumed to be heterosexual . . . frequently prevail if they show that they have been sexualized; merely showing gender-based but nonsexualized conduct . . . is usually not sufficient."[144]

Perhaps the courts should not be faulted for grounding sexual harassment on sexual, rather than gender-based conduct, for they have faced a number of outside commentators urging them to do just this. The EEOC's own test premises liability on "conduct of a sexual nature."[145] Furthermore, a number of feminist theorists have justified the claim on its sexual overtones. Catharine MacKinnon, for example, has argued that sexual harassment should be defined according to its "unwanted imposition of sexual requirements."[146]

Of course, there is nothing pleasant about inappropriate or unwelcome sexual overtures, and it is understandable that the courts would enforce Title VII to prohibit sexual advances in the workplace. This is the quid pro quo prong of Title VII, which makes it illegal to ground employment on the performance of sexual favors. But what of the HWE test, which penalizes speech and actions that deny equal opportunity? Why is it that sexualized banter or horseplay warrant judicial intervention when other offensive topics often go untouched? Certainly, pornography and obscenity may be restricted under the First Amendment, but offensive, sexualized speech does not necessarily reach the level of obscenity. Is there something worse about sexual topics, something that makes this type of expression worse than, say, racist speech?

Actually, yes, if American cultural history is a guide. According to several observers, America is preoccupied with sexualized content, a process in which collective prudishness leads to the repression of sexual expression.[147] Indeed, our approach to sex is almost contradictory. On one hand, many of our movies and television programs are full of titillation, but this fixation is due in part to our uncomfortableness with sexuality, a prudishness that alternately manifests itself in waves of censorship.[148] For years advocates have sought to regulate sexual expression, from the somewhat comical attempts to seize the novels of Henry Miller,[149] to the Reagan-era Task Force on Pornography.[150] Admittedly, pornography is an unusual issue, bringing together social conservatives offended by sexual content with feminists concerned about the secondary effects of sexual violence. But the history of sexual regulation in this country makes it easier to understand why the courts would enjoin sexually hostile expression over other offensive themes.

If anything, judges may view sexualized expression as "locker room talk," the kind of boasting and braggadocio that men have traditionally enjoyed at Friar's Club roasts and towel-slapping sessions. But when the talk reaches a mixed audience—when "ladies" are exposed to such coarseness—male judges take umbrage. They may censure sexual speech not because it targets or discriminates against women but because women are a "weaker sex" of workers who need to be sheltered from vulgarity in public life. We have seen a similar approach before in the labor cases of the early twentieth century. As *Muller v.*

Oregon[151] and its progeny pronounced, women are more "delicate" than men and need to be shielded from harm in the workplace. Admittedly, this is a strange sentiment to confront over eighty years later, but one need only read the feminist literature of the 1990s to see that the charge still reverberates. Even among feminist activists, some accuse others of "asking to be protected from society. . . . [defeatists who are] just re-enforcing society's opinion that all women are victims and need protection."[152] Whether or not this depiction of women is correct—and I for one would disagree with its presumption—it may have some resonance in explaining the courts' conflicting approach to HWE and hate speech. Considering that Title VII claims arise from the rough and tumble of the shop floor and not among the ivy-protected walls of the Ivory Tower, it is possible that the courts have stepped in to shield women from sexual speech in the workplace where they permit other offensive expression in different contexts.[153]

SOCIALLY CONSTRUCTED LAW

What, then, do the hate speech and sexual harassment cases tell us? On one level they show that it is possible to distinguish the decisions from one another. Surveying Michigan's Interpretive Guide, for example, one finds it difficult to disagree with Judge Cohn's conclusion in *Doe* that the speech policy was applied too broadly. Yet many of the hate speech decisions lack the ring of judicial clarity, especially when compared to the courts' contradictory treatment of HWE claims under Title VII. Both the Michigan and Wisconsin speech policies shared similar terms with HWE prohibitions, a commonality true for many other college hate speech codes. If these schools had applied their policies conservatively—limiting enforcement to severe or pervasive hate speech—would the courts have let them pass? I am not so sure. Whether motivated by advocates or responding to the different connotations of hate speech and sexual harassment, I suspect the courts might have continued to treat hate speech and HWE differently.

I do not mean to say that judges act capriciously or that they routinely ignore precedent. To the contrary, the traditional model of adjudication has resonance. But as suggested earlier, one cannot ignore the influence of political, social, and cultural pressures on judicial decision-making, a process that serves to construct constitutional law—and most particularly free speech jurisprudence—by its social utility. That is certainly the case here, where extralegal factors also played a role in the hate speech and sexual harassment decisions. As others have predicted, the "Supreme Court will inevitably hear a case in which hostile environment law and First Amendment prerogatives conflict,"[154] but already the courts appear willing to punish sexual harassment when it involves speech. That the courts would place one form of content regulation (HWE) over another (hate speech) begs the question why, and it is difficult to justify the disparity on jurisprudential grounds. Maybe the courts are uneasy with speech regulation, judges fantastically trying to convince themselves that HWE does not restrict expression. Or, perhaps the courts have implicitly assessed the value of speech regulations, evidently rating sexual harassment rules higher than hate speech restrictions.[155] Either way, the courts have been far from consistent in their approach to regulating hateful and discriminatory speech, be it racist or sexist.

While They Slept

On March 30, 1995, newspaper headlines declared that hate speech regulations were dead. After six years of litigating over university hate speech codes, a California superior court confirmed what four other courts before it had ruled—that collegiate hate speech codes, and in this case Stanford's policy, were constitutionally suspect.[1] In the wake of the Stanford decision, many commentators rejoiced. Nat Hentoff, a long-time critic of hate speech codes, hailed the end of a doctrine that had suffered from "fundamental weakness[es]." The *Arizona Republic* delighted that "the First Amendment has been reinstated on America's college campuses." And the *Rocky Mountain News* opined that hate speech codes were now "dead letters—unenforced law."[2]

As happy as the critics were at their apparent victory, had they celebrated too soon? Had the speech code "movement" truly been silenced, or were critics unwittingly taking refuge in a line of case law that would fail to hold up? To be sure, under a traditional model of judicial precedent and impact—that legal decisions command public action and affect public opinion—one might have expected schools with suspect speech policies to amend or rescind their rules. From a California superior court all the way up to the highest court of the land, the judiciary appeared to be sending a unified message about the impropriety of restrictive speech codes at public colleges and universities. For that matter, given the courts' influence beyond public bodies, and given the importance

Table 5.1. Speech Codes in 1997 (intervals at 95 percent confidence level)

Type of Speech Policy	Frequency	(%) Range of Estimate
No speech policy	54	45–63
Fighting words	4	1–5
Verbal harassment	19	12–26
Verbal harassment against minorities	11	5–17
Offensive speech	12	6–18

that many Americans ascribe to the First Amendment, we might also have expected many private schools to follow suit.

The trend, however, was just the opposite. Returning to the sample of 100 schools surveyed earlier, tables 5.1 and 5.2 present data on speech codes at these institutions as of 1997, two years after *Corry* and a full five years following the Supreme Court's decision in *R.A.V.* As these data indicate, the percentage of schools with speech policies actually jumped following the court cases. Indeed, the greatest rise was seen among the most restrictive speech codes, those that prohibited offensive expression.

Although the rise may not be as dramatic when taking into account the confidence intervals, the number of speech policies clearly rose following the court decisions, with the largest percentage jump coming from the most restrictive speech policies. Moreover, as table 5.3 indicates, the vast majority of schools with constitutionally suspect speech policies kept theirs on the books in the face of contrary legal precedent. Table 5.4, too, provides a closer look at the various strategies that schools followed. There, "offending policies" reflect those speech restrictions considered unconstitutional by the relevant court cases—verbal harassment of minorities and offensive speech—while "non-offending policies" cover fighting words and generic verbal harassment, restrictions that were still permitted after the decisions. While a majority of schools maintained speech policies neither before nor after the court cases, almost a quarter of institutions either retained offending policies or adopted new ones following these decisions.

That the courts' decisions had neither a powerful impact nor compelled widespread compliance is hardly novel, for as chapter 2 explained, the calculus to comply is a complex proposition. Two of the leading theorists of judicial impact, Bradley Canon and Charles Johnson, identify several factors that affect the process, including interpreting, implementing, consumer, and secondary populations.[3] The interplay of these influences explains why some de-

Table 5.2. Change in Speech Codes, 1987–92 to 1997

Type of Speech Policy	Net Change in Frequency (%)
No speech policy	–11
Fighting words	+3
Verbal harassment	+4
Verbal harassment against minorities	–3
Offensive speech	+8

cisions are accepted and followed (such as tax rulings) and others are not (for example, *Brown v. Board of Education*).[4]

In the case of college hate speech codes, the question is why so many schools chose to ignore the terms, if not the spirit, of the courts' rulings. Initially it is important to define what it means for a school to comply or not with the courts' decisions. Returning a moment to table 5.4, not all of the schools there made a decision to accept or reject the emerging precedent. To comply with judicial holdings is to bring a school's policies into line with the courts' rules. Noncompliance, by contrast, means permitting speech policies that conflict with the cases. Thus, table 5.4 distinguishes between "offending policies"— those whose terms conflict with the courts' holdings—and "nonoffending policies," those that were not touched by the cases.

Given these terms, a school that complied with the courts' rulings would have removed an offending policy, replacing it either with a nonoffending policy or none at all. By contrast, noncompliance reflected two possibilities. Certainly, a school failed to comply with the decisions when it adopted an offending policy even after the cases, but schools that kept offending policies on the books were also in noncompliance. Put another way, noncompliance includes acts of both commission and omission.

In addition, there are several schools that were not faced with a compliance decision. Those schools that regulated fighting words or generic verbal harassment—institutions with "nonoffending policies" in table 5.4—were not affected by the court cases. Putting aside jurisdictional issues of a school's private/public status, the holdings did not reach speech codes less restrictive than those covering verbal harassment of minorities. As a result, schools with nonoffending policies did not confront the question of whether to comply with the courts' decisions.

The preceding discussion notwithstanding, I do not mean to put too fine a point on the distinction between compliance and noncompliance. To be

Table 5.3. Percentage of Questionable Speech Codes That Went Unchanged

Category	% Unchanged
Verbal harassment of minorities	78
Offensive speech	66

sure, under technical rules of judicial precedent only those parties to a lawsuit are required formally to comply with the holding. In the case of hate speech codes, then, just four schools—Michigan, Wisconsin, Central Michigan, and Stanford—would have been subject to judicial sanctions had they not amended their policies in light of the court decisions against them. But compliance also has a broader meaning, encompassing an individual's or entity's response to a new and contradictory legal rule. That is the case here, where a host of elite institutions were faced with the issue of whether to bring their own policies or administrative processes into line with judicial precedent that seemed to invalidate their approach. This is an attenuated process, more so than even the school prayer[5] or civil rights[6] case studies chronicled in years past. Unlike those examples, just a handful of colleges and universities would have been subject to an adverse declaratory judgment had they not amended or removed their speech policies in light of the court decisions.[7] Yet what makes this a case of legal compliance is the fact that the issue at hand concerns the First Amendment. Even if many of the schools were not technically bound by the court decisions, collegiate leaders still sought to keep their institutions within the bounds of free speech norms, and as a whole they recognized the persuasive authority of the speech code decisions. Indeed, the fascination of the speech codes is the way in which individuals—and in this instance nongovernmental institutions—may seek to comply as much with the spirit of a new legal rule as with the explicit precedent itself. Put another way, this is likely a case where the shadow cast by formal law[8] has more symbolic influence than the underlying case law or the formal legal order.[9]

QUALITATIVE EXPLANATIONS

The response of schools to the hate speech cases evidences a variety of motives, but together they illustrate a common point—that the ultimate power of constitutional decisions and norms is found not in court rulings but in the response, acceptance, and interpretation of those holdings in civil society. In the case of hate speech codes, schools sat on their hands, added new measures, or modified provisions, but only a handful of institutions responded as

Table 5.4. Schools' Actions Following Court Cases

Schools' Actions	Estimated Percentage of Schools (%)	Estimated Number of Schools (*n*)
Kept offending policy	14	193
Adopted offending policy	9	124
Removed offending policy	2	28
Kept nonoffending policy	17	235
Adopted nonoffending policy	6	83
Removed nonoffending policy	0	0
No policy before *and* after court cases	51	704

Note: Due to rounding, percentages do not sum to 100.

a traditional model of precedent would predict, by eliminating their "offending" policies. A much greater number ignored, evaded, or directly challenged the courts' authority.

This divergent response provides fertile ground for examining the process by which individuals and institutions interpret, implement, and ultimately establish constitutional norms in civil society. In chapter 2 I characterized this concept as mass constitutionalism, positing that informal law often has more persuasive power than does codified constitutional law. In this chapter I examine the response of schools to such formal law as a way of dissecting the development of mass constitutionalism. Although few schools directly challenged the courts, many more tinkered with or evaded the developing case law, in the process setting up divergent constitutional norms and interpretations on campus that would later spread within civil society.

To examine this process I have focused on schools that removed, maintained, or added an offending speech policy after the series of contrary holdings. Although it would certainly be interesting to examine schools with fighting words or other nonoffending speech policies, the courts did not condemn these policies, and resultantly they do not directly raise an issue of constitutional compliance. As a result, I have examined three types of schools: those that removed an offending hate speech policy, those that maintained an offending hate speech policy, and those that developed a new offending hate speech policy. Table 5.4 estimates these categories as comprising, respectively, 2 percent, or 28 schools; 14 percent, or 193 schools; and 9 percent, or 124 schools nationwide. Within the stratified sample of 100 schools, there were 5 institutions that removed an offending speech policy, 22 that kept an offending speech policy, and 5 that created a new offending speech policy.

The Appendix discusses the intricacies of case selection and the methods of qualitative research employed, including the need to use monikers for most institutions and subjects. In short, I was able investigate each of the 32 schools through a variety of news coverage, with detailed research reserved for seven such institutions. As was true of the schools chronicled in chapter 3, the institutions presented here were not chosen with any ideological goal in mind. They were selected as representative of the larger set of 32 colleges and universities that removed, maintained, or added an offending speech policy after the series of contrary decisions.

The secondary research and campus visits were quite successful at illuminating the various approaches identified in the quantitative results. Here, schools that complied with the court decisions fell into three distinct groupings: those whose policies had been challenged in court, those that decided on their own that the speech codes were unworkable, and one that abided by the court decisions by removing its hate speech policy in light of the adverse legal precedent. By contrast, schools that maintained their offending speech policies—an approach I label passive noncompliance—did so generally out of a calculation by collegiate officials that the symbolic advantages of keeping the policies on the books outweighed the scant chance that they would be challenged in court. Finally, schools that adopted new offending speech policies—a decision I call active noncompliance—fell into two categories. Some consciously tried to evade the court decisions, drafting policies they thought would just skirt the court decisions. Others, though, were delayed diffusers, adopting policies in the face of contrary precedent to catch up with what they believed had become the norm in higher education.

Compliant Schools

Table 5.4 suggests that 2 percent of schools nationwide removed offending speech policies between 1992 and 1997; in the stratified sample there were five such cases. The five schools include a mix of private and public institutions, both large and small, and all well known to most observers of American higher education. But of the five institutions, only three made the decision in light of the court cases, and in fact, two were directly subject to court challenges over their speech codes. Because the machinations of these cases have been well publicized, I can identify the two institutions by name: the University of Michigan and Stanford University. Both are world-class institutions with large and diverse undergraduate and graduate enrollments. Each was also politically charged, boasting a collection of liberal and conservative student activists. The two schools that acted independently of the court cases are both elite, private institutions, with student bodies that are predominantly white. Although each is primarily a liberal arts college, the two also maintain graduate programs. Like both Michigan and Stanford, the two schools are known for battles over identity politics, having sponsored minority studies departments, gay/lesbian groups, and alternative, conservative student newspapers, while also having experienced considerable student protest over divestment. The fifth school, which neither acted independently of the courts nor was compelled by a court order to rescind its speech policy, is a public institution. Predominantly white and undergraduate, it nonetheless has a long history of liberal political activism. While few would call it elite—the school accepts over 80 percent of all applicants—the institution maintains a good academic reputation.

That each of these five institutions rescinded its offending speech policy between 1992 and 1997 does not mean that they all chose to comply with the courts' constitutional decisions. Compliance, again, suggests a reaction to judicial precedent—whether explicit or indirect—in which an institution changes its policies or procedures to conform to the prevailing legal order.[10] However, the two liberal arts colleges rescinded their speech codes with little consideration of the court cases. Instead, they responded to considerable backlash, both on campus and in the press, over the enforcement of their policies. At the smaller of the schools a student was charged with racial and sexual harassment following a drunken rage of epithets. Student services staff sought to discipline him for his behavior, but the student responded with an orchestrated media campaign accusing school officials of selective enforcement in punishing him for the content of his speech. Coverage became so great that the school's president felt obliged to respond, claiming that the institution was holding the student accountable for his behavior, not his speech. However, the student was able to marshal allies from the faculty, who took pen in hand to chastise the school and its president for adopting a "politically correct" attitude in restricting undesirable messages on campus. The fact that the student also faced possible suspension for his slurs (and past behavioral problems) gave some credence to the charge that the school was over-reacting.

The ensuing firestorm seems to have had little influence on the handling of the initial case, but school administrators certainly took a lesson from the situation in considering future discipline. College policy was changed to ensure that students' actions, and not their speech, were open to sanction, and there has not been a case since in which speech has been targeted. A high-level official goes so far as to say "we don't have a hate speech policy." What drove this change is more difficult to determine, although the court decisions do not appear to have played a role. At the highest level, officials maintain that college policy has been "recast" in light of the school's "long-standing commitment to free speech norms." But those who implement student discipline acknowledge that practices have been changed to focus exclusively on student behavior. Similarly, while the college's former president declaims any influence from the media firestorm, faculty and student services personnel note the severe beating the school took in the press—and from alumni—during the prior case and acknowledge that top administrators were under tremendous pressure to change policy.

At the other institution administrators proposed a new speech policy designating zones around campus in which different standards for speech applied. For example, free speech would reign in the student commons, but greater restrictions would apply in residence halls. On paper the policy may have had merit, but students reacted negatively to the new plan, drawing chalk lines across campus and openly deriding college officials for "treating [them] like children." Their protests quickly caught the attention of the national press, a dynamic that had as much to do with the substance of the controversy as it did with the fact that the school is an elite and well-known institution. In fact, students took full advantage of their window of news coverage, painting administration officials as paranoid foes of open discourse and their own followers as champions of free speech and civil liberties. In the end their strategy was successful. The policy had been championed by middle-level administrators, who saw the proposal as an opportunity to set clear rules for an issue—hate speech and violence—that had vexed other institutions. But with few such incidents on campus, it was difficult to overcome the growing exasperation of top officials who feared the negative press attention and continuing protests on campus. About a month after its inception, the policy was retired.

It would be a mistake to count these schools as reaching compliance decisions. Although they did rescind their policies after the bulk of the court cases, the holdings were not part of their calculus. Rather, their decisions reflected a cost-benefit calculation, with the costs of internal strife and negative press attention outweighing any benefits that administrators may have anticipated in the quality of campus life or the expectations for racial, gender, or ethnic relations at the school. It is also instructive that the ultimate decision-makers were top administrators, specifically the institutions' presidents, who overruled middle-level officials who had pushed for the policy initiatives. This is a dynamic unique to large organizations (be they private or public) and one that reflects the different constituencies of officials at varying level of responsibilities within the organization. At lower levels—in this case in student services—administrators were concerned about the quality of student life and multicultural relations on campus. Officials in the upper echelons of collegiate administration shared some of these interests, but they had other constituencies to accommodate, including alumni, prospective students and their families, and national opinion makers. They were also up against a wall of advocates—either the suspected student who marshaled faculty support or the student demonstrators who "chalked" the campus—who were determined to provoke press coverage and attempt to force the administrators' hands.

As scholars have noted in other contexts,[11] advocates can be crucial in affecting policy decisions, especially when, as here, top officials did not confront protests from the speech codes' supporters. On one level the speech policies may not have been that popular on these campuses, but it is also instructive that their prime proponents were lower-level administrators, who may have recognized the danger in opposing ultimate supervisors who fretted over the speech policies. I was unable to uncover data that elucidate this question, and as an academician I am well aware that faculty and students often show little trepidation in challenging top administrators. But when the proponents of a policy are nonunionized staff—a group that is neither served by the institution nor is protected from recrimination by tenure—it is plausible that some would mute their opposition when convinced that top administrators intend to rule the other way.

If the actions of these two schools do not represent compliance decisions, the reactions of the University of Michigan and Stanford University are the most obvious form of compliance. Both schools were defendants in hate speech cases, and each faced a judicial order to rescind or revise its speech policy. That they would comply with a direct ruling is not that surprising, since as parties to the suits they were subject to direct "legal coercion."[12] Still, it is interesting that neither institution chose to appeal the trial judge's verdict, a determination that while similar to that of the University of Wisconsin in *UWM Post* contrasts with the strategy of Central Michigan University in *Dambrot.*

Here their decisions appear to be a combination of a utility calculus coupled with the policy preferences of senior administrators. Like both of the elite institutions that rescinded their speech policies during this time, Michigan and Stanford had suffered through a plethora of negative, national news coverage over their speech codes. Michigan took the brunt of the criticism since its policy was the first to be challenged and one of the most restrictive codes, but Stanford also took considerable heat for its speech code. The fact that the author of Stanford's policy, Professor Thomas Grey, wrote extensively about the rule's rationale, only fueled attention of the policy.[13] In some sense, then, by the time that the *Doe* and *Corry* decisions came down, senior administrators at the two schools were tired of the notoriety that their schools had engendered.

Moreover, at least at Michigan, university leadership was in transition at the time of *Doe*. The search committee had successfully recruited a new president, and the interim president, who had presided over the development of the contested speech policy, was able to move on. There were also personnel changes in the university's General Counsel's Office, the result of which had new administrators looking at the policy in a different light. Some came to agree with Judge Cohn in *Doe* that the explanatory guide for its policy was overreaching, and others simply wanted the controversy to "go away." As a result, the university's response was to amend its policy, to narrow the code's scope so that it was similar to a general harassment policy. This change reflected the policy preferences of new administrators as well as their cost-benefit calculation that whatever influence the existing policy might exert in creating a communitarian environment on campus would be overshadowed by the bad press and hard feelings of continued litigation. There had been no groundswell of support from faculty or students for the contested speech policy, and any fears that removing the code would "send the wrong signal" to women, minorities, and others likely to be protected by its terms, were relieved by the university's decision to maintain a narrower semblance of a speech policy.

In this sense, then, officials at both Michigan and Stanford had a compliance decision to make—whether to comply with a court order or to challenge the ruling by either appealing its terms or seeking to evade its implications. However, the fifth school to comply had an even more difficult decision to make—whether to respond to a growing body of legal precedent by removing or amending its offending speech policy. This university, a large public institution, has a history of activism but sits in an increasingly conservative area. It is also a school that relies on a state agency for its legal representation. While faculty and administrators were already beginning to question the propriety of the school's speech policy at the time of the court cases, upper-level administrators were pushed to rescind the policy by the state's legal counsel. Senior officials in the Attorney General's Office had little sympathy for hate speech policies—seeing them as offshoots of a "political correctness" movement—and the growing number of court cases gave them the ammunition to declare to university administrators that the policy had to be revised or removed to comport with developing constitutional doctrine. The university, in turn, substituted a fighting words policy for the earlier version to satisfy the Attorney General's Office.

It might have been possible for university administrators to contest the legal advice, but here bureaucratic pressures or interorganizational politics explain the school's decision to comply. Campus leaders recognized that lawyers at the Attorney General's Office were tightly tied to state legal and political leaders, and realizing that the institution depended upon the continued good will of those figures for its appropriations, university officials were unlikely to evade the legal advice even if they disagreed. The fact that faculty, staff, and students were already questioning the policy's appropriateness made the decision to comply all the easier.

Noncompliant Schools

At first blush it may seem surprising that such a small number of schools with an offending speech policy would remove it, and more shocking still that even a smaller number would act in response to the court decisions. Such intransigence contradicts the traditional model of judicial authority and begs the question why so many schools would ignore the spirit and terms of the court rulings. To some observers the answer undoubtedly lies in a broad coalition of support for the speech codes—that a virtual cacophony of liberal and activist groups would have lined up behind the hate speech policies.[14] But student and faculty activists did not have legal responsibility for the codes, nor would they be called to court to defend the policies. That task fell to university administrators, whose commitment to the speech codes was balanced with other organizational considerations that varied by campus.

The variety of such concerns also explains the diversity of approaches between schools. As table 5.4 indicates, almost 25 percent of schools nationwide failed to comply at some level with the court decisions. But there is a distinction between schools that kept an offending policy on the books and those that added new ones. I call this dichotomy the difference between active and passive noncompliance, for it takes more administrative action and consumes more organizational energy and human capital to adopt a new policy than simply to keep an existing one on the books. Moreover, as the research shows, the decision to retain an offending speech code reflects different motives from the determination to adopt new policies. This distinction revolves around several competing pressures, including the policy preferences of administrators, their perception of support and opposition for the speech codes, the likelihood of a court challenge, the level of campus activism, alumni reactions, and the relative prestige of each school.

Passive Noncompliance

By far, the majority of noncompliant schools chose simply to keep their offending speech policies on the books. Together they total 14 percent of the sample, but as table 5.3 points out, between two-thirds and three-quarters of schools with offending policies in 1987–92 still had them as of 1997. The overwhelming reason for their noncompliance was utilitarianism. As chapter 3 explains, many college speech codes were created with instrumental or organizational goals in mind. Developed primarily by deans, presidents, or other high-level administrators, the speech policies were designed to counteract unpleasant racial incidents on campus—allowing administrators to assure on- and off-campus audiences that things were "under control"—or as a reaction by less-prestigious institutions to keep up with their more renowned peers in higher education. In only a few cases did deans or administrators promote speech policies because they *personally* believed in the codes' merits. Nor were many policies advanced by faculty or students. The policy-making process at most schools was a top-down operation, with administrators acting to serve organizational interests.

So too, the decision to continue the speech policies reflected a combination of utilitarian calculus and policy preferences by institutional leaders. In this case the benefits of hate speech codes were symbolic, for few if any schools have actively enforced their hate speech policies. Nevertheless, as several administrators reminded me, one should not mistake symbolism for impotence. Although her speech policy has rarely been used, one dean of students at a northeastern liberal arts college told me that the policy "sets a standard on campus. It gives us something we can point our finger to in the catalog to remind students of the expectations and rights we all have in the community." This sentiment was repeated by a former college president, who claimed that "we didn't set out to enforce the policy punitively but to use it as the basis for our educational efforts at respecting individuality."

If there were symbolic benefits to the hate speech policies, administrators also feared the symbolic costs of removing the speech codes. Here the operative word was "signal," in that collegiate officials worried that rescinding any type of antidiscrimination policy would send a message to ethnic and racial minorities that they were no longer as welcome on campus. When coupled with the scant possibility of legal action to challenge the speech codes, administrators were content to leave their policies in place.

This calculation was no more pronounced than at the two schools I visited in this category, "Plains University" and "Middleberg College," both of which were introduced in chapter 3. Following the adoption of its hate speech policy in 1990, the Plains code has largely fallen off the campus radar screen. Decisions about the speech policy have consistently been the province of upper-level administrators, the issue having never aroused much faculty or student ardor. Part of the reason may be that student protestors never sought speech policies, but it is instructive that the speech code has not been invoked in over a decade of its existence.

So, why then would Plains administrators retain their hate speech policy? When asked, both the university's attorneys and top officials in student services say they were aware of contrary legal precedent and considered it persuasive. Were top officials willfully blind to the decisions, did they personally favor the speech policy, or were there other more pressing matters? The answer must come somewhat second-hand, for the university's chancellor throughout this period—the individual who was ultimately responsible for the decision—has moved on to another position outside of academe and was unavailable for the research. Nonetheless, interviews with university counsel, top administrators in student services, former leaders in faculty senate, and a former aide to the trustees suggest that the chancellor was concerned about "stirring up protest" if the policy were removed. Said the dean of students, "we had just gone through three or four years" in which minority students regularly questioned whether the university was committed to their presence on campus. Regardless of the chancellor's position on the policy, whether students had even pushed for the policy, hate speech codes have been interpreted elsewhere as protection for minorities. As a result, "there is a risk in the signal you send when you change policies," and Plains did not want to do that.

Still, what about the threat of a declaratory judgment against the policy? Since the state's attorney general openly opposed the policy, might an enterprising student or conservative group challenge the policy in court? Yes, say respondents, but again net utility has counseled against a policy change. University counsel reports that Plains has rarely, if ever, been sued for a declaratory judgment. Moreover, since the speech code has fallen off the campus agenda—if it had ever been a priority—counter activism was unlikely. Put simply, said a student services staff member, there was little legal exposure from the policy, but administrators worried about "opening a can of worms" if they tinkered with it.

The experience at Middleberg College was a little different, for while the school still retained its hate speech policy, the college's dean changed the enforcement strategy out of personal concerns for the policy's reach. That he did not remove the policy, however, reflects a campus consensus that the hate speech code has symbolic value.

As detailed in chapter 3, Middleberg adopted its hate speech policy in August of 1989, following a fiery debate in the college senate. Given the code's controversial beginnings, it is surprising that opposition has been fairly mute since the policy's adoption. Deans, faculty, and student services staff credit the code with "articulating community standards" so that "people can measure their behavior and the behavior of others against" it. Enforcement actions have been rare. A prior ombudsperson recalls three cases from the 1997–98 academic year, but these all turned on action, not expression, and concerned alleged age discrimination, reverse racism, and sexual harassment. Still, with the exception of one faculty member (who calls himself "a strict libertarian") all of those interviewed agree that the policy has been a success. As one person explained, "You have to understand that 'enforced' is a funny word to use at [Middleberg]. 'Discipline' is informal here. The goal of 'policy' is to set standards of behavior," which are often resolved through informal networks.

Still, the policy's acceptance lies in more than its enforcement record, for the speech rules had been eclipsed by the policy's prohibitions on sexual harassment. To be sure, the code includes prohibitions against verbal harassment of racial and ethnic minorities, but the policy was originally seen as affecting sexual harassment, not hate speech. Indeed, one of the policy's prime proponents, a women's studies professor, says she is "surprised" that the policy would be labeled a hate speech policy. Her reaction is particularly confusing when she reports that the college worked closely with its outside counsel in drafting the policy. While their specific advice is not available, most recall the attorneys' admonition that the policy was "too far-reaching" and ought simply to have tracked Title VII's language against sexual harassment.

That the College did not adopt this advice does not mean that similar concerns went unraised later. In the year following the policy's adoption the college recruited a new dean of the college, a scholar who calls himself a "free speech advocate" and who believes the college's speech policy was adopted "without elaborate consideration of what it would mean to implement it." The dean reports that in the mid-1990s he, the college president, and the college as a whole were trying to decide "what did this policy mean, what kind of statements are covered, what should we do when incidents arise?" His own concern—as well as one he ascribes to the president and some faculty—was that the code was "excessively cushioning debate." In turn, he proposed that the college "back away from the more egregious restrictions on speech" with "subtle changes in tonality." The policy was never rewritten, nor were there proposals for "legislative or judicial changes" in college policy. Rather, in keeping with much of Middleberg's culture, the dean initiated informal discussions between himself, the president, and other members of the college community to redefine collective understandings of the policy's reach. Practically, this meant that administrators would be less likely to invoke the policy (and faculty, staff, and perhaps students would be less likely to file charges) when verbal taunts were not especially persistent or severe.

Still, if the dean were so opposed to speech limitations, why did he not push to amend or remove the policy's *terms*? He reports that he was aware of the various court cases against collegiate speech codes, and he agreed with their overall message. Instead, he and the college president made a utility calculation. Like the chancellor at Plains University, they were concerned about the message sent to students, staff, and faculty if they minimized or removed the harassment policy so soon after it had been adopted. As a private school they did not fear legal action over the policy's constitutionality, and with so few enforcement actions the threat of any lawsuit about the code was minimal. Rather, the potential cost was campus protest and the loss of good will. Since the policy was seen as largely covering sexual harassment, any change to the policy—even if on a different issue—might be misinterpreted as condoning sexist behavior. Given the campus uproar five years earlier, both officials were determined not to repeat the debate and protest over sexual harassment. So, they took a middle ground. Moved by a reexamination of the policy's merits, they crafted a new and informal understanding for enforcement practices. But to stave off "collateral protest" from this change, they retained the policy's terms in the college's handbook.

Active Noncompliance

There is an important difference between an individual or organization's passive decision not to alter its behavior in light of contrary legal precedent and its active choice to undertake new actions or policies that contradict judicial authority. As table 5.4 pointed out, 9 percent of schools engaged in active noncompliance, having adopted new or expanded speech policies that conflict with the five court cases. Of these institutions there were five in my sample of 100 schools, and I visited four of them for qualitative research.

Evaders

Among the four schools, I found two distinct motives for new speech policies, explanations that I call "evader schools" and "delayed diffusers." Evaders sought to finesse the cases, believing they were binding or at least persuasive, but still trying to find a way to create an expansive speech policy. Delayed diffusers, by contrast, were not trying to sidestep the decisions so much as they were motivated by a larger, lagged desire to bring their schools "into the mainstream of higher education policy." Administrators at the evaders, institutions that included both public and private schools, had a sophisticated understanding of constitutional law. They knew that their schools were either bound by the First Amendment, or had voluntarily chosen to follow First Amendment doctrine, and they were not only aware of the relevant court decisions but also sought to draft policies that did not overtly contradict those norms. But, while they wanted to minimize the contradictions between their policies and the court decisions, they were also willing to "push the envelope," so to speak, to achieve other organizational interests.

One of these schools is a large, public research institution with agricultural roots, which I call Agrarian University. Agrarian sits in a conservative region and state, a fact that may explain the dearth of political activism on campus. Nearly half of the student body is female, but only 5 percent of students are minority. The school does not maintain a women's studies or minority studies department, nor did it experience divestment protest.

Agrarian adopted its speech code in 1989 for many of the same reasons as did Plains University. The state board of regents had begun to survey other state systems, and believing that racial harassment was the next potential wave of litigation under Title VII, ordered institutions to create policies to protect against such incidents and the liability they presented. At Agrarian drafting went to a collective of an affirmative action officer, a university attorney, and representatives of the provost's office. Together, they modeled their policy on Title VII's protection against sexual harassment. But by extending the rule to speech and expression while also limiting the bases on which a violation would be found (e.g., race and ethnicity), officials were arguably doing that which *R.A.V.* eventually prohibited—punishing certain messages as being worse than others.

Participants recall few incidents in which the policy was ever invoked, and archived documents do not identify any others, save one. In 1991–92 a faculty member was charged under the policy for racist speech in the classroom. Many of the facts remain confidential, but it is clear that the faculty member threatened litigation over the denial of his First Amendment rights, and the university privately settled the case with him. The case strengthened the view of the university's attorneys that Agrarian's hate speech policy was unconstitutional. The attorneys had been tracking the *Doe* and *UWM Post* decisions in 1989 and 1991 and increasingly came to believe that their own policy "had constitutional weaknesses." Analyzing the faculty member's potential court challenge, they concluded that he probably had standing to challenge the entire policy, and that the policy might very well be overturned by the courts.

The attorneys recommended to the president and provost that the university substantially rewrite, if not totally rescind the policy, and in fact, the revision that followed was prompted, said a dean, "by the recently developing case law regarding First Amendment limitations on universities' regulation of speech." But while the same administrator claimed that the resulting policy modification "should be capable of withstanding constitutional scrutiny," an attorney who was closely involved says that the changes were at best a band-aid, designed to give the appearance that the university was "still affirmatively and aggressively addressing the issues of racial and ethnic harassment in the University community," while at the same time reducing the chances that the policy would be challenged. As this person acknowledges, the policy that emerged in 1994 "was still unconstitutional," if not more so. Where before the policy covered expression based on "race, ethnicity, or racial affiliation," the revised edition not only engaged in content discrimination, but it used vague and potentially over-broad terms such as "degrade, demean or stigmatize." The difference, however, was that the revised policy was limited to slander, libel, or obscenity. Thus, while the policy violated *R.A.V.* for its content discrimination and *Doe* and *UWM Post* for its vague terms, the types of potential cases had been narrowed, meaning that the policy would only rarely be invoked.

Those close to the policy deliberations say this crafting was deliberate, and that it was done "above the deans' level." Essentially, officials were making a cost-benefit determination similar to those at schools that engaged in passive noncompliance. Since the university had been under investigation by the U.S. Department of Education in the late 1980s for cases of race discrimination, administrators were hypervigilant about signs that the university might retreat from its equal opportunity policies. As the transmittal memorandum for the policy stated, "we have taken the position that the university can and will continue to enforce a policy prohibiting racial and ethnic harassment to the fullest extent the law allows, even if it might be simpler and less legally risky to completely eliminate our policy." But at the same time, the policy quite clearly took a legal risk; it was still unconstitutional. Administrators had attempted to evade the court decisions with legal craftsmanship. While still standing against messages of racial and ethnic hatred, the policy's reach had been sufficiently limited so that few, if any, cases would arise to create a legal challenge.

The other school to evade the courts' rulings is an elite private institution with a religious affiliation, a school I call St. Ann's College. St. Ann's is a small, liberal arts college, split roughly in half between men and women, and containing about 5 percent of minority students. Although St. Ann's has none of the traditional signs of progressive politics—there being no women's studies, minority studies, or gay/lesbian organizations on campus—both faculty and admissions personnel describe the college as "unusually activist and progressive" for a parochial institution.

As a private, religious school, St. Ann's is not subject to First Amendment doctrine. Nonetheless, administrators expressed a strong allegiance to the First Amendment, each offering several bases for college policy to track First Amendment norms. The school's existing policy was written as late as 1997, but its evolution traces to a change in administrative philosophy for student services. Through the mid-1990s, the dean of student's office had been run by a minister, a former high school principal who had the title of "Dean of Discipline."

The arrival of a new president for the institution spawned a change in student affairs, and the institution moved to what the current dean of students calls a "professional student services model." As part of that turn, staff were hired with graduate training in student services, many of whom belonged to professional associations for student affairs personnel. Their recruitment also invigorated veteran administrators at the school, as officials sought to apply the "best professional practices" to student services. One of these "practices," the associate dean says, was antidiscrimination policies that maintain "an environment of civility that is free from disparagement, intimidation, harassment, and violence of any kind." However, it was not until 1996 that administrators sought to enforce such norms through a punitive policy. Their goal was not only to address the cultural changes on campus that would lead to harassment claims but also to move the college, and especially student services, from a parochial to a professional model of administration. To do so, officials contracted with three consultants in higher education law and policy to draft a rule with sufficient breadth but that remained within constitutional bound. One dean who was involved is quite clear that the school sought a policy that would be consistent with the First Amendment.

What the school got was a policy that seemed to evade the court decisions, a result that an administrator confirms in his description of the consultants. The experts "knew the law well" and tried to "go as far as possible" in preventing harassing speech while still not running afoul of the cases. For example, in its description of characteristics that may invite harassment, the policy says these "attributes include, but are not limited to: race or ethnic origin, gender, physical or mental disability, age, religion, economic class, and sexual orientation." The use of inclusive but not limiting language, of course, avoids content discrimination. But the policy trips up in its definition of harassment, which it describes as physical contact or verbal comments that "degrade the status of another human being." Given the holdings in *Doe, UWM Post, Dambrot,* and *Corry,* "degrading speech" would likely be considered vague and over broad. For that matter, the policy also covers "offensive pictures or 'jokes,'" a restriction that would assuredly be found unconstitutional if challenged in court.

When asked about the consultants' recommendations, an administrator who worked with them admits that the experts have "gotten slammed" in court on similar policies written for other institutions, and officials at the school are still debating how, and under what circumstances, they should enforce their own policy. Nevertheless, three veteran student services officers acknowledge that the college endorsed, if not encouraged, the consultants to "finesse" the law by pushing the policy's reach as far as practical given the case law. Even more, the college's enforcement pattern suggests that administrators have been willing to apply the policy beyond now-established First Amendment limits. When asked if the hate speech policy would apply to a student who claimed in a classroom debate that "women belong in the home"—a factual situation akin to that in *Doe*—the dean of students agreed that the message would be covered as discriminatory speech.

Nor is this a hypothetical case. In the late 1990s officials charged a student with hate speech for distributing a flyer decrying the "sin of homosexuality." Whatever the goodness of their intentions, such restrictions are inconsistent with First Amendment law. In fact, the student filed suit against St. Ann's charging the school with censorship. College attorneys were quick to discount the case as frivolous since St. Ann's is private and therefore is not bound by the First Amendment. But rather than defend the policy in court, the school settled with the student. Their reason, according to both the affirmative action officer and the assistant dean of students, was the president's concern for public relations—his sense that the school would court untold bad press for "being on the wrong side of the First Amendment." Although neither official was responsible for the ultimate decision to settle, they both recognize the pressures now on them when administering the college's hate speech policy. On one hand, the college is committed to rooting out discrimination and has given them broad discretion to apply, or threaten to apply, the policy widely and vigorously. Yet, on the other hand they are wary of the president's support should they actually approach or exceed the boundaries of the First Amendment. In a sense, they say, St. Ann's experience reflects a strategy of evasion—looking for a balance that allows them to cast the policy widely but enforce it in ways that do not court legal or public complaint.[15]

Delayed Diffusers

The remaining group of schools to actively disregard the court decisions involves what I call delayed diffusers. They are not technically in noncompliance, for as private schools they are immune from First Amendment doctrine. Moreover, unlike the private institution chronicled as an "evader," these schools have neither considered themselves bound by the First Amendment nor have sought in the past to follow First Amendment doctrine. Within the study sample two schools fit this category, and I visited them both. The two are conservative religious institutions, located in different parts of the country but similar in appearances. The first, which I call Cherrydale College, is a small liberal arts institution tucked away in a rural hamlet. Without a national reputation, Cherrydale recruits students primarily from a three-state region or from members of its denomination. The school is over 95 percent white, with a 2 to 1 ratio of female to male students. Alcohol is forbidden on campus, which, the dean of students says, makes the campus atmosphere "respectful." But even faculty who disagree with the school's (and the region's) conservatism do not consider Cherrydale "repressive." The dean of students acknowledges that Cherrydale students have been known to take the one-hour drive to a big state school and "party" for the weekend.

The second school, which I call Ezekiel College, is virtually the same size as Cherrydale and is also located in a remote area about one hour from the nearest metropolitan area. Over 95 percent of the students are white, although male and female students are evenly matched. Almost all of Ezekiel's recruitment comes from within its denomination, with the academic dean acknowledging that one of Ezekiel's (relatively) unstated goals is to help "proper Christian young people" find suitable mates. Unlike the other schools visited, Ezekiel's rules for student behavior are extremely strict. Dancing was only recently permitted on campus, with the current rule discouraging entertainment that "detract[s] from spiritual growth and break[s] down proper moral inhibitions and reserve." Other rules follow in the same spirit, resembling those that were last in place at secular institutions in the 1950s.

To put these schools in the category of noncompliance may seem odd, since as conservative religious institutions the top administrators at each school felt allegiance to a higher power than judicial precedent. But here their actions bring together notions of judicial impact and compliance decisions. In both cases the schools adopted hate speech policies as a way to move into the mainstream of higher education administration. Each had recently hired student affairs deans with secular backgrounds, and, much like policy entrepreneurs, these new administrators "promoted policy ideas," "articulated policy innovations," and "energized the diffusion process" by which their new schools sought to become more professional and less provincial.[16] At Cherrydale the president recruited a new assistant dean of students with an eye toward grooming him for the deanship when the incumbent retired. The new hire came from a prestigious public institution in the East, where he had become active in one of the professional associations for student services. He took the job, he says, "because it was clear that [Cherrydale] was looking to upgrade student services and I could make a real difference in merging the academic and extracurricular sides of campus."

At the time he was hired, Cherrydale's outside lawyers had noticed that the school did not have an antidiscrimination policy, and they began work on a rule that would apply to the college's employees. The assistant dean of students says that he, the then-dean of students, and the school's counselor worked to expand the policy and apply it to Cherrydale's students too. By the fall of 1994 they had succeeded in crafting a policy that, among other things, forbade jokes that "belittle or demean an individual's or group's sex, race, color, religion, or national origin." They did not face objection from the college's outside counsel, which coincidentally had changed from a local to a regional law firm during the time and which "passed on the policy" because Cherrydale is a private school. The then-assistant dean of students says he was aware of the *Doe, UWM Post,* and *R.A.V.* cases at the time, but in his view, "we had civility goals to achieve" and the cases were not dispositive.

The process was surprisingly similar at Ezekiel College, which over a seven-year period had appointed three presidents. The result was to consolidate institutional power in the dean of the college, the vice president for business, and the dean of students. Two of these men, the academic and student deans, were both hired at about the same time and from secular institutions. Although Ezekiel already had many rules for student conduct, the dean of students undertook to include one more—a provision that would punish students for racial harassment or discrimination. Again, Ezekiel's student handbook was already a model in content restrictions—students being subject to prohibitions on vulgarity, for example—but the dean himself championed the racial harassment provision. No other administrator with whom I spoke would call the rule a "hate speech code," labeling it, instead, a "policy of inclusion" or "diversity," but the dean (who has since retired) allows that it is "substantially similar" to hate speech policies at other institutions. Several faculty members agree that the policy may be termed a hate speech code, but as one cautioned, "It's a misnomer to think of [Ezekiel] policy as 'anti-hate.' This is a conservative, Christian school. Policy here is written with the goal of promoting Christian conduct."

Maybe so, but the author of the policy, the now-retired dean of students, says that "diversity and acceptance" were behind his initiative. Was Ezekiel experiencing a rash of racial violence or harassment? No, say all interviewed. Was the college's purpose even to become more "tolerant" of campus members who did not already subscribe to the Code of Student Conduct? No, too, admit those most closely involved. Rather, says the former dean of students, the racial harassment policy was designed to put the college on record as castigating that which had troubled other institutions—*racial* intolerance—as well as moving the college "into the mainstream" of student services by adopting a policy that seemed to be "advancing" at other well-known schools.

The dean of students found support for the policy with the dean of the faculty, and together they advanced the policy to Ezekiel's president. Presenting it as a "professional, almost legal requirement," they also managed to bypass the faculty, who, all without tenure, were reluctant to tangle with an issue that was clearly backed by top administrators. Like his counterpart at Cherrydale, Ezekiel's president was supportive of the policy, reflecting as it did the administration's interests in diversifying the institution. In the officials' view, hate speech codes were an important ingredient in this process. Not only would the policies make clear that racial and ethnic minorities were welcome on campus, but with new administrators itching to apply the professional standards they had learned elsewhere, antiharassment codes would bring the schools into line with the "best practices" of other, more distinguished institutions.

At first the creation of these policies does not seem to make sense. If officials were trying to adopt the best professional practices, why would they embrace policies that had already been found to be unconstitutional? The answer is not simple, but their actions return us to the interplay between mass constitutionalism and formal constitutional law. While these schools are not technically in noncompliance with the court decisions—being neither bound by the First Amendment nor historically having followed it—they have declined to follow the spirit of the holdings. Considering that the five hate speech cases were publicized widely, that their rulings were understood within academe and publicized by the popular press, their reach presumably went beyond the technical limits of jurisdictional application. These became decisions about the proper limits of hate speech, not simply anonymous disputes involving a few schools or a midwestern city. To disregard these cases, then, was to ignore the implications, nay the impact, of the courts' decisions and to set up alternative legal meanings in their place. Administrators at these schools may not have seen themselves as directly flaunting the authority of the courts, but their aspirations and policy preferences served to establish new legal norms on campus that differed from the formal legal order.

One of the features that makes this dynamic so interesting is its relation to the converse situation found in the area of equal opportunity and affirmative action. As Lauren Edelman has argued, the "institutionalization process" of equal employment and affirmative action practices within private organizations made them "somewhat immune from changes in the political environment."[17] Yet this process was just the converse for collegiate hate speech codes. Here the institutionalization process had made policies immune to the changing formal law. As schools developed these policies in the late 1980s to the early 1990s there arose an administrative constituency for the policies' preservation and enforcement. Whether reflecting the policy preferences of administrators or simply the utilitarian calculus that more was to be gained from the codes than lost, American academe seems to have accepted that the policies have value. At the very least, this norm sets up interests on one side of the scale that are resistant to removing the policies but for direct judicial enforcement. When those enforcement actions did not materialize, the persuasive impact of the courts' hate speech decisions have not been enough to overcome the interests that schools and their officials have in the speech policies.

6

The Triumph of Hate Speech Regulation

The new millennium has seen another organized attack against college hate speech policies, this time by the Foundation for Individual Rights in Education (FIRE). Led by its founders Alan Kors and Harvey Silverglate, FIRE in 2003 successfully challenged Shippensburg University in Pennsylvania for a speech policy that, according to FIRE, chilled the rights of students "to freely and openly engage in appropriate discussions of their theories, ideas and political and/or religious beliefs."[1] The suit presaged FIRE's launch of Speechcodes.org, a Web site that purported to "catalog[ ] speech codes at public and private colleges and universities across the country." According to FIRE, the lawsuit and new Web site represent an "unprecedented national campaign that will end—through legal action and through public exposure—the scandal of unconstitutional censorship at America's public college and university campuses and that will force private institutions to choose between liberty and tyranny."[2]

FIRE is not alone in contesting college hate speech regulation. In 2001, conservative activist David Horowitz crafted a highly controversial advertisement against reparations for slavery and sent the ad to a selection of newspapers at the most prestigious and liberal colleges across the country.[3] The ad drew a firestorm of protest at many schools, with several newspapers refusing to run the ad and others apologizing to their readers for having inflamed the campus community. Despite his protestations to the contrary—

according to Horowitz "this kind of censorship . . . should send chills up anybody's spine"[4]—Horowitz appeared delighted with the response. Known as a "rightist rabble-rouser," Horowitz used the controversy to jump-start his "'Freedom Tour' of campus lectures," reveling, as he said, in "my 15 minutes of fame."[5]

FIRE is correct that many schools still retain their hate speech policies, some of them challenging or even overstepping constitutional norms. A reexamination of the 100 schools chronicled in chapters 3 and 5 finds that most still have the same speech rules on the books in 2004 that they maintained seven years earlier. But this fact does not tell the whole story, for FIRE's claims are by turns both too broad and too narrow. FIRE has taken to rating college speech policies, claiming that upwards of two-thirds of public campuses have unconstitutional policies.[6] This number, however, is an exaggeration. Among other things FIRE does not distinguish between enforceable rules and exhortative statements; it confuses examples with definitions; and it takes statements out of context.

A good example is FIRE's charge that the University of Michigan's Policy and Guidelines Regarding Electronic Access to Potentially Offensive Material is unconstitutional for stating that "individuals should not be unwittingly exposed to offensive material by the deliberate and knowing acts of others." At best this line is ambiguous—the debate being whether the policy is restricting expression that the offender knows is offensive or material that the offender believes a recipient would find offensive. The context of the policy, however, should answer this question in favor of Michigan, especially considering that the policy applies only to computer systems administrators, not to students or faculty. More shocking is FIRE's exclusion of a line in the policy that clearly supports free speech and open expression: "[S]ystem administrators will have to guard against making judgments as to the appropriateness of the content of another person's work. Research and instruction take many forms and may not be restricted through censorship." Indeed, such luminaries as Robert O'Neil, director of the Thomas Jefferson Center for the Protection of Free Expression and former president of the University of Virginia, have contested FIRE's claims and estimates. Says O'Neil, "I just can't believe there are anything like that number of genuine speech codes."[7]

THE LARGER WAR

For all its focus on the precise number of college hate speech policies, FIRE risks missing the larger point that it is losing the war over hate speech regulation in general. Rather than being considered an unconstitutional pariah, hate speech restrictions are increasingly the norm among influential institutions of civil society, including higher education, the news media, and Internet service providers. Even as FIRE and its compatriots have won legal battles in court, the informal law of speech regulation has prospered. This, then, is the ultimate irony; adopted largely for utilitarian or instrumental purposes, the speech codes have had the very effect on mass constitutionalism and speech norms that their opponents originally feared. Without a court case won or a statute passed, the bounds of free speech have been reinterpreted and a new norm spread in civil society.

Initially, some of the evidence may appear to the contrary. Throughout the qualitative research I found few schools that had actively enforced their hate speech policies, the highest rate constituting one case per year. Part of the reason, says a former college president, is that "adopting policies is easier than acting on actual cases. . . . Policies are non-action," which most college administrators prefer, he says. "Usually, the least action a president can take is to adopt a policy. The adoption does nothing." Action, by contrast, "scares everyone, not just the actor."

Yet the very adoption of hate speech policies has influenced behavior on several campuses. This point was repeated to me by many administrators at the schools I visited, who reported the rise of a "culture of civility" that eschews, if not informally sanctions, hateful speech. "Don't mistake symbolism for impotence," they regularly reminded me. Symbols shape and reflect social meaning, providing cues to the community about the range of acceptable behavior. Adopting a hate speech policy, then, could have persuasive power even if it were rarely enforced. Consider the dean of students at a northeastern liberal arts college, who spoke proudly of her school's hate speech policy. Had the policy been formally invoked, I asked. "Rarely," she told me, but the measure "sets a standard on campus. It gives us something we can point our finger to in the catalog to remind students of the expectations and rights we all have in the community." This sentiment was repeated by the president of a well-known institution, who claimed that "we didn't set out to enforce the policy punitively but to use it as the basis for our educational efforts at respecting individuality." Still another administrator admitted that, "while we've rarely used the policy formally, it does give support to students who believe their rights have been violated. They'll come in for informal mediation and point to the policy as the reason for why the other person must stop harassing them."

Sociologists would call this process norm production—that symbolic measures can condition and order behavior without the actual implementation of punitive mechanisms.[8] Hate speech policies set an expected standard of behavior on campus; college officials employ orientation sessions, extracurricular programs, and campus dialogue to inculcate and spread the message; and over time an expectation begins to take root that hate speech is unacceptable and should be prohibited. Of course, this mechanism makes regulation a self-policing exercise—colleges need not take formal or punitive action—but the effect is to perpetuate a collective norm that sees hate speech as undesirable and worthy of prohibition. Moreover, considering the isomorphic tendencies of college administrators, the creation of speech policies—or speech norms—at respected and prestigious institutions has a "trickle down" effect throughout academe. Again, sociologists would call this process normative isomorphism, but most people know the phenomenon as "keeping up with the Joneses."[9] If Harvard, Berkeley, or Brown passes measures against hate speech, then institutions lower in the academic food chain are likely to take note and follow suit. If prestigious institutions advance campus norms that eschew hate speech, then both peer and "wannabe" institutions are likely to consider and replicate such informal rules. Indeed, this is the very fear of FIRE and its compatriots—that if PC policies are not checked now, their message will spread throughout academe infecting other campuses. What FIRE fails to say, but undoubtedly must be thinking, is that informal law and mass constitutionalism are at stake if the spread of speech regulation is not curbed. FIRE can hang its hat on *R.A.V., Doe, UWM Post,* and the other court cases in which judges have overturned college hate speech policies, but as hate speech regulation continues to flourish on college campuses, informal speech norms are at stake throughout the larger bounds of civil society.

Whatever one thinks of FIRE and its agenda, its supporters are like the old-fashioned fire brigade that excitedly shows up at a burning building only to toss paltry pails of water on the inferno. Hate speech regulation has already crossed the firebreak between academe and the rest of civil society and is well on its way toward acceptance in other influential institutions. The initial signs are found in surveys of incoming college freshmen. Shortly after *R.A.V.,* researchers began asking new freshmen whether they believe that "colleges should prohibit racist/sexist speech on campus."[10] In a 1993 survey, 58 percent of first-year students supported hate speech regulation, a number that has stayed steady and even grown a bit in the years following. By 1994, two-thirds of incoming freshmen approved of hate speech prohibitions, with more recent results leveling off around 60 percent.[11] Unfortunately, there are not similar surveys before 1993 to compare these results against, but it is a safe bet that support would have been minimal through the mid-1980s when the issue had not yet achieved salience. More to the point, the surveys show that support for speech regulation is achieved *before* students ever set foot on campus. If, as the codes' opponents claim, colleges are indoctrinating students in favor of speech regulation, the influence has reached beyond campus borders. New students are being socialized to this norm in society even before they attend college.

So too, surveys of the general population show an increasing queasiness with hate speech and a greater willingness to regulate such expression privately, especially when communicated over the Internet. In 1991, at the height of the speech code controversy, the CBS News/New York Times Poll asked the following question of American adults:

> Some universities have adopted codes of conduct under which students may be expelled for using derogatory language with respect to blacks, Jews, women, homosexuals and other groups of students. Which of the following comes closest to your view about this?
>
> A. Students who insult other students in this fashion should be subject to punishment; or
>
> B. The Bill of Rights protects free speech for these students, and they should not be subject to punishment.

Among respondents, 60 percent agreed that hate speech deserved punishment; only 32 percent believed that the Bill of Rights should protect such expression, with 8 percent undecided.[12]

In 1994 the National Opinion Research Center (NORC) took the issue beyond campuses, asking a national sample whether, "under the First Amendment guaranteeing free speech, people should be allowed to express their own opinions even if they are harmful or offensive to members of other religious or racial groups." At the time, 63 percent of respondents agreed, although only 21 percent did so strongly.[13] However, when NORC dropped a direct reference to the First Amendment, asking whether "people should not be allowed to express opinions that are harmful or offensive to members of other religious or racial groups," respondents were split almost evenly in their opinions. Forty-one percent supported such restrictions, 44 percent opposed them, and the remainder were either neutral or unsure.[14]

Both the CBS News/New York Times and NORC surveys were conducted in the early 1990s, as the speech code controversy was being played out on the front pages of major media. If respondents at the time seemed comfortable with different rules for separate venues—approving of hate speech measures on campus but split over regulations in larger society—this divergence seemed to narrow by the end of the decade. In 1999 the Freedom Forum conducted a State of the First Amendment Survey. Among its several questions, the Forum queried:

> I am now going to read you some ways that people might exercise their First Amendment right of free speech. . . . [Do you believe that] people should be allowed to use words in public that might be offensive to racial groups?[15]

Even with the explicit reference to the First Amendment and the right of free speech, researchers found that 78 percent of respondents disagreed with the exhortation to open discourse. Indeed, an amazing 61 percent of respondents strongly disagreed with the statement, indicating a presumed willingness to regulate or restrict racial hate speech.[16] The Freedom Forum has repeated this survey annually, and although support for hate speech regulation has dropped a bit, the level still hovers around two-thirds assent.[17]

The results from the Freedom Forum's surveys are in line with other polling data about hate speech involving computers and the Internet. In 1999, National Public Radio, the Kaiser Foundation, and Harvard's Kennedy School of Government teamed up to query Americans' attitudes about government. As part of that survey, researchers asked two questions about online hate speech. Finding that over 80 percent of respondents believed that hate speech on the Internet was a problem,[18] the survey asked whether "the government should do something about" these attacks against a person's "race, religion, or ethnicity." Nearly two-thirds of respondents believed the problem required governmental action,[19] a number consistent with the 60 percent of respondents in a study by Princeton Survey Research Associates who agreed that "the government should put major new restrictions on the Internet to limit access to pornography, hate speech, and information about bomb-making or other crimes."[20]

We should be careful not to overstate these results. The surveys do *not* show that Americans have become less supportive of the First Amendment, for other polling reflects continued attachment to open discourse and free speech.[21] Moreover, many of these surveys are limited to a specific mode of hate speech—expression over the Internet. For that matter, the Freedom Forum's surveys consistently show that respondents oppose a formal law prohibiting hate speech, presumably preferring that regulation be handled informally.[22] Yet there has been a significant change afoot, a sizeable shift in popular norms of free speech as the line dividing valuable speech from harmful expression has been moved. Open discourse is still important, respondents appear to say, but just as fighting words may be restricted, there seems to be a burgeoning sense that hate speech, and particularly racist speech, warrants proscription.

MEDIA COVERAGE AND POLICIES

It is always a chicken-and-egg question whether media depictions influence public attitudes or if changes in public mores or customs affect media depictions. Regardless of which factor precedes the other, the shift in public opinion has been mirrored in media treatment of hate speech. As the data in table 6.1 indicate, media coverage of college hate speech policies has waned over time. With speech policies no longer novel, it may be that the national press corps simply lost interest in collegiate speech codes and chose not to cover them. So, too, opponents may have believed that they had won the battle against speech regulation and ceased their frontal assault. Without the prospect of controversy or confrontation to sell a story, reporters may have avoided the topic.[23]

It is also possible, however, that media coverage has dropped because the terms of the codes are themselves increasingly accepted. A content analysis of magazine coverage finds more positive coverage of college hate speech codes since the initial court cases. In 1990, when only *Doe* had been decided, 80 percent of magazine stories on the speech codes were unfavorable, with the remaining 20 percent neutral. Three years later, shortly following *R.A.V.*, the stories continued to speak unfavorably of the speech codes. But while none of the stories was favorable, the ratio between unfavorable to neutral had moved to 45 to 55. Remarkably, by 1996 a quarter of the stories portrayed the speech codes favorably. A narrow majority of the stories was still unfavorable, but for the first time in six years the codes received some positive coverage. Table 6.2 presents these data.

Table 6.1. Annual Press Coverage of College Hate Speech Codes

Year	Magazines Newspapers	Major Newspapers	Other Service	Television	Wire	Total
1988	0	0	0	0	0	0
1989	0	13	14	0	6	33
1990	10	25	27	0	4	66
1991	17	159	221	6	20	423
1992	20	121	192	7	24	364
1993	40	197	254	16	25	532
1994	29	151	256	47	25	508
1995	36	126	207	17	12	398
1996	16	51	97	5	1	170
1997	11	35	87	6	4	143

Table 6.2. Content Analysis of Magazine Coverage (percentage)

Year	Favorable	Unfavorable	No Viewpoint
1990	0	80	20
1993	0	45	55
1996	25	56	19

Was this changing coverage a sign that hate speech regulation had become more accepted in society? Certainly, magazines represent reflective coverage, especially when compared to broadcast media or newspapers whose daily format often eschews analysis over an assembly-like reporting of events. Moreover, the stories in table 6.2 were largely devoid of opinion pieces or editorials whose screed might have tipped the content analysis. The change in tone, thus, may have reflected a more general familiarity with or acceptance of hate speech regulation as journalists took pen to ink (or keyboard to computer) to report the matter. As Anna Quindlen has said, media "do not make social policy, only reflect it once it moves convincingly from the fringe into the mainstream."[24]

In this respect, it is interesting that many media outlets now restrict hate speech on their own. The most common examples are newspapers and broadcast media that no longer air racial epithets. The O. J. Simpson trial showcased this dilemma, as many news organizations struggled with whether, and how, to depict Mark Fuhrman's slurs against "niggers." CNN began by saying the "n-word" or "racial epithet" on its broadcasts, only later choosing to air the word in its entirety, but several other journalists chose not to repeat the slur.[25] The *St. Petersburg Times* and *The State* in South Carolina "took the route of many newspapers when they decided to use 'n——' or other euphemisms for every reference to 'nigger' that appeared in news stories about Fuhrman."[26] Of course, journalists might well have excised the term as profane, using the cloak of a "family newspaper" to edit out coarse language of all stripes. Indeed, in September of 2003, many newspapers refused to print a Doonesbury comic on masturbation, concerned "that the mention of certain words *per se* . . . might offend some readers."[27] But in considering the word "nigger," editors sounded remarkably like the critical race theorists who had thundered against racial hate speech a few years earlier. "I know [the word's] power," said a managing editor of a southern paper, "because I know history and how it would be used. It was meant to degrade people."[28] "Pain" and "history" figured prominently in journalists' explanations. "I talked to a colleague," said another editor, who reported that, 'Every time I see that word in print, it's a slap in my face.' . . . It's not the paper's place to be slapping our readers."[29] People may be "saying it in their living rooms," said an observer, "but that doesn't mean they want to read it on the front page of the *New York Times*." If anything, "repeated use of 'nigger' may make its use more common but no less devastating."[30]

The Fuhrman flap is only one of many occasions in which reporters and journalists must make subjective decisions about potentially offensive expression. Several papers have adopted policies to handle racial slurs, deciding "to use them only in direct quotations if they are essential to the story."[31] Said Matthew Storin, editor of the *Boston Globe*, "in most cases 'nigger' should not be used."[32] Other papers have applied such logic in refusing to name sports mascots. The *Minneapolis Star Tribune* and the *Oregonian*, for example, refuse to print "racist Native [American] mascots" and names. Explained Tim McGuire, editor of the *Star Tribune*, "the decision to stop using mascots was based on a 'humane gesture to my fellow man.'" In 2001 the *Kansas City Star* stopped printing the Cleveland Indians' mascot, Chief Wahoo. Echoing McGuire's rationale, Mark Zieman of the *Star* said, "Chief Wahoo is a ridiculous, offensive, racist caricature. We would be ashamed to run it as an editorial cartoon or comic strip, so why should we repeatedly publish it in the sports pages of our newspaper?"[33]

This hesitance to print hate speech is also seen in newspapers' advertising policies, where another study of mine found that up to one-half of the nation's top papers refuse ads containing hate speech. A year after the September 11 attacks, more than one hundred newspapers were randomly sent one of three mock issue ads about the implications of 9/11. Of the ads, one was neutral, suggesting the legacy of September 11 must be a greater commitment to American ideals of equality and freedom; a second ad was highly liberal, arguing that American arrogance had brought on the attacks; and a third ad was ultraconservative, advocating that America tighten its immigration policy. The ads were timed to coincide with either Thanksgiving or Christmas of 2002, shortly after the first anniversary of the attacks.[34]

We had expected that a paper's editorial stance would affect its decision to accept or reject an ad, but instead most papers were willing to consider a variety of ideological messages. Where papers rejected ads, they pointed to language that they claimed was analogous to hate speech. Consider the mock ad that advocated curbs on immigration. The ad text said:

> It has now been a year since the attacks of September 11th. The President has led a war against Al Qaeda. Congress has passed laws to root out terrorists. These are all admirable.
>
> The problem is that they do not go far enough. Call it political correctness, but no one is willing to point the finger where it ought to go. American citizens

> did not carry out the September 11th attacks. Foreign terrorists did. They were not your neighbors. They were visitors or would-be immigrants.
>
> The answer ought to be obvious. If we want to make America safer we need to make our borders more secure by tightening the rules for immigration. We now know that many of the September 11th terrorists used loopholes in the immigration laws to stay in the U.S. and plan their attacks. Some used student visas to attend flight schools; others received multiple tourist visas to remain in the U.S. That just gives terrorists time on our shores to coordinate their plans.
>
> We need to crack down on the revolving visa system and make it harder for foreigners to immigrate to the U.S. Up to now the INS has treated visa applicants relatively equal. That has to stop. The Swedes and Thais are not trying to attack us. All of the terrorists came from the Middle East. It is time to limit visitors from these countries and to ensure that the Government is screening applicants very carefully from that part of the world.
>
> Is this putting up a brick wall around America? Perhaps. But what is more dangerous, would-be terrorists roaming inside the U.S. or stuck outside? You be the judge. Join us in an effort to enact smart immigration laws. Protect America by keeping dangerous foreigners where they belong: out of the U.S.
>
> —The Partnership to Protect America

According to the papers, the offending language came in the third line of the fourth paragraph: "The Swedes and Thais are not trying to attack us. All of the terrorists came from the Middle East." How was this hate speech, we asked? Because the language seemed to "disparage a group on the basis of its religion or ethnicity," papers replied. But the text did not mention Islam or Arabs, we countered. "Maybe, but it's implied," an ad executive said. Explained another quite adamantly, "I will not publish this. It's offensive, incendiary, and it picks on people's religion." Almost all of the ad executives described their decisions as an "editorial judgment." Said the advertising director of a paper in the Northwest, "Although this may not be news, where we offer greater latitude to quote newsmakers, we want to encourage open debate in our paper. . . . It's good for the community and good for sales. . . . But free speech doesn't mean singling someone out because of his race."

It is remarkable that one-third of the papers that received this ad rejected it as hate speech, but follow-up interviews with advertising executives discovered that roughly *half* of the participating papers have some policy, whether written or informally understood, that prohibits ads with hate speech. How do papers define hate speech? There was some variation, and not everyone used the exact term "hate speech," but the collective focused on "offensive" or "derogatory" language directed at a person or group because of its race, gender, ethnicity, or religion. Some newspapers were incredibly precise. An official of a major national paper said definitively that he would not print "hate speech." When asked to define the term, he answered, "gratuitously offensive on race, ethnicity, religion, gender, and possibly sexual orientation." Interestingly, his paper was willing to publish the mock ad, since he believed that the text had not reached this threshold. But there are many more situations in which his paper—and papers like this well-respected national journal—would prohibit public dissemination of hate speech. Papers were not rejecting the ad because it was profane, obscene, or controversial; they took issue with its perceived attack against a minority group's immutable characteristics. Indeed, their reasoning seemed almost synonymous with the purported theory of college hate speech codes—speech that attacks people on the basis of their minority characteristics serves no useful function and only acts to inflict unnecessary pain.

If newspapers—one of the "old line" media—are willing to reject hate speech in their opinion ads—the new, online media impose even greater restrictions on hate speech. This may be surprising to many, since the Internet has been touted as "the ultimate soapbox," allowing users "to communicate their viewpoints to the world."[35] Yet many Internet service providers explicitly restrict hate speech. None is more adamant about this prohibition than America Online (AOL), which states in its Rules of User Conduct that users may not:

> upload, post or otherwise distribute [content that] victimizes, harasses, or degrades an individual or group of individuals on the basis of religion, gender, sexual orientation, race, ethnicity, age or disability.[36]

Another major Internet player, Verizon Online, includes similar language in its Website Use Agreement, threatening to:

> deny Service to you, or immediately to terminate your Service for material breach, if your use of the Service or your use of an alias or the aliases of additional users on your account, whether explicitly or implicitly, and in the sole discretion of Verizon . . . espouses, promotes or incites bigotry, hatred or racism.[37]

Unlike some of the college speech policies, Internet service providers are often willing to enforce the terms of these rules. AOL has blocked users from such screen names as "uranigger," "uraraghead," and "uratowelhead."[38] Although a quick search by the Institute for the Study and Prevention of Hate Crimes found such aliases as "urafaggot" available or already in use, a representative for AOL called the screen name a mistake that slipped past the company's filters. Said the spokesman, Nicholas Graham:

> We have zero tolerance for hate speech on the service, anywhere on the service. So, whether it's on chat rooms or message boards, if we are made aware of hate speech, we will actively remove it, and we will reprimand the member who posted it.[39]

As if to prove Mr. Graham's point, AOL quickly removed a message board about Rosie O'Donnell's talk show when it was quickly flooded with disparaging remarks about the actress's sexual orientation.[40] Nor is AOL alone in its regulation of the Internet. The very fact that the Web is world wide puts Americans in touch with European practices that not only prohibit hate speech but also penalize providers and users for its dissemination.[41]

THE MASS CONSTITUTIONALISM OF HATE SPEECH REGULATION

If hate speech regulation is alive and well, how widespread and accepted is its practice? Certainly, no one would claim that the norm has been codified in the formal law, for the courts have been abundantly clear that public bodies may not prohibit hateful "expressions based on the underlying message."[42] With the exception of sexual harassment law, measures that impose "special prohibitions on those speakers who express views on the disfavored subjects of 'race, color,'" and the like are considered constitutionally suspect.[43] But, by the same token, hate speech regulation is hardly a fringe perspective, relegated to the realm of unaccepted moral views. Hate speech measures have become a part of informal law, as a critical mass of civil society has accepted the notion of hate speech regulation. This is not to say that hate speech rules are uniformly popular or that the public supports legislation to prohibit hateful expression. Quite the contrary, for as FIRE has shown, there are many detractors uneasy at what they consider a "scandal" of intellectual "tyranny."[44] Nonetheless, there is a growing sense in civil society, especially among its most influential institutions like academe and the media, that hate speech is not only inappropriate and dangerous but that it ought to be prohibited, if only through informal mechanisms.

How is it that I can make this claim when almost no court has upheld a hate speech code? Part of the answer turns on the definition of a hate speech policy, for if the category includes rules that prohibit sexually demeaning expression, the kind that would lead to a hostile work or educational environment, several courts have sustained measures that prevent and punish harassment. But as chapter 4 argued, there is a disparity in American law between sexual harassment policies, which the courts largely accept even when applied to expression, and other measures that address hateful speech based on race, ethnicity, or sexual orientation. The latter category has largely been panned by the courts. Indeed, the closest that American law comes to punishing hate speech is hate crimes legislation, which imposes a "penalty enhancement" if a suspect picks his victim "because of the race, religion, color, disability, sexual orientation, national origin or ancestry of that person."[45]

In some ways hate crimes legislation is recompense by the courts for their prohibition of hate speech measures. The leading case, *Wisconsin v. Mitchell,*[46] was decided by the U.S. Supreme Court in 1993, a year following the Court's contrary decision about hate speech in *R.A.V. v. City of St. Paul.*[47] The Court's reasoning in *Mitchell* also struck some as overly solicitous, to the point of contradictory. As the Wisconsin Supreme Court had ruled, hate crimes violate "the First Amendment directly by punishing what the legislature has deemed to be offensive thought."[48] This decision would appear to confirm the courts' traditional dichotomy between speech and acts, but the U.S. Supreme Court muddied the waters by penalizing hateful intentions in one context but not another. Under the Court's reasoning, public bodies may not punish a man for a racist tirade, but if the same person attacks another because of his race—and, more particularly, if the aggressor confirms his intentions by spewing racial epithets during the attack—the defendant may face a heightened penalty on account of his racist motives.

Whether this dichotomy is adequately explained by the courts' traditional speech-act distinction, hate speech regulation generally meets a hostile reception in the courts. For that matter, much of the polling data I have presented repudiates hate speech without necessarily supporting formal, legal prohibition of the same. Is it possible, then, that the traditional model of law has prevailed here? Whatever people privately think of hate speech, has the formal law effectively forbidden its punishment?

I do not doubt that hate speech regulation is largely prohibited under the formal Constitution, just as I do not question that the formal law has both compulsory and persuasive power. But, formal and mass constitutionalism are not mutually exclusive territories. They entwine each other, sharing power and competing for authority over the minds and actions of the public. In the case of hate speech regulation, opponents undoubtedly control the formal law, but hate speech measures flourish in civil society, the idea of speech regulation having taken hold in mass constitutionalism. With academe, the media, and Internet service providers willing to tamp down hate speech—with majorities of the public now concluding that a person's right to speak should give way when the message is racist or offensive—the informal law of mass constitutionalism exerts influence over civil society.

We might also reexamine those polls that reflect reluctance to codify hate speech prohibitions. Laura Beth Nielsen has done a superb job of studying the public's response to street harassment, interviewing hundreds of people to understand their views of hate speech as well as their proposed response to the problem. Like much of what is reported here, Nielsen finds large majorities who "have strong normative reactions against most offensive speech. They are willing to say that they find it offensive and morally wrong to make racist or sexist comments to strangers in public."[49] So, too, just as in the polls from the Freedom Forum, most of Nielsen's subjects "are not in favor of limiting such speech" in formal law.[50] But Nielsen wisely probed further to understand why respondents simultaneously abhor hate speech yet reject its formal prohibition. Her findings help to elucidate the relationship between formal and mass constitutionalism.

"Contrary to the popular depiction of Americans as overly litigious"—of an American society that must rely on judicial decrees to establish rights and order behavior—Nielsen presents a public with "a pragmatic skepticism about law as a remedy for offensive public behavior." As she explains, "only a small proportion of the individuals I interviewed, most of whom are white men, cite freedom of speech as the principal rationale for exempting public speech from legal regulation." Much larger numbers grounded their response "in a lay realism about the law and what it can be expected to accomplish." Some distrust the state. Still others—primarily white women and people of color—are skeptical "about the law as a remedial tool" or "are unwilling to be defined as victims, which they think would happen if they invoked the law to 'protect' them."[51]

The result is a political divide, where, as Nielsen says, the traditional First Amendment theory of hate speech "remains firmly in control of legal and political institutions."[52] But, just as important are the countervailing legal or constitutional norms that exist, and are practiced, in civil society by a public that is skeptical about the courts' powers. People do not tolerate hate speech, they do not acknowledge a right to offensive public speech, because the courts have declared the First Amendment requires as much. To the contrary, large numbers of the public reject a right to hate speech and believe that they are entitled to be free from hurtful invective. In this respect, they have the support of several influential institutions of civil society, which reinforce the norm that hate speech is to be prohibited and informally enforce these ideas through their policies and practices.

My point, then, is not that hate speech regulation has triumphed *over* the formal law but that it triumphs *in the face of* formal constitutionalism. What we see is a battle in the contact zone between formal and informal law, between formal and mass constitutionalism. Traditional legal theory tells us that formal law should prevail, that if one wants to secure constitutional rights he appeals to and wins the support of legal institutions, including the courts and legislatures. But what mass constitutionalism—and the hate speech debate—reveal is that legal and constitutional norms may exist in place of, in the face of, or alongside the formal law. More than being inert or symbolic, the informal law may guide and inform mass understandings, expectations, and practices in a way that formal law cannot command. This is particularly true when, as Nielsen's work shows, the debate between mass and formal constitutionalism remains stuck in the contact zone not because people reject the underlying constitutional norm but because they have doubts and suspicions about the formal law's ability to enforce that doctrine and protect them.

Another way to understand these developments is to borrow from the concept of legal pluralism, which is a heuristic that helps to explain "a situation in which two or more legal systems coexist in the same social field."[53] Originally applicable to the interplay between indigenous and colonial law, the theory has been broadened more recently to include "informal systems in which the processes of establishing rules, securing compliance to these rules, and punishing rulebreakers seem natural and taken for granted, as occurs within families, work groups, and collectives."[54] The notion of legal pluralism is that persuasive or even compulsory social power is shared between competing legal systems, even if one of those systems lacks formal codification.

The same is true in many ways for the relationship between formal and mass constitutionalism. The formal law may set a floor of rights expectations, the courts' decisions may even secure support or compliance on particular questions. But when an issue is highly salient, when formal legal decrees conflict with strongly held views of elites or the mass public, formal constitutionalism gives ground as the informal norms of mass constitutionalism increasingly hold sway in civil society.

The triumph of hate speech regulation, then, is the success of a competing legal system in the face of formal law. The courts may have spoken on the subject, rejecting attempts to punish racial or ethnic hate speech, but a countervailing norm has taken root in mass constitutionalism, replicating itself in the institutional activity of civil society and in the process influencing public attitudes about the scope of constitutional norms and free speech rights. What may have begun as an instrumental, intra-academic exercise has not been dispatched by its critics. In the early morning of a new century, the norm of hate speech regulation has grown to challenge the formal Constitution.

Appendix

Methodology and Data Sources

Research was based on both quantitative and qualitative methods, using a random, stratified sample of 100 four-year colleges and universities. Schools were drawn from the 1987 *Classification of Institutions of Higher Education* produced by the Carnegie Foundation. The Carnegie listing is the most complete and unbiased source of tertiary educational institutions in the United States, and its 1987 report was contemporaneous to the rise of the first college hate speech codes. Although the Carnegie list also includes two-year institutions (generally community colleges) and specialized institutions (music schools and the like), the study was limited to those schools that offered a traditional baccalaureate program.[1]

The sample was stratified to account for the higher frequency of speech codes among large research universities and well-known liberal arts colleges, meaning that 30 percent of the sample comes from research universities, 20 percent from doctorate granting institutions, 20 percent from comprehensive universities, 20 percent from liberal arts colleges I, and 10 percent from liberal arts colleges II. The selected schools include the following:

Where a school's state is not clear from its name, the state's abbreviation is added.

American University (DC)
Auburn University (AL)
Beloit College (WI)
Bethany College (WV)
Brandeis University (MA)
Brown University (RI)

California State University–Long Beach
Case Western Reserve University (OH)
Central State University (OK)
Chapman College (CA)
Claremont McKenna College (CA)
Clark College (GA)
College of Great Falls (MT)
College of the Holy Cross (MA)
College of Mt. St. Joseph (OH)
Davis Elkins College (WV)
Denison University (OH)
Drury College (MO)
Duke University (NC)
D'Youville College (NY)
Emmanuel College (MA)
Emory University (GA)
Fitchburg State University (MA)
Florida State University
Georgetown University (DC)
Georgetown College (KY)
Goddard College (VT)
Johns Hopkins University (MD)
Hamilton College (NY)
Hamline University (MN)
Haverford College (PA)
Idaho State University
Illinois Institute of Technology
Indiana/Purdue University at Indianapolis
Indiana State University
Kansas State University
Kent State University (OH)
Kings College (PA)
Knox College (IL)
Linfield College (OR)
Luther College (IA)
Massachusetts Institute of Technology
Messiah College (PA)
Middlebury College (VT)
Mississippi State University
Monmouth College (IL)
Moorehead State University (MN)
Mt. Holyoke College (MA)
New York University
North Carolina Central University
North Carolina State University
North Carolina Wesleyan
Northwest Nazarene College (ID)
Northwestern University (IL)
Nova University (FL)
Oglethorpe College (GA)
Old Dominion University (VA)
Park College (MO)
Queens College (NC)
Regis College (MA)
Rice University (TX)
Ripon College (WI)
Roanoke College (VA)
St. Ambrose College (IA)
Smith College (MA)
Southern Illinois University
Southern Methodist University (TX)
Stanford University (CA)
Sul Ross University (TX)
State University of New York–Binghamton
State University of New York–Stony Brook
Texas Woman's University
Thomas More College (KY)
Tufts University (MA)
University of Arizona
University of California–Berkeley
University of California–Santa Barbara
University of California–Santa Cruz
University of Florida
University of Hawaii
University of Kansas
University of Maryland–Baltimore County
University of Massachusetts–Amherst
University of Michigan
University of New Hampshire
University of New Mexico

University of Northern Colorado
University of Oklahoma
University of Oregon
University of Puget Sound
University of San Francisco
University of Tampa
University of Texas–Arlington
University of Tulsa
Wagner College (NY)
Wesley College (DE)
West Virginia University
Western Michigan University
Western Washington University
Williams College (MA)

QUANTITATIVE RESEARCH

Dependent Variable

Nearly 50 variables were collected from these schools to evaluate against the development of college hate speech codes. Foremost was the dependent variable—whether a school had adopted a hate speech code, and if so how restrictive it was. In this respect, the research was aided by an earlier study conducted at Vanderbilt University's First Amendment Center, where researchers collected speech policies from a variety of public colleges and universities.[2] Of course, the present research is different from Vanderbilt's work—being both descriptive and explanatory—but the scale used in the earlier estimate provided an excellent base.

Vanderbilt's researchers used six ordered categories to code university speech policies. The rankings were on a sliding scale, with each step intended to reflect decreasing comportment with First Amendment norms. The present research borrows from that scale, dropping only Vanderbilt's code for obscenity policies. Although one can imagine several instances in which obscene expression is speech (without also being fighting words), most instances of obscenity involve actions, drawings, or exhibitions rather than speech. Consequently, college policies were classified according to the following categories:

0. Did not adopt speech policies
1. Punished fighting words
2. Banned verbal abuse or harassment
3. Forbade verbal abuse or harassment against minorities
4. Proscribed offensive, demeaning, or stigmatizing speech

Starting from the top, it is self-evident that a school averts First Amendment concerns by avoiding speech policies. The next step, fighting words, recognizes that courts have carved out limited areas of expression that state actors may proscribe. According to *Chaplinsky v. New Hampshire,* public entities may prohibit words "which by their very utterance inflict injury or tend to incite an immediate breach of the peace."[3] Over time the courts have cut the definition of fighting words in half, forbidding only those words that "incite an immediate breach of the peace," but the prohibition presumably still exists.[4]

The next category skirts the line of constitutionality, as verbal abuse falls into the common law category of harassment, which itself is a narrow, subjective basis to restrict expression. However, when codes distinguish verbal abuse by its racial/sexual/ethnic message, these policies almost certainly contradict current law.[5] Finally, offensive expression, to the extent that it does not reach fighting words, is constitutionally protected. Any measures that restrict such expression are unconstitutional on the grounds of over-breadth and/or vagueness.[6]

Hate speech codes were estimated over two different time periods. The first encompassed 1987–92, reflecting the period from the codes' initial appearance on college campuses to their potential death knell following the Supreme Court's decision in *R.A.V. v. City of St. Paul* in 1992. Codes were also measured in 1997, two years after *Corry v. Stanford*. The research was only concerned with hate speech codes adopted during this ten-year period, from 1987 to 1997. If a school already had a speech policy on the books before 1987 (one school), it was coded as null. For that matter, if a school adopted a policy after 1987 but rescinded it before 1992 (two schools), it was coded as reflecting the more restrictive policy in the first estimate. These decisions mean that the data may slightly overstate the number of speech codes up to 1992 (because two had been rescinded) but understate those that were still valid later. (A school coded as zero for adopting a policy prior to 1987 remained as that in the later data unless it created a new policy.)

Independent Variables

As the text indicates, several hypotheses have been advanced for the rise of college hate speech codes. These hypotheses, whether primary or alternative, involve many constructs, including at least the following:

- Philosophical priming from:
  - Feminism
  - Critical race studies
  - Postmodernism
  - Deconstructionism
  - Critical legal studies
- The percentage of students, faculty, staff, or administrators who were:
  - African American

    - Other racial or ethnic minorities
    - Women
    - Gay/lesbian
- Prior anti-apartheid protest on campus
- Political liberalism on campus
- Racial or ethnic violence on campus
- Previous adoption of a campus sexual harassment policy
- Influence from conservative activists on campus
- Schools' characteristics, including:
    - Size
    - Public/private status
    - Religious affiliation or control
    - Percentage of students who were full-time
    - Percentage of students who were undergraduates
    - Percentage of students from in-state
- Campus penchant for codifying student rules
- Outside influence from:
    - Alumni
    - State legislators
    - Political climate of a school's surrounding community or state

Several of these constructs were easy to represent with variables. A school's size and in-state enrollment, for example, came from either the 1989–90 Integrated Post Secondary Education Data System (IPEDS) that schools must file with the U.S. Department of Education or the *Barron's Guide to Colleges*. All racial, ethnic, and gender data on an institution's students, faculty, staff, or administrators were taken from IPEDS and the Equal Employment Opportunity Commission's 1991 EEG-6 Campus Survey. In addition, schools willingly shared their policy manuals, permitting a determination of those institutions that had developed sexual harassment policies in advance of hate speech codes (as well as an analysis of the speech policies themselves).

Other variables required more creativity. The influence of feminism was represented by the presence of a women's studies department on campus, while the presence of African American, Latino American, or ethnic studies departments reflected the influence of Critical Race Studies.[7] Even recognizing that these are imperfect measures, the members of such departments are more likely to support the philosophies under consideration than would faculty in other departments. Moreover, there was sufficient variation among schools in sponsoring these departments.

Postmodernism and deconstructionism were not represented in the quantitative analysis, their adherents spread widely throughout many humanities and social science programs. The qualitative research, however, considered such influences. The presence of a law school was noted in the quantitative research, even though law schools can be bastions of feminism, CRS, or of course, critical legal studies. To some extent this variable was included to direct the qualitative research. By regressing this variable with those for women's and minority studies it was possible to focus on the potential influences for the underlying identity philosophies. These, in turn, were drawn out in the qualitative interviews.

Schools do not report the number of gays and lesbians on campus, so the analysis utilized a dummy variable to measure whether a school maintained a gay and/or lesbian student organization between 1987 and 1992. Understandably, this variable is not the same as measuring a group's numerical status among students, faculty, and administrators, but it is axiomatic that such an organization would not exist unless a school had a sufficient number of students who openly identified themselves as gay or lesbian. Moreover, gay/lesbian student groups are often aided by faculty or administrators who are themselves "out."

The study used three different college guides to obtain data on gay and lesbian collegiate organizations: *Barron's, The College Board College Handbook,* and *The Gay and Lesbian Guide to College.* Whenever one of the guides indicated that a college maintained a gay/lesbian group, the school was coded as such. Admittedly, there was a problem of measurement consistency within this variable, but such data were not readily reported in the early 1990s. It was, thus, worth the risk of incongruity to ensure that the sample noted all schools in the sample that had gay/lesbian groups. All together, the sources identified 33 such schools out of the sample of 100.

Many of the colleges in the study divested from their South African holdings during the late 1980s, but the operative variable identified schools that experienced campuswide protest against apartheid, the kind that might have prepared activists for a later campaign for speech codes. Three sources were utilized to identify such schools: Lexis/Nexis, the Investors Responsibility Research Service in Washington, D.C., and the American Committee on Africa in New York City. The latter two organizations kept records on campus divestment and protest, and each group allowed me access to their reports and files.

Commentators often linked the speech codes to liberal campuses, suggesting that students and faculty at such schools reacted negatively to national changes in civil rights policy and organized to push campus measures to protect racial and ethnic minorities. Unfortunately, there are no national studies of the political ideology of faculty or students on individual campuses. Each year the Cooperative Institutional Research Program at UCLA produces a national survey titled *The American Freshman,* but they do not release information on individual schools. Similarly, the American Association of University Professors no longer conducts attitudinal surveys of its members, nor does it release information on individual schools.

Instead, the research drew from the finding of Ladd and Lipset that a school's academic standing is positively linked to the liberalness of its faculty:

> Surveys of professors . . . all agree that achievement in higher education, however, measured, has been associated with more liberal-to-left views on a wide array of social and political issues. . . . The "top" of the academic community is more liberal than the "bottom," not because its members are more advantaged in salary, research opportunities, and various prerequisites of academic life, but seemingly because *within* the group role and orientations are closer to those of the ideal intellectual.[8]

Ladd and Lipset do not claim that prestigious academicians are intrinsically more liberal than other colleagues. Rather, they say, the kind of critical questioning associated with prestigious academic work is closely connected with liberal political beliefs. This finding is most helpful because it represents campus liberalness apart from variables measuring the influence of racial minorities. Several national studies indicate that African Americans and some Latino communities are more liberal on average than whites,[9] but a general liberalness score permits the ranking of campuses as a whole.

Under Ladd and Lipset's approach, a school's academic standing is synonymous with its prestige. Just as a prestigious school draws faculty who are questioning, insightful, and open-minded, it attracts students who are inquisitive, tolerant, and creative. Prestige was represented in two ways in the research, incorporating both the *Barron's* rankings of schools as well as listings from the *Yale Daily News Insiders Guide to College.* The former roughly evaluates the collective academic abilities of a school's student body, while the latter reflects outside esteem for a college or university. Of course, *Barron's* rankings rely in part on standardized test scores, which have been criticized for failing to measure students' academic abilities. But the intent here was to represent quantitatively the notion of ability—and thus prestige—among students and faculty. Although some faculty may question the value of standardized tests, many more may not, and prospective students rarely do.[10] Further, the *Barron's* rating also includes the high school class rank of incoming students. This measure does not present the same concerns as do standardized tests.

Incidents of campus ethnoviolence were determined by news coverage, scouring Lexis/Nexis, the *Readers Guide,* the *Chronicle of Higher Education,* and the archives of the Center for Applied Study of Ethnoviolence, which subscribed to three clipping services between 1985 and 1992 and graciously allowed me access to its files. In this way, I was able to secure stories about a variety of schools, both well known and relatively obscure. Of note, the variable reflects *off-campus* coverage of incidents, figuring that mainstream media would only cover serious incidents and not minor scrapes that might make a campus paper. Using a dummy variable, incidents were coded positively if they occurred on or near campus, or if they directly involved a member of the campus community. Incidents were also evaluated for their timing, since only antecedent events could influence the adoption of a hate speech policy.

Although the codes' critics focused on progressive activists, an alternative hypothesis explains the development of hate speech policies by campus conservatism, with conservatives either seeking codes to ban indecent language or provoking liberals who offered PC policies out of fear of rising conservative support on campus. Again, no national surveys measure the ideology of faculty or students on individual campuses, nor would the inverse of the prestige variables be sufficient here, for the alternative constructs imply pockets of conservative activists on campus. Instead, two different variables were employed. Building on research that shows fraternity and sorority members are appreciably more conservative than are other students,[11] the study estimated the percentage of each campus' study body that was "Greek." In addition, the study considered whether a school maintained an alternative, conservative student newspaper.

Any penchant for codifying student rules ought rightly to turn on the number of administrative or behavioral policies each school had adopted, but unfortunately these data are not standardized; what one school considers an administrative policy others call an academic rule. Instead, the study compared the percentage of each school's annual budget it spent on student services in 1992, on the presumption that a rise in campus procedural rules required additional student services personnel to administer them. To account for the different spending priorities between research universities and teaching colleges,[12] mean student expenditures were calculated for each Carnegie category of schools. The mean scores were then compared against the actual expenditures for schools in their respective categories.

A similar approach was used to compare the influence of outside groups on collegiate policy. Public schools were ranked by the percentage of their operating budgets that came from state sources, while private institutions were compared by the proportion of their budgets dependent on annual contributions. Both sets of data are reported in *Higher Education Revenues and Expendi-*

tures. Recognizing that schools might also have responded to the political climate of their environs, the study compared the 1988 presidential vote from each school's congressional district and state. Those areas where the Democrat had majority support were presumed to be more liberal than those jurisdictions where the Republican candidate won.

STATISTICAL TESTS

Traditionally, one would compare the dependent variable—the hate speech codes—against a collection of independent variables that represent a coherent model. Here, however, the critics' explanation for speech codes involved up to 19 variables,[13] which is too many to evaluate at once given the limited sample size. Instead, each independent variable was compared against the speech codes by either a contingency table or a bivariate correlation to deduce its statistical significance. For these purposes, the dependent variable was evaluated continuously as well as in four dichotomous models,[14] with the best statistical significance for an independent variable used to estimate its explanatory power. Table A.1 reports the statistical significance of these relationships:

Table A.1. Statistical Correlations between Independent Variables and College Hate Speech Codes

Independent Variable	Level of Statistical Significance
Independent Variables Statistically Significant at or below the .05 Level	
Anti-apartheid protest	.013
Barron's Guide	.048
Black studies department	.008
Full-time students	.028
Gay/lesbian	.047
Graduate students	.037
Minority studies department	.014
Women faculty	.028
Yale Guide	.003
Independent Variables Not Statistically Significant at the .05 Level	
Annual contributions	.762
Asian administrators	.153

(continued)

Table A.1 *(continued)*

Independent Variable	Level of Statistical Significance
Asian faculty	.666
Asian staff	.261
Asian students	.427
Black administrators	.526
Black faculty	.354
Black staff	.596
Black students	.219
College vs. university	.868
Conservative newspaper	.075
Fraternities/sororities	.477
Racial/ethnic incident	.443
In-state students	.218
Latino administrators	.562
Latino faculty	.768
Latino staff	.757
Latino students	.976
Latino studies department	.072
Law school	.089
Minority administrators	.304
Minority faculty	.445
Minority staff	.608
Minority students	.109
Students on-campus	.189
Presidential vote–CD	.962
Presidential vote–State	.464
Public/private status	.962
Religious affiliation	.965
Religious control	.316
Sexual harassment policies	.233
Size	.428
State contributions	.220
Student services staff	.711
Women administrators	.537
Women staff	.927
Women students	.146
Women's studies department	.082

Table A.2. Univariate Logistic Regression—No Speech Policy vs. Any Speech Policy

Variable	Estimate	Standard Error	Δ Probability
Anti-apartheid protest	.902*	.420	.22
Barron's Guide	1.192	.424	.29
Black studies program	.332	.428	—
Full-time students	.037*	.018	.40
Gay/lesbian group	.516	.429	—
Graduate students	.001	.018	—
Minority studies program	.348	.422	—
Women faculty	–.047*	.022	–.57
Yale Guide	.299*	.158	.14

* = Statistically significant at the .05 level

Those variables that indicated a statistically significant connection at the .05 level were then tested against the speech codes in univariate regression analysis to confirm their connection. Both Ordinary Least Squares (OLS) and Logit regressions were conducted, with the dependent variable coded dichotomously in the latter tests. (Three different dichotomous pairs were tested, including no code vs. any code; offensive speech policies vs. all others; and policies prohibiting offensive speech and verbal harassment of groups vs. all others.) OLS may not have been precisely applicable in this situation, since the categories for hate speech policies are not strictly continuous, although the results from both OLS and Logit were analogous. Nonetheless, tables A.2, A.3, and A.4 report the results from Logit.

Following the univariate regressions, statistically significant variables were grouped to test in multivariate Logit models. For example, from table A.2 the speech codes (split into dichotomous pairs between no speech code and any speech policy) were regressed on the variables representing anti-apartheid protest, the *Yale Guide,* the percentage of female faculty, and the percentage of full-time student enrollment. Surprisingly, none of the multivariate regressions yielded statistically significant results, a predicament that is explained by the fact that many of the independent variables in tables A.2, A.3, and A.4 are collinear with each other. In fact, nearly 80 percent of the bivariate relationships between these variables reflect multicollinearity (no table shown).

QUALITATIVE DATA

Rather than employing factor analysis to tease through the quantitative relationships, the study turned to qualitative research to complete the inquiry. Cer-

Table A.3. Univariate Logistic Regression—Offensive Speech Policies vs. All Others

Variable	Estimate	Standard Error	Δ Probability
Anti-apartheid protest	1.75*	.793	.18
Barron's Guide	.479*	.238	.24
Black studies program	1.61*	.656	.22
Full-time students	.070	.042	—
Gay/lesbian group	1.20	.630	—
Graduate students	.048*	.024	.39
Minority studies program	1.50*	.654	.11
Women faculty	–.076*	.044	–.57
Yale Guide	2.57*	1.06	.19

* = Statistically significant at the .05 level

Table A.4. Univariate Logistic Regression—Offensive Speech and Verbal Harassment of Groups vs. All Others

Variable	Estimate	Standard Error	Δ Probability
Anti-apartheid protest	1.04*	.449	.22
Barron's Guide	.252	.166	—
Black studies program	.648	.453	—
Full-time students	.042*	.021	.35
Gay/lesbian group	.441	.454	—
Graduate students	.017	.019	—
Minority studies program	.511	.449	—
Women faculty	–.045	.026	—
Yale Guide	1.13*	.465	.23

* = Statistically significant at the .05 level

tainly, the quantitative tests were useful, narrowing the potential factors behind the speech codes, but even the variables uncovered failed to identify the likely actors behind the speech codes nor explain their motives. To investigate these questions—and to understand how schools responded to the contrary judicial decisions—the study employed a variety of qualitative techniques. First, a subset of schools was selected from the sample of 100 for more intensive inquiry. To examine the initial adoption (or rejection) of speech codes, the study employed four paired samples of institutions. In one pair the schools had rejected speech codes, in two others the schools had adopted speech codes, and in a final pair the schools differed in their adoption of hate speech policies.

At each school the qualitative inquiry was a mix of secondary research and personal interviews. I began by searching Lexis/Nexis and then closeted myself in college archives to review past campus newspapers, local coverage of campus events, as well as reported deliberations from campus committees and relevant administrative offices. My intention was to become well versed in the events that occurred on campus before meeting those who would characterize the events and provide their own interpretations.

The interviews were semistructured, snowball style lasting between 30 to 60 minutes. At each campus I spoke with 10 to 25 people, including faculty, staff, and administrators who were involved in, or familiar with, their campus's consideration of hate speech policies. I did not, however, interview students. Since the secondary research was conducted between 1996 and 2000, most of the students who had been on campus at the time of speech code deliberations were gone and inaccessible. The omission of students excludes the perspectives of an essential part of any school's community, but, in the study's defense I was still able to reach the other three bulwarks of a campus—its faculty, staff, and administrators.

A similar form of qualitative research was used to investigate the response of schools to the court cases invalidating hate speech codes. Here, though, inquiry focused on the sample's 32 schools that changed a speech policy or added a new code that would have run afoul of the new precedent. Of these 32 institutions, 5 removed a speech policy that conflicted with the new precedent, 22 retained codes that arguably conflicted with it, and 5 enacted new policies that contradicted the court decisions. Of course, only public institutions (and private schools in California) were required to comply with these judicial decisions, but as chapters 3 and 5 explain, collegiate leaders at private schools also spouted support for First Amendment principles and recognized the persuasive authority of the speech code decisions.

I was able to investigate each of the five schools that removed a questionable policy, if only because many of these institutions had been fully covered by both national and local press, and some of the schools had already been dissected by earlier research.[15] Nonetheless, I also utilized a series of phone interviews at two of the schools to fill in chronological gaps from the secondary coverage.

There were few prior studies investigating the 22 schools that retained their suspect speech policies, and I was able to conduct secondary research on each of them through Lexis/Nexis. Because of time and resource constraints, though, I was only able to visit two of these schools for in-person interviews. Here I selected institutions that shared characteristics the quantitative data linked to the development of speech codes. Finally, I both conducted secondary research and visited four of the five institutions that adopted restrictive speech policies in the face of contrary legal precedent. (The fifth institution was excluded because the school was undergoing a change of administration at the time of study, and staff and top officials were unable to meet.)

I rarely confronted an unwilling subject during the interviews, and in the few cases where individuals refused I navigated around their intransigence by interviewing others who had worked with them. The same was true when academic administrators were reluctant to disclose much, if any, information in the interviews. Fortunately, I was able to find faculty and other staff who were willing to explain the stories their administrators balked at discussing.

One of the strict conditions of the research was that I would not name interviewees or their institutions. Even when I asked subjects to comment on the conclusions of other interviewees I never quoted from the original source. As a result, I have used pseudonyms throughout much of the book for both institutions and individuals. In only two cases do I make an exception, where, as with the University of Michigan and Stanford University, institutional decision-making was meticulously detailed in open court. My goal in using pseudonyms is not to be obtuse but rather to ensure that an enterprising reader cannot link an official's description or quotation with the name of his or her school, thereby revealing the individual's identity and breaking the terms of confidentiality.

Notes

Unless otherwise noted, all Web sites herein were accessed in July 2004.

Introduction

1. "U. of North Texas Professor's Remark Angers Black Students," *Chronicle of Higher Education,* October 10, 1997, A8.

2. Ibid.

3. "UNT Professor Placed on Leave after Remark on Minority Students," *Austin American-Statesman,* October 1, 1997, B2.

4. "U of North Texas," *Chronicle of Higher Education,* A8.

5. Ibid.

6. "UT Professor Blasts Efforts for Diversity on Campus," *Houston Chronicle,* September 11, 1997, A25.

7. *Hopwood v. Texas,* 78 F.3d 932 (5th Cir. 1996).

8. "Jackson Leads Rally; UT Law Professor Softens Comments," *San Antonio Express-News,* September 17, 1997, A1.

9. Mary Ann Roser, Andy Alford, and Dave Harmon, "UT Racial Harassment Policy Unconstitutional, Lawyer Says," *Austin American-Statesman,* November 14, 1997, A1.

10. "Jackson Leads Rally," *San Antonio Express-News,* A1.

11. Roser, Alford, and Harmon, "UT Racial Harassment Policy Unconstitutional," A1.

12. Bradford P. Wilson, "Politicizing Academic Freedom, Vulgarizing Scholarly Discourse," *Chronicle of Higher Education,* December 19, 1997, A52.

13. Alan Charles Kors and Harvey A. Silverglate, *The Shadow University: The Betrayal of Liberty on America's Campuses* (New York: Free Press, 1998), front flap.

14. See, e.g., George Will, "Curdled Politics on Campus," *Newsweek,* May 6, 1991, 72; William Safire, "Linguistically Correct," *New York Times,* May 5, 1991, Sec. 6,18; Charles Krauthammer, "Annals of Political Correctness," *Washington Post,* February 8, 1991, A18; Peter Edelman, "Imposing Sanctions on Racist Speech," *Manhattan Lawyer,* May 23, 1989, 12.

15. Kors and Silverglate, *Shadow University,* front flap.

16. *Bair v. Shippensburg University,* 280 F. Supp. 357, 361 (M.D. Pa. 2003).

17. *Corry v. Stanford University,* No. 740309 (Cal. Super. Ct. filed Feb. 27, 1995); *Doe v. University of Michigan,* 721 F. Supp. 852 (E.D. Mich. 1989); *The UWM Post v. Board of Regents of the University of Wisconsin System,* 774 F. Supp. 1163 (E.D. Wis. 1991); *Dambrot v. Central Michigan University,* 55 F.3d 1177 (6th Cir. 1995).

18. *R.A.V. v. City of St. Paul, Minnesota,* 505 U.S. 377 (1992).

19. Dinesh D'Souza, *Illiberal Education: The Politics of Race and Sex on Campus* (New York: Free Press, 1991), 13.

20. These institutions include Bowdoin College, Bowling Green State University, the City University of New York, Harvard University, Kennesaw State University, the University of California–Riverside, the University of Connecticut, the University of Illinois, the University of Massachusetts, and the University of Pennsylvania.

21. Avern Cohn, "Life on Campus Really Ain't So Bad," *Michigan Law Review* 98 (2000): 1551.

22. In California, the so-called Leonard Law holds private colleges and universities to the terms of the First Amendment. Named for its sponsor, Bill Leonard, the statute is unusual among states and was adopted in direct response to the rise of collegiate hate speech codes. The statute forbids "private postsecondary educational institution[s]" from "subjecting any student to disciplinary sanctions solely on the basis of . . . speech or other communication that, when engaged in outside the campus . . . is protected from governmental restriction by the First Amendment to the United States Constitution or Section 2 of Article 1 of the California Constitution" (Calif. Educ. Code § 94367 (1992)). The Leonard Law does, however, exempt schools controlled by a religious organization to the extent these terms "would not be consistent with the religious tenets of the organization" (id.).

23. Kors and Silverglate, *Shadow University,* front flap.

24. Linda J. Sax, Alexander W. Astin, William S. Korn, and Kathryn M. Mahoney, *The American Freshman: National Norms for Fall 1996* (Los Angeles: Higher Education Research Institute, 1996); "Fact File. This Year's Freshmen at 4-Year Colleges: A Statistical Profile," *Chronicle of Higher Education,* January 26, 2001, 48–49.

25. *R.A.V.,* 505 U.S. at 389.

26. Richard B. Saphire, "The Constitutional Status of Hate Speech: Comments on Delgado and Stevancic," *Northern Kentucky Law Review* 23 (1996): 500.

27. Steven G. Gey, "The Unfortunate Revival of Civil Republicanism," *University of Pennsylvania Law Review* 141 (1993): 808. Some might even say that judges apply their own attitudes when deciding cases (Jeffrey A. Segal and Harold J. Spaeth, *The Supreme Court and the Attitudinal Model* [New York: Cambridge University Press, 1993]), or reflect popular opinion in their decisions (Gregory Caldeira, "Courts and Public Opinion," in

American Courts: A Critical Assessment, ed. John B. Gates and Charles A. Johnson [Washington, D.C.: Congressional Quarterly Press, 1990]).

28. Keith E. Whittington, *Constitutional Construction: Divided Powers and Constitutional Meaning* (Cambridge: Harvard University Press, 1999).

29. Stuart A. Scheingold, *The Politics of Rights: Lawyers, Public Policy, and Political Change* (New Haven: Yale University Press, 1974); Patricia Ewick and Susan Silbey, *The Common Place of Law: Stories from Everyday Life* (Chicago: University of Chicago Press, 1998); David M. Engle and Frank W. Unger, *Rights of Inclusion: Law and Identity in the Life Stories of Americans with Disabilities* (Chicago: University of Chicago Press, 2003).

30. Richard Delgado, "Words That Wound: A Tort Action for Racial Insults, Epithets and Name Calling," *Harvard Civil Rights–Civil Liberties Law Review* 17 (1982): 133.

31. 29 C. F. R. 1604.11; Barbara Lindemann and David Kadue, *Primer on Sexual Harassment* (Washington, D.C.: Bureau of National Affairs, 1992).

32. See, e.g., *Rubin v. Ikenberry,* 933 F. Supp. 1425, 1445–47 (C.D. Ill. 1996).

33. For a more detailed discussion, consider Jon Gould, "Title IX in the Classroom: Academic Freedom and the Power to Harass," *Duke Journal of Gender, Law & Policy* 6 (1999): 61–81.

34. For a serious analysis of the hate speech controversy, consider Milton Heumann and Thomas W. Church, with David P. Redlawsk, *Hate Speech on Campus: Cases, Case Studies, and Commentary* (Boston: Northeastern University Press, 1997); and Samuel Walker, *Hate Speech: The History of an American Controversy* (Lincoln: University of Nebraska Press, 1994).

Chapter One

1. ABC's *Nightline,* "'Political Correctness' on U.S. Campuses," May 13, 1991.

2. *Doe v. University of Michigan,* 721 F. Supp. 852 (E.D. Mich. 1989).

3. *Jacobellis v. Ohio,* 378 U.S. 184, 197 (1964).

4. Indeed, some claim that hate speech cannot be defined, instead representing "a placeholder for contested meanings" (Amy Adler, "What's Left? Hate Speech, Pornography, and the Problem of Artistic Expression," *California Law Review* 84 [1996]: 1499–572).

5. Samuel Walker, *Hate Speech: The History of an American Controversy* (Lincoln: University of Nebraska Press, 1994), 8.

6. According to the Supreme Court in *Chaplinsky v. New Hampshire,* 315 U.S. 568, 572 (1942), fighting words are "those which by their very utterance inflict injury or tend to incite an immediate breach of the peace."

7. Walker, *Hate Speech,* 8.

8. Richard Delgado and Jean Stefancic. "Cosmopolitanism Inside Out: International Norms and the Struggle for Civil Rights and Local Justice," *Connecticut Law Review* 27 (1995): 773–88.

9. Online at http://www.purelyrics.com/index.php?lyrics=vzgoujpq.

10. Savage Love, online at http://www.theonionavclub.com/avclub2810/avfeature_2810.html (accessed October 2, 2002).

11. Ibid.

12. *Dambrot v. Central Michigan University,* 839 F. Supp. 477, 479 (E.D. Mich. 1993), *reversed,* 55 F.3d 1177 (6th Cir. 1995).

13. There is some debate about whether the terms are equivalent. In *Dambrot* the District Court considered whether the players had been using "nigga" or "niggah," a different pronunciation that carries a positive connotation when compared to "nigger." Nonetheless, testimony suggested that African Americans would use the former expressions themselves, while whites were often presumed by listeners to mean the latter (*Dambrot,* 839 F. Supp. 477).

14. Consider, for example, Heather Moos, "N-word results in double standard," *Daily Trojan,* February 19, 1997, 4–5.

15. Episode 145, "The Yada Yada," April 24, 1997.

16. Baptists Are Saving Homosexuals (http://www.bettybowers.com/bash.html).

17. Consider, Mayo Moran, "Talking about Hate Speech: A Rhetorical Analysis of American and Canadian Approaches to the Regulation of Hate Speech," *Wisconsin Law Review,* 1994:1425–514; Richard A. Glenn and Otis H. Stephens, "Campus Hate Speech and Equal Protection: Competing Constitutional Values," *Widener Journal of Public Law* 6 (1997): 349–384; Laura Leets, "Responses to Internet Hate Sites: Is Speech Too Free in Cyberspace?" *Communication Law & Policy* 6 (2001): 287–317. Charles Lawrence, one of the most prolific writers on hate speech, has criticized those who would oppose restrictions on "intentional face-to-face insults" (Charles R. Lawrence III, "The Debates over Placing Limits on Racist Speech Must Not Ignore the Damage It Does to Its Victims," *Chronicle of Higher Education,* October 25, 1989, B1).

18. Moos, "N-word," 4–5.

19. Delgado and Stefancic, "Cosmopolitanism Inside Out," 782.

20. Nikki Finke, "Vanity Too Fair: Michael Ovitz's Gay Problem," *LA Weekly,* July 5–11, 2002, online at http://www.laweekly.com/ink/02/33/news-finke.php.

21. Richard Delgado, "Zero-Based Racial Politics and an Infinity-Based Response: Will Endless Talking Cure America's Racial Ills?" *Georgetown Law Journal* 80 (1992): 1879–90.

22. Richard Delgado and Jean Stefancic, *Must We Defend Nazis? Hate Speech, Pornography, and the New First Amendment* (New York: New York University Press, 1997).

23. The International Convention on the Elimination of All Forms of Racial Discrimination, March 7, 1966, art. 4, 660 U.N.T.S. 195, 218; International Covenant on Civil and Political Rights, December 19, 1966, art. 19, 999 U.N.T.S. 171.

24. Eric Stein, "History against Free Speech: The New German Law against the 'Auschwitz'—and Other—'Lies,'" *Michigan Law Review* 85 (1986): 277–324.

25. *R. v. Andrews,* [1990] 3 S.C.R. 870 (Can.); *R. v. Keegstra,* [1990] 3 S.C.R. 697 (Can.).

26. Consider Henry Ford. As much as he may be revered for the introduction and mass production of the automobile, Ford was also infamous for his anti-Semitic articles in the *Dearborn Independent* as well as the dissemination of his diatribe, *The International Jew: The World's Foremost Problem* (http://www.wordiq.com/definition/Henry_Ford).

27. *Texas v. Johnson,* 491 U.S. 397 (1994); *Bond v. Floyd,* 385 U.S. 116 (1966); *Cohen v. California,* 403 U.S. 15 (1971) (First Amendment bars punishment of antiwar protestor for wearing jacket that said "Fuck the Draft" because of the expressive content of the message.)

28. As one commentator rightly points out, there is "no expression that is protected or unprotected under all circumstances. A political speech may be prohibited by regulations prohibiting noise in an intensive-care unit, and obscenity may not be prohibited by a law that distinguishes among obscene expressions based upon their political content" (Kingsley R. Browne, "Title VII as Censorship: Hostile-Environment Harassment and the First Amendment," *Ohio State Law Journal* 53 [1991]: 481–550). The point is that, absent a compelling basis, speech may rarely be restricted while actions are open to regulation.

29. Under the Supreme Court's three-part test in *Miller v. California,* 413 U.S. 15 (1973), obscenity is defined as (a) portraying sexual conduct in a patently offensive way; (b) appealing to the prurient interest; and (c) lacking any artistic, literary, scientific or political value.

30. *Brandenburg v. Ohio,* 395 U.S. 444 (1969); *Schenck v. United States,* 249 U.S. 47 (1919).

31. *Terminiello v. Chicago,* 337 U.S. 1 (1949).

32. *Beauharnais v. Illinois,* 343 U.S. 250, 251 (1952).

33. In its consideration of the Nazis' proposed march in Skokie, Illinois, the U.S. Court of Appeals for the Seventh Circuit concluded that *Beauharnais* was impertinent because it "turns quite plainly on the strong tendency of the prohibited utterances to cause violence and disorder" (*Collins v. Smith,* 578 F.2d 1197, 1204 (7th Cir. 1978)).

34. Milton Heumann and Thomas W. Church, with David P. Redlawsk, *Hate Speech on Campus: Cases, Case Studies, and Commentaries* (Boston: Northeastern University Press, 1997), 152.

35. "Student at Brown Is Expelled under a Rule Barring 'Hate Speech,'" *New York Times,* February 12, 1991, A17.

36. Ibid.

37. "Academic Index," *Lingua Franca,* October 1991, 5. *Nightline,* "'Political Correctness' on U.S. Campuses" used the latter figure.

38. Kansas State University "Racial and/or Ethnic Harassment Policy."

39. "Fighting words" has a defined meaning in constitutional law. Its import will be explained shortly.

40. Emory University "Policy Statement on Discriminatory Harassment."

41. Its rule lists race, ethnicity, religion, gender, sexual orientation, ancestry, age, marital status, handicap, and veteran status as worthy of protection.

42. Under these policies a university could punish a black student who verbally demeans a white classmate because of his race. But the history of civil rights legislation suggests that antidiscrimination measures are generally enacted to protect minority members of the community, not the majority.

43. 42 U.S.C. § 2000e-2.

44. Barbara Lindemann and David Kadue, *Primer on Sexual Harassment* (Washington, D.C.: Bureau of National Affairs, 1992), 10.

45. 29 C.F.R. 1604.11.

46. Cynthia L. Estlund, "Freedom of Expression in the Workplace and the Problem of Discriminatory Harassment," *Texas Law Review* 75 (1997): 688–777. The Court's reluc-

tance is especially notable when one considers that a number of amici curiae encouraged the justices to address the First Amendment issues.

47. *The UWM Post v. Board of Regents of the University of Wisconsin System,* 774 F. Supp. 1163 (E.D. Wis. 1991).

48. *Widmar v. Vincent,* 454 U.S. 263, 274 (1981).

49. See, among other cases, *Cohen v. San Bernardino Valley College,* 92 F.3d 968 (9th Cir. 1997).

50. Estlund, "Freedom of Expression," 775. I offer this quotation not because it is correct but because of the perspective it evidences. In fact, the U.S. Court of Appeals for the Eleventh Circuit reminds us that academic freedom is not an independent First Amendment right (*Bishop v. University of Alabama,* 926 F.2d 1066 (11th Cir. 1991)).

51. *UWM Post,* 774 F. Supp. 1163.

52. Except in California, where under the "Leonard Law" (Calif. Educ. Code § 94367 (1992)) private schools are subject to the First Amendment as well.

53. See Dinesh D'Souza, *Illiberal Education: The Politics of Race and Sex on Campus* (New York: Free Press, 1991); and Walker, *Hate Speech.*

54. As determined using Lexis/Nexis.

55. Nancy Gibbs, "Bigots in the Ivory Tower," *Time,* January 23, 1989, 104; Jonathan Yardley, "On Campus, Civil Rights and Wrongs," *Washington Post,* March 23, 1987, C2; Allan R. Gold, "Campus Racial Tensions—and Violence—Appear on Rise," *New York Times,* February 21, 1988, sec. 4, 6.

56. As determined using Lexis/Nexis.

57. Editorial, "A New Racism," *The Nation,* January 10, 1987, 1.

58. "Racism Rearing Head on College Campuses," *UPI,* March 11, 1989.

59. Bill Nichols, "A Controversial Plan to Require College Students to Study Racism Comes to a Head Monday," *Gannett News Service,* April 2, 1989.

60. Jon Wiener, "Reagan's Children: Racial Hatred on Campus," *The Nation,* February 27, 1989, 260.

61. Elaine El-Khawas, *Campus Trends 1989* (Washington, D.C.: American Council on Education, 1989).

62. This term comes from the Center for Applied Study of Ethnoviolence, a descendant of the National Institute against Prejudice and Violence. It is an all-encompassing phrase, referring to violence against groups defined by race, gender, ethnicity, or sexual orientation.

63. Part of Ehrlich's difficulty is that he released a study at that time showing that 20 percent of college students faced racial abuse on campus. Although Ehrlich seems quite credible, one might reasonably ask if the release of his study was intended to feed the media's preoccupation with a "crisis" of collegiate racism.

64. Howard Ehrlich interview, 1997. All of the quotes from Ehrlich come from this interview.

65. George Curry, "Racial Climate Turns Cool on Campuses," *Chicago Tribune,* February 17, 1987, A1.

66. Ken Myers, "Conventioneers Argue Pros, Cons of Restrictions on Hate Speech," *National Law Journal,* January 28, 1991, 4.

67. George Curry, "Federal Rights Agency Hopes to Find Its Lost Credibility in Violence Study," *Chicago Tribune,* January 18, 1987, Perspective 4.

68. George Curry, "Rights Group Ties Reagan, Race Tension," *Chicago Tribune,* January 15, 1987, A3.

69. Zillah R. Eisenstein, *The Female Body and the Law* (Berkeley: University of California Press, 1988), 152, 160.

70. Edwin Meese III, *With Reagan* (Washington, D.C.: Regnery Gateway, 1992), 316–20.

71. *Wards Cove v. Atonio,* 493 U.S. 802 (1989); *Richmond v. Croson,* 488 U.S. 469 (1989).

72. "Racism Rearing Head."

73. Everett Carll Ladd Jr. and Seymour Martin Lipset, *The Divided Academy: Professors and Politics* (New York: McGraw-Hill, 1975), 36.

74. El-Khawas, *Campus Trends 1989.*

75. See Cecilia A. Ottinger, ed., *Higher Education Today: Facts in Brief* (Washington, D.C.: American Council on Education, 1987).

76. Ladd and Lipset, *Divided Academy,* 191.

77. Telephone interviews with Dinesh D'Souza and George Will, 1997.

78. Will interview.

79. D'Souza interview.

80. Will interview.

81. See Alexander W. Astin, Kenneth C. Green, William S. Korn, Marilynn Schalit, and Ellyne R. Berz, *The American Freshman: National Norms for Fall 1988* (Los Angeles: Higher Education Research Institute, 1988).

82. Constance L. Hays, "Yale Shanty Burns and Alumnus Is Held," *New York Times,* June 6, 1988, B1; "Students Rally at Dartmouth," *UPI,* February 14, 1986; "Vandalism Probed at Knox College," *UPI,* May 16, 1986; "Students Rebuild Shanties," *UPI,* February 6, 1987; "Students to Erect Protest Shanty," *UPI,* February 9, 1987; "Fire Damages Shanty at Johns Hopkins," *Washington Post,* February 24, 1987, B3.

83. According to a brochure of the Madison Center obtained by the University Conversion Project, the Center had supported seventy-one alternative, conservative college newspapers.

84. Ralph Reed later became executive director of the Christian Coalition, an organization founded by the one-time presidential candidate and televangelist, Pat Robertson; David Binder and Andrew Rosenthal, "Conservative Limelight," *New York Times,* January 19, 1989, B12.

85. Gregor W. Pinney, "Racial Problems to Be Aired on Campuses Statewide," *Minneapolis Star Tribune,* October 29, 1992, B8; Joseph Berger, "Deep Racial Divisions Persist in New Generation at College," *New York Times,* May 22, 1989, A1; "'Prejudice' against White Students," *Newsweek,* April 23, 1990, 78; Mike Williams, "White Students Group Causing a Stir at UF," *St. Petersburg Times,* February 20, 1990, 4B; Carol Innerst, "College

Whites Fight 'Favoritism,'" *Washington Times,* April 26, 1990, A1; Valerie Richardson, "'Whites' Seek Multicultural Niche," *Washington Times,* March 28, 1992, A1.

86. "'Prejudice' against White Students," 78.

87. Joseph Berger, "Scholars Attack Campus 'Radicals,'" *New York Times,* November 15, 1988, A22.

88. See Ottinger, *Higher Education Today.*

89. Keith Richburg, "Fewer Blacks Finding Way to College," *Washington Post,* July 6, 1985, A1.

90. "Regional News—Ann Arbor, Michigan," *UPI,* March 31, 1985.

91. Charles Goldsmith, "U Mass Report Laments Minority Efforts," *UPI,* March 6, 1989.

92. Lena Williams, "Officials Voice Growing Concern over Racial Incidents in U.S. Campuses," *New York Times,* December 15, 1986, A18.

93. El-Khawas, *Campus Trends 1989.*

94. Ibid.

95. Ibid.

96. David Dent, "Reassessing the Roots: The Resurgence of Black Colleges," *Playboy,* June, 1989, 74.

97. El-Khawas, *Campus Trends 1989.*

98. K. Edward Renner, "Racial Equity and Higher Education," *Academe,* January/February, 2003, online at http://www.aaup.org/publications/Academe/2003/03jf/03jfrenart.htm.

99. For example, consider Michael Weisskopf, "Chinese Press Blames Mao for Political Chaos," *Washington Post,* December 23, 1980, A1. As Stanley Fish says, PC "originated on the left . . . in a kind of self-mocking way by people interested in raising consciousness about parts of our vocabulary that are saturated with implicit racism and sexism" (Arlynn Presser, "The Politically Correct Law School: Where It's Right to Be Left," *ABA Journal,* September 1991, 52–56).

100. "Remember When Men Were Men and Women Were Women," *UPI,* February 24, 1986.

101. D'Souza, *Illiberal Education,* 195.

102. Reed Way Dasenbrock, "We've Done It to Ourselves: The Critique of Truth and the Attack on Theory," in *PC Wars: Politics and Theory in the Academy,* ed. Jeffrey Williams (New York: Routledge, 1995).

103. See for example, George Will, "Curdled Politics on Campus," *Newsweek,* May 6, 1991, 72; William Safire, "Linguistically Correct," *New York Times,* May 5, 1991, sec. 6, 18; Charles Krauthammer, "Annals of Political Correctness," *Washington Post,* February 8, 1991, A18.

104. John Leo, "The Academy's New Ayatollahs," *U.S. News & World Report,* December 10, 1990, 22; Richard Bernstein, "The Rising Hegemony of the Politically Correct," *New York Times,* October 28, 1990, sec. 4, 1.

105. Lee Dembart, "At Stanford, Leftists Become Censors," *New York Times,* May 5, 1989, A35.

106. Thomas L. Jipping, "What Washington Can Do to Protect Campus Free Speech," *Heritage Foundation Reports* (June 12, 1991).

107. One student sent a computer message to an Iranian faculty member declaring "Death to All Arabs!! Die Islamic Scumbags!" Others yelled epithets at their classmates including "piece of shit nigger" and "fat-ass nigger" (*UWM Post v. Wisconsin,* 774 F. Supp. at 1168).

108. Mari J. Matsuda, Charles Lawrence III, Richard Delgado, and Kimberle Williams Crenshaw, *Words That Wound: Critical Race Theory, Assaultive Speech, and the First Amendment* (Boulder, CO: Westview Press, 1993), 1, 3.

109. Mari J. Matsuda, "Public Response to Racist Speech: Considering the Victim's Story," *Michigan Law Review* 87 (1989): 2320, 2336.

110. Richard Delgado, "Words That Wound: A Tort Action for Racial Insults, Epithets, and Name Calling," in Matsuda, Lawrence, Delgado, and Crenshaw, *Words That Wound,* 89.

111. Steve France, "Hate Goes to College," *ABA Journal,* July 1990, 44.

112. Matsuda, "Public Response to Racist Speech," 2336.

113. Walker, *Hate Speech,* 163.

114. Kent Greenawalt, *Speech, Crime, and the Uses of Language* (New York: Oxford University Press, 1989), 298.

115. Walker, *Hate Speech,* 111–12.

116. *Cohen v. California,* 403 U.S. 15 (1971); *Gooding v. Wilson,* 405 U.S. 518 (1971); *Edwards v. South Carolina,* 372 U.S. 229 (1963).

117. Telephone interview with Nadine Strossen, 1997.

118. For a brief review of the range of these articles, consider George Will, "Liberal Censorship," *Washington Post,* November 5, 1989, C7; "Universities Take Care," *The Economist,* February 2, 1990, 20; and Leo, "Academy's New Ayatollahs," 22.

119. D'Souza interview.

120. Will, "Curdled Politics," 72.

121. Safire, "Linguistically Correct," sec. 6, 18.

122. Many came from Delgado, Matsuda, Lawrence, and Strossen, although Duke's Katharine Bartlett, Yale's Stephen Carter, Chicago's Cass Sunstein, and Boalt's Robert Post all weighed in (among others) (Katharine T. Bartlett and Jean O'Barr, "The Chilly Climate on College Campuses: An Expansion of the 'Hate Speech' Debate," *Duke Law Journal* [1990]: 574–86; Stephen Carter, "Does the First Amendment Protest More Than Free Speech?" *William and Mary Law Review* 33 [1992]: 871–94; Cass R. Sunstein, "Words, Caste, Conduct," *University of Chicago Law Review* 60 [1993]: 795–844; Robert C. Post, "Racist Speech, Democracy, and the First Amendment," in *Speaking of Race, Speaking of Sex: Hate Speech, Civil Rights and Civil Liberties,* ed. Henry Louis Gates, Anthony P. Griffin, Donald E. Lively, Robert C. Post, William B. Rubenstein, and Nadine Strossen [New York: New York University Press, 1994]).

123. Nat Hentoff, syndicated columnist for the *Village Voice,* wrote regularly about the perils of hate speech restrictions, with the occasional guest columnist at other papers providing the counterpoint.

124. Based on an analysis of 458 editorials identified by Lexis/Nexis.

125. Walker, *Hate Speech,* 143.

126. Ibid.

127. Ibid., emphasis added.

128. Elaine Povich, "ACLU Joins Hyde in Free-Speech Fight," *Chicago Tribune,* March 12, 1991, A16.

129. As Hyde said, "The ACLU, for all of our differences—and they are legion—nonetheless is a premier defender of free speech. I'm pleased that they are going to stand with me on this one" (ibid.).

130. Hearing of the Committee on Labor and Human Resources, United States Senate. University

Responses to Racial and Sexual Harassment on Campuses, September 10, 1992.

131. Ibid.

132. California's action could not change the law in other states. Private institutions remain exempt from the First Amendment outside of California.

133. Calif. Educ. Code § 94367 (1992).

134. D'Souza interview.

Chapter Two

1. For a brief review of the range of these articles, consider George Will, "Liberal Censorship," *Washington Post,* November 5, 1989, C7; "Universities Take Care," *The Economist,* February 2, 1990, 20; and John Leo, "The Academy's New Ayatollahs," *U.S. News & World Report,* December 10, 1990, 22.

2. Gerald Rosenberg, *The Hollow Hope: Can Courts Bring About Social Change?* (Chicago: University of Chicago Press, 1991); Patricia Ewick and Susan S. Silbey, *The Common Place of Law: Stories from Everyday Life* (Chicago: University of Chicago Press, 1998); Stuart A. Scheingold, *The Politics of Rights: Lawyers, Public Policy, and Political Change* (New Haven: Yale University Press, 1974); Larry Kramer, *The People Themselves: Popular Constitutionalism and Judicial Review* (New York: Oxford University Press, 2004).

3. Mark Graber, Law and Courts listserv, January 16, 2004.

4. See Kramer, *The People Themselves.*

5. See Lee C. Bollinger and Geoffrey R. Stone, eds., *Eternally Vigilant: Free Speech in the Modern Era* (Chicago: University of Chicago Press, 2002).

6. Richard A. Posner, "The Speech Market and the Legacy of *Schenck,*" in *Eternally Vigilant,* ed. Bollinger and Stone, 121.

7. Robert Post, "Reconciling Theory and Doctrine in First Amendment Jurisprudence," in *Eternally Vigilant,* ed. Bollinger and Stone, 161.

8. Post, "Reconciling Theory and Doctrine," 166. Of course, Meiklejohn and Post differ in an important respect. Whereas Meiklejohn's approach posits the state as a neutral moderator of public debate, "distinguishing between relevant and irrelevant speech, abusive and nonabusive speech," Post's "participatory perspective emphasizes the autonomy of individual citizens," seeing public discourse as the ultimate "'Hyde Park,' filled with 'unregulated talkativeness'" (ibid., 167).

9. Ibid., 176.

10. Posner, "The Speech Market," 121.

11. Ibid., 121, 122.

12. Stanley E. Fish, *There's No Such Thing as Free Speech: And It's a Good Thing, Too* (New York: Oxford University Press, 1994).

13. Stanley E. Fish, "First Amendment Opportunism," in *Eternally Vigilant,* ed. Bollinger and Stone, 198.

14. "'There Is No Such Thing as Free Speech': An Interview with Stanley Fish," *Australian Humanities Review* (1988), online at http://www.lib.latrobe.edu.au/AHR/archive/Issue-February-1998/fish.html.

15. See Post, "Reconciling Theory and Doctrine."

16. Posner, "Speech Market," 145.

17. "Excerpts: Easy Virtue," *Columbia Journalism Review,* March/April 1994, online at http://archives.cjr.org/year/94/2/books-fish.asp.

18. See Karl N. Llewellyn, *Jurisprudence: Realism in Theory and Practice* (Chicago: University of Chicago Press, 1962).

19. Peter Gabel and Duncan Kennedy, "Roll Over Beethoven," *Stanford Law Review* 36 (1984): 1–54.

20. Jane E. Larson, "Women Understand So Little They Call My Good Nature 'Deceit': A Feminist Rethinking of Seduction," *Columbia Law Review* 93 (1993): 374–472. According to Larson, sexual fraud involves such cases as breach of the promise to marry and the reckless transmission of sexually transmitted diseases. Larson also claims that gender bias explains the courts' reluctance to enforce sexual fraud.

21. It is possible that male lawmakers and jurists would have come to see the need for these protections on their own. But it was politically empowered women who pushed to remove a victim's sexual history from the consideration of rape cases. Ultimately, they reached a compromise with "law and order" legislators who sought to prosecute rapists.

22. "The First Amendment says in no equivocal language that Congress shall pass no law abridging freedom of speech, press, assembly or petition. The activities of this [House] Committee [on Un-American Activities], authorized by Congress, do precisely that, through exposure, obloquy and public scorn" (*Barenblatt v. United States,* 360 U.S. 109, 140 (1958)).

23. For more detailed discussion, consider Martin H. Redish, "Taking a Stroll through Jurassic Park: Neutral Principles and the Originalist-Minimalist Fallacy in Constitutional Interpretation," *Northwestern University Law Review* 88 (1993): 165–74; Martin H. Redish, "Advocacy of Unlawful Conduct and the First Amendment: In Defense of Clear and Present Danger," *California Law Review* 70 (1982): 1159–200.

24. Gerald N. Rosenberg, "Protecting Fundamental Political Liberties: The Constitution in Context." Paper presented at the Annual Meeting of the American Political Science Association, Washington, D.C. (1988).

25. Fish, *There's No Such Thing as Free Speech,* 110.

26. *R.A.V. v. City of St. Paul, Minnesota,* 505 U.S. 377, 426–27 (1992).

27. *Texas v. Johnson,* 491 U.S. 397 (1989); *Bond v. Floyd,* 385 U.S. 116 (1966); *Cohen v. California,* 403 U.S. 15 (1971).

28. Indeed, it "often has been argued that the most defining characteristic of what it means to be human is the symbol-creating and symbol-transmitting capability." Franklyn S. Haiman, *"Speech Acts" and the First Amendment* (Carbondale: Southern Illinois University Press, 1993), 9.

29. Ibid.

30. *Plessy v. Ferguson,* 163 U.S. 537 (1896); *Brown v. Board of Education,* 347 U.S. 483 (1954) (*Brown I*); *Brown v. Board of Education,* 349 U.S. 294 (1955) (*Brown II*).

31. *Beauharnais v. Illinois,* 343 U.S. 250 (1952); *Johnson,* 491 U.S. 397; *Collins v. Smith* is an appellate case from the Seventh Circuit, but most observers believe the Supreme Court endorsed its approach in refusing to grant the decision certiorari (*Collins v. Smith,* 578 F.2d 1197 (7th Cir. 1978), *cert. denied,* 446 U.S. 911 (1980)).

32. An example here would be the Supreme Court's decisions permitting capital punishment. When the Court reopened capital punishment to the federal and state governments in *Greg v. Georgia,* 428 U.S. 153 (1976), it immediately created significant changes in the criminal justice system. New offices were set up to handle capital cases, increased resources were appropriated to handle the expanding caseload, and lawmakers took up their legislative pens to extend the number of crimes eligible for the death penalty.

33. For example, it is said that the Supreme Court's decision in *Roe v. Wade,* 410 U.S. 113 (1973) (along with the development of the birth control pill) helped to drive the sexual revolution and with it women's independence. As women were able legally to choose abortion over pregnancy, an unplanned pregnancy no longer relegated them to a life inside the home (Kristin Luker, *Abortion and the Politics of Motherhood* [Berkeley: University of California Press, 1984]).

34. For a model of judicial impact consider Bradley C. Canon and Charles A. Johnson, *Judicial Policies: Implementation and Impact* (Washington, D.C.: Congressional Quarterly Press, 1999).

35. Ronald J. Lipkin, Law and Courts listserv, January 17, 2004; Graber, Law and Courts listserv.

36. Sue Davis, "Book Review of *Constitutional Interpretation: Textual Meaning, Original Intent and Judicial Review,*" *Law and Politics Book Review* 10 (2000): 261.

37. Keith Whittington, *Constitutional Interpretation: Textual Meaning, Original Intent, and Judicial Review* (Lawrence: University Press of Kansas, 1999), 10.

38. Craig R. Ducat, "Book Review of *Constitutional Construction: Divided Powers and Constitutional Meaning.*" *Law and Politics Book Review* 9 (1999): 452.

39. *Goodrich v. Department of Public Health,* 798 N.E.2d 941 (Mass. 2003).

40. Rachel Gordon, "Newsom's Plan for Same-Sex Marriages," *San Francisco Chronicle,* February 11, 2004, A1.

41. *Lockyer v. San Francisco,* 33 Cal. 4th 1055 (2004); Law and Courts listserv discussions from early 2004.

42. Larry Kramer, "We the People: Who Has the Last Word on the Constitution?"

Boston Review, February/March, 2004, online at http://www.bostonreview.net/BR29.1/kramer.html.

43. See Rosenberg, *Hollow Hope.*

44. In *Judicial Policies,* Canon and Johnson describe four populations that affect the impact and implementation of a court's decision: interpreting, implementing, consumer, and secondary populations.

45. Valerie J. Hoekstra and Jeffrey A. Segal, "The Shepherding of Local Public Opinion: The Supreme Court and Lamb's Chapel," *Journal of Politics* 58 (1996): 1079–102.

46. Ibid.

47. See Elliott E. Slotnick and Jennifer A. Segal, *Television News and the Supreme Court: All the News That's Fit to Air?* (New York: Cambridge University Press, 1988).

48. Hoekstra and Segal, "The Shepherding of Local Public Opinion."

49. Jeffrey J. Mondak, "Policy Legitimacy and the Supreme Court: The Sources and Contexts of Legitimation," *Political Research Quarterly* 47 (1994): 675–92; David Adamany, "Legitimacy, Realigning Elections, and the Supreme Court," *Wisconsin Law Review,* 1973:790–846.

50. Mondak, "Policy Legitimacy and the Supreme Court"; Gregory A. Caldeira and James L. Gibson, "The Etiology of Public Support for the Supreme Court," *American Journal of Political Science* 36 (1992): 635–64.

51. True opposition must be knowing. Although one might claim that judicial decisions are unaccepted if people engage in *any* behavior inconsistent with the courts' rulings, the courts have little to fear unless people are aware that their behavior contradicts the law. For example, some civics groups and businesses occasionally place solicitations in private mailboxes despite statutes and case law forbidding the practice (*U.S. Postal Service v. Council of Greenburgh Civic Associations,* 453 U.S. 114 (1981)). Yet these people may be unaware they are violating the law and may, in fact, change their behavior if informed of existing statutes or cases. Because the courts (or at least the Supreme Court) retain a residual level of diffuse support, individuals may be persuaded to follow a judicial decree if educated about it. Even when people disagree with the substance of a decision, their respect for the judiciary's institutional legitimacy may override such opposition and convince them to tolerate and follow a ruling (Mondak, "Policy Legitimacy and the Supreme Court").

52. See William K. Muir, *Prayer in Public Schools: Law and Attitudinal Change* (Chicago: University of Chicago Press, 1967).

53. Rosenberg, *Hollow Hope.*

54. This process is ably described in Malcolm Gladwell's *The Tipping Point* (Boston: Little Brown, 2000), 7, where he explains the process by which "ideas and products and messages and behaviors spread just like viruses do."

55. Paul Lopes and Mary Durfee, eds., "The Social Diffusion of Ideas and Things," *The Annals of the American Academy of Political and Social Science* 566 (1999): 8–12.

56. *Boy Scouts of America v. Dale,* 530 U.S. 640 (2000).

57. Princeton Survey Research Associates. Poll conducted June 29–30, 2000. Pollsters surveyed 752 adults, with a margin of error ± 4 percent.

58. Online at http://www.scoutingforall.org.

59. These include the United Church of Christ, the Religious Society of Friends (Quakers), the Reform Jewish Movement, and the Unitarian/Universalists (http://www.scoutingforall.org).

60. Online at http://www.scoutingforall.org.

61. Robert L. Lineberry, "Review of William G. Domhoff's *Who Really Rules? New Haven and Community Power Revisited,*" *Journal of Politics* 42 (1980): 875–76.

62. See Robert A. Dahl, *Pluralist Democracy in the United States: Conflict and Consent* (Chicago: Rand-McNally, 1967); and *Dilemmas of Pluralist Democracy: Autonomy vs. Control* (New Haven: Yale University Press, 1982).

63. See Benjamin Ginsberg and Ins Chang, *Captive Public: How Mass Opinion Promotes State Power* (New York: Basic Books, 1988); and Benjamin Ginsberg, *Consequences of Consent: Elections, Citizen Control, and Popular Acquiescence* (Reading, MA: Addison-Wesley, 1982).

64. Doris Graber, "Book Review of *The Captive Public: How Mass Opinion Promotes State Power,*" *Political Science Quarterly* 102 (1987): 129–30.

65. Charles H. Franklin and Liane C. Kosaki, "Republican Schoolmasters: The U.S. Supreme Court, Public Opinion, and Abortion," *American Political Science Review* 83 (1989): 752.

66. James A. Stimson, Michael B. Mackuen, and Robert S. Erikson, "Dynamic Representation," *American Political Science Review* 89 (1995): 543–65.

67. Alan D. Monroe, "Public Opinion and Public Policy, 1980–1993," *Public Opinion Quarterly* 62 (1998): 6–28.

68. See William Mishler and Reginald Sheehan, "The Supreme Court as a Counter-Majoritarian Institution? The Impact of Public Opinion on Supreme Court Decisions," *American Political Science Review* 87 (1993): 87–101; and Michael W. Link, "Tracking Public Mood in the Supreme Court: Cross-Time Analyses of Criminal Procedure and Civil Rights Cases," *Political Research Quarterly* 48 (1995): 61–78. For an alternative explanation consider Helmut Norporth and Jeffrey Segal, "Popular Influence on Supreme Court Decisions," *American Political Science Review* 88 (1994): 711–16.

69. Of course, it is possible for people to support gay rights and still believe that private organizations should be allowed to limit their membership as they see fit. This, undoubtedly, was the argument behind the amicus brief of Gays and Lesbians for Individual Liberty in *Dale.* But the public's reaction to *Dale* turned less on the rights of private groups—much of the public discussion saw the Boy Scouts as akin to a civics organization—than on the compatibility of policies opposing homosexuals with the promotion of good citizenship.

70. Rosenberg, *Hollow Hope.*

71. Bradley C. Canon, "The Supreme Court as a Cheerleader in Politico-Moral Disputes," *Journal of Politics* 54 (1992): 638.

72. Ibid.

73. Ibid.

74. Canon mentions all but gay rights, but then gay rights was not as salient in 1992 when he wrote than it is today (ibid.).

75. At the same time, the opposition may be tempered by the tendency of law enforcement bodies to implement any "bright line" rules that the courts establish for their operations.

76. *Johnson,* 491 U.S. 397; *Cohen,* 403 U.S. 15.

77. John Anthony Maltese, "Book Review of *Rights Talk: The Impoverishment of Political Discourse,*" *Law and Politics Book Review* 3 (1993): 7–8.

78. Mary Ann Glendon, *Rights Talk: The Impoverishment of Political Discourse* (New York: Free Press, 1991), 103.

79. Rosenberg, *Hollow Hope;* Muir, *Prayer in Public School.*

80. Jonathan Rauch, "Conventional Wisdom: Rediscovering the Social Norms That Stand between Law and Libertinism," *Reason Online,* February, 2000, online at http://reason.com/0002/fe.jr.conventional.shtml.

81. E-mail correspondence with Patricia Ewick.

82. Ewick and Silbey, *The Common Place of Law,* 22–23.

83. Ibid., 21.

84. Rauch, "Conventional Wisdom."

85. In fact, this event took place in 2001 when Alabama Chief Justice Roy Moore unveiled "a 5,280-pound monument dedicated to the Ten Commandments" in the Supreme Court's rotunda (Freedom Forum, "'Ten Commandments Judge' Erects Monument in State Supreme Court," August 5, 2001, online at http://www.freedomforum.org/templates/document.asp?documentID=14557). In 2002 a U.S. District Court ordered the removal of the monument from court grounds (*Glassroth v. Moore,* 242 F. Supp. 2d 1067 (M.D. Ala. 2002)).

86. Ewick and Silbey, *The Common Place of Law,* 21.

87. There is a long tradition of scholarship that suggests public opinion or political processes actually command the "generalized approval" of the courts (C. Neal Tate, "Personal Attribute Models of the Voting Behavior of U.S. Supreme Court Justices: Liberalism in Civil Liberties and Economics Decisions, 1946–1978," *American Political Science Review* 75 [1981]: 355–67), with judges responding to changed social expectations in setting formal constitutional rules. The Supreme Court's decision in *Planned Parenthood v. Casey,* 505 U.S. 830, 850 (1992) is a good example, where the majority effectively acknowledged that its decision was adopted with one eye on public opinion, noting that judges must take account of "what history teaches are the traditions from which [America] developed as well as the traditions from which it broke. That tradition is a living thing. A decision of this Court which radically departs from it could not long survive, while a decision which builds on what has survived is likely to be sound."

88. Kramer, *The People Themselves.*

89. Correspondence with Michael McCann, 2004.

90. Ibid.

91. In California, state law also extends the doctrine to private educational institutions (Calif. Educ. Code § 94367 (1992)).

92. Stanley Fish, "The Free Speech Follies," *Chronicle of Higher Education,* June 13, 2003, C3.

93. Michael A. de Yoanna, "Palestinian Visit Draws Fire," *Colorado Daily,* August 23, 2002, online at http://www.forthofer.com/pressCoverage/CODailyOnAshrawi20020823.html (accessed October 2, 2002).

94. In Fish, "Free Speech Follies."

95. Richard L. Abel, *Speaking Respect, Respecting Speech* (Chicago: University of Chicago Press, 1999), 180.

96. Fish, "Free Speech Follies."

97. Dennis Chong, "How People Think, Reason, and Feel about Rights and Liberties," *American Journal of Political Science* 37 (1993): 869.

98. Vincent Blasi, "The Pathological Perspective and the First Amendment," *Columbia Law Review* 85 (1985): 449–514, 456.

99. Elliott L. Richardson, "Freedom of Expression and the Function of Courts," *Harvard Law Review* 65 (1951): 54.

100. Haiman, *"Speech Acts" and the First Amendment,* 85.

101. In this context, I mean to strip morality of its theological connotations. I use the term as Haiman intends, to represent the views of a society that certain acts or behaviors are wrong, no matter what epistemological system the society uses to reach that conclusion (ibid.).

102. As already noted, Jane Larson ("Women Understand So Little They Call My Good Nature 'Deceit'") makes a compelling case that sexual fraud should be treated on the same par as business fraud and ought to be legally actionable. Further, there was a time when a breach of promise to marry found a receptive judiciary. But as Larson herself admits, there is not presently sufficient agreement that this misdeed deserves legal standing.

103. To be sure, gambling is regulated by law, but the point is to prevent cheating, not to eliminate its practice.

104. See Ronald S. Burt, "The Social Capital of Opinion Leaders," *The Annals of the American Academy of Political and Social Science* 566 (1999): 37–54; and Paul Lopes and Mary Durfee, eds., "The Social Diffusion of Ideas and Things," *The Annals of the American Academy of Political and Social Science* 566 (1999): 8–12.

105. Duncan J. Watts, "Networks, Dynamics, and the Small-World Phenomenon," *American Journal of Sociology* 105 (1999): 493–527.

106. Paul J. DiMaggio and Walter W. Powell, "The Iron Cage Revisited: Institutional Isomorphism and Collective Rationality in Organizational Fields," *American Sociological Review* 48 (1983): 147–60.

107. See William J. Bennett, *Why We Fight: Moral Clarity and the War on Terrorism* (New York: Doubleday, 2002); *The Broken Hearth: Reversing the Moral Collapse of the American Family* (New York: Doubleday, 2001); and *The De-Valuing of America: The Fight for Our Culture and Our Children* (Touchstone Books, 1994).

108. See Craig Reinarman, *Social Movements and Social Problems: "Mothers Against Drunk Drivers," Restrictive Alcohol Laws, and Social Control in the 1980s* (Berkeley: University of California Press, 1985).

109. On July 26, 1948, President Harry Truman issued Executive Order 9981 desegregating the armed forces.

110. One day before a House vote on the Civil Rights Act, proponents of Title VII amended the legislation to add "sex" as a protected basis. They did so with the help of Title VII's opponents, "who hoped that the inclusion of 'sex' would highlight the absurdity

of the effort as a whole and contribute to its defeat" (Susan Estrich, "Sex at Work," *Stanford Law Review* 43 [1991]: 813–61).

111. As Brown says, "Contrary to its insistence that it speaks in the name of the political, much feminist anti-postmodernism betrays a preference for extrapolitical terms and practices. . . . [Will feminist activists] give up substituting Truth and Morality for politics? Are we willing to engage in struggle rather than recrimination, to develop our faculties rather than avenge our subordination with moral and epistemological gestures, to fight for a world rather than conduct process on the existing one?" (Wendy Brown, *States of Injury: Power and Freedom in Late Modernity* [Princeton: Princeton University Press, 1995], 48).

112. Frances Kahn Zemans, "Legal Mobilization: The Neglected Role of the Law in the Political System," *American Political Science Review* 77 (1983): 690–703, 700.

113. Michael W. McCann, "Reform Litigation on Trial," *Law and Social Inquiry* 17 (1993): 715–43.

114. This term comes from resource mobilization theory advanced by John D. McCarthy and Mayer N. Zald ("Resource Mobilization Theory," in *Social Movements in an Organizational Society,* ed. Mayer N. Zald and John D. McCarthy [New Brunswick, NJ: Transaction Books, 1987]). It refers to a coordinating group that organizes movement members and keeps them networked. In McCann's work (*Rights at Work: Pay Equity Reform and the Politics of Legal Mobilization* [Chicago: University of Chicago Press, 1994]), groups such as the Women's Equity Action League, the Coalition of Labor Union Women, and the Washington Federation of State Employees all represent central social movement organizations. Other such groups include the NAACP for the civil rights movement and NARAL for the abortion rights movement.

115. McCann, *Rights at Work,* 5.

116. A good example is the political process model of social movements, which envisions people organizing to fight against political processes that are closed to them (Doug McAdam, *Political Process and the Development of Black Insurgency, 1930–1970* [Chicago: University of Chicago Press, 1982]). But even so, this theory still contends that movement activists pressure government officials to obtain their demands. They do not organize simply for the sake of protesting conditions. Movement actors know where to make their voices heard.

117. Zemans, "Legal Mobilization," 700.

118. McCann, *Rights at Work,* 8.

119. Martha Minow, "Interpreting Rights: An Essay for Robert Cover," *Yale Law Journal* 96 (1987): 1861–2.

120. Zemans, "Legal Mobilization," 697.

121. John D. McCarthy and Mayer N. Zald, "Resource Mobilization and Social Movements: A Partial Theory," *American Journal of Sociology* 82 (1977): 1217–18.

122. McAdam, *Political Process and the Development of Black Insurgency.*

123. Mari J. Matsuda, "Legal Storytelling: Public Response to Racist Speech, Considering the Victim's Story," *Michigan Law Review* 87 (1989): 2358.

124. Matsuda first advanced this argument (ibid., 2325), which was later reprinted in Mari J. Matsuda, Charles Lawrence III, Richard Delgado, and Kimberle Williams Crenshaw,

Words That Wound: Critical Race Theory, Assaultive Speech, and the First Amendment (Boulder, CO: Westview Press, 1993).

125. Matsuda, "Public Response to Racist Speech," 2357.

126. *Pemberthy v. Beyer,* 800 F. Supp. 144 (D.N.J. 1992); *Karins v. City of Atlantic City,* 152 N.J. 532 (1998); *Aguilar v. Avis Rent-A-Car,* 50 Cal. App. 4th 28 (1st Dist. 1996); *Williams v. Tri-County Metro Transportation District of Oregon,* 153 Or. App. 686 (1998); *Lam v. University of Hawaii,* 1991 U.S. Dist. Lexis 20572 (D. Hawaii); *Doe v. Hartz,* 970 F. Supp. 1375 (N.D. Iowa 1997).

Chapter Three

1. Milton Heumann and Thomas W. Church, with David P. Redlawsk, *Hate Speech on Campus: Cases, Case Studies, and Commentary* (Boston: Northeastern University Press, 1997); John Arthur and Amy Shapiro, *Campus Wars: Multiculturalism and the Politics of Difference* (Boulder, CO: Westview Press, 1994).

2. Dinesh D'Souza, *Illiberal Education: The Politics of Race and Sex on Campus* (New York: Free Press, 1991); Alan Charles Kors and Harvey A. Silverglate, *The Shadow University: The Betrayal of Liberty on America's Campuses* (New York: Free Press, 1998), 2.

3. As the appendix explains in greater detail, the speech codes were first estimated from 1987 to 1992. This time reflects the period from the codes' initial appearance on college campuses to their potential death knell following the Supreme Court's decision in *R.A.V. v. City of St. Paul,* 505 U.S. 377 (1992). Chapter 5 reports the estimates from 1997, two years after the last college speech code case, *Corry v. Stanford.*

4. *Chaplinsky v. New Hampshire,* 315 U.S. 568, 572 (1942).

5. See *Gooding v. Wilson,* 405 U.S. 518 (1972).

6. See Samuel Walker, *Hate Speech: The History of an American Controversy* (Lincoln: University of Nebraska Press, 1994).

7. Ibid.

8. Except, of course, in California, where private, non-parochial schools are also bound by the terms of the First Amendment (Calif. Educ. Code § 94367 (1992)).

9. Jay Matthews, "The Perils of Campus Candor," *Washington Post Magazine,* November 10, 2002, W18.

10. Kors and Silverglate, *The Shadow University,* front flap.

11. John D. McCarthy and Mayer N. Zald, "Resource Mobilization and Social Movements: A Partial Theory," *American Journal of Sociology* 82 (1977): 1222.

12. Ibid.

13. In this context, I equate political liberalness with support for civil rights policies, particularly affirmative action.

14. See John W. Kingdon, *Agendas, Alternatives, and Public Policies* (New York: HarperCollins, 1995).

15. J. Craig Jenkins and Craig M. Eckert, "Channeling Black Insurgency: Elite Patronage and Professional Social Movement Organizations in the Development of the Black Movement," *American Sociological Review* 51 (1986): 812–29.

16. I first encountered this term in a paper of a graduate school classmate, Barbara Walter, although I have yet to see it expanded much since then.

17. Mancur Olson, *The Logic of Collective Action: Public Goods and the Theory of Groups* (Cambridge: Harvard University Press, 1965), 5–6.

18. Ibid.

19. See Mary Ann Glendon, *Rights Talk* (New York: Free Press, 1991).

20. Michael McCann, "Legal Mobilization and Social Reform Movements: Notes on Theory and Its Applications," *Studies in Law, Politics, and Society* 11 (1991): 234.

21. Paul Burstein, "Legal Mobilization as a Social Movement Tactic: The Struggle for Equal Employment Opportunity," *American Journal of Sociology* 96 (1991): 1201–25, quote on page 1209.

22. Mari J. Matsuda, "Public Response to Racist Speech: Considering the Victim's Story," *Michigan Law Review* 87 (1989): 2325.

23. Heumann and Church, with Redlawsk, *Hate Speech on Campus,* 125–252.

24. That is, three different sets of logistic regressions were conducted. The first compared schools that created hate speech policies against those than had not. The second regression compared schools that had created offensive speech policies—terms that assuredly violated the spirit of the First Amendment—against schools that either had eschewed speech codes or had written policies whose terms were not as restrictive as the offensive speech codes. The third regression applied the same methodology but moved policies banning verbal harassment of groups from the constitutional to constitutionally suspect category. The intention here was not to distinguish between policies that violated the specific tenets of formal doctrine—say, by coding public and private schools' policies differently—but to reflect those policies that comported with the spirit of constitutional law and those that did not.

25. Actually, this relationship is explained by an intervening factor—the academic prestige of an institution—which correlates with both the creation of speech codes and the percentage of female faculty. It is still an unfortunate fact, as confirmed by the analysis conducted for this project, that the percentage of female faculty is lower at highly prestigious schools than it is at less-regarded institutions.

26. See Everett Carll Ladd Jr. and Seymour Martin Lipset, *The Divided Academy: Professors and Politics* (New York: McGraw-Hill, 1975).

27. Paul J. DiMaggio and Walter W. Powell, "The Iron Cage Revisited: Institutional Isomorphism and Collective Rationality in Organizational Fields," *American Sociological Review* 48 (1983): 147–60.

28. Under assault law, a person can be found guilty if he intends to put another under the threat of harm. While assault law is generally addressed to actions, it would make sense also to extend it to situations where a person uses speech to threaten injury.

29. Terrance Sandalow, "Academic Freedom and Tenure: A Preliminary Report on Freedom of Expression and Campus Harassment Codes," *Academe* 77 (1991): 23–26.

30. Ibid.

31. The "Global Sullivan Principles of Social Responsibility" take their name from the Reverend Leon Sullivan, an African American pastor, who created "a code of conduct for human rights and equal opportunity for companies operating in South Africa," online at http://www.globalsullivanprinciples.org.

32. Explaining President Fleming's actions, the court in *Doe v. Michigan* said, "the

Acting President recognized at the time that the proposed policy would engender serious First Amendment problems," but reasoned that "just as an individual cannot shout 'Fire!' in a crowded theater and then claim immunity from prosecution for causing a riot on the basis of exercising his rights of free speech, so a great many American universities have taken the position that students at a university cannot by speaking or writing discriminatory remarks which seriously offend many individuals beyond the immediate victim, and which, therefore detract from the necessary educational climate of a campus, claim immunity from a campus disciplinary proceeding. I believe that position to be valid" (*Doe v. Michigan,* 721 F. Supp. 852, 855 (E.D. Mich. 1989)).

33. "Civility restraints" are a set of ground rules that say open dialogue rests on an assumption of decorum, that free speech is impossible in an atmosphere of personal attack (Cynthia L. Estlund, "Freedom of Expression in the Workplace and the Problem of Discriminatory Harassment," *Texas Law Review* 75 [1997]: 688–777).

34. Steve France, "Hate Goes to College," *ABA Journal* 76 (1990): 44.

35. This point is discussed extensively in chapter 4.

Chapter Four

1. *Doe v. University of Michigan,* 721 F. Supp. 852 (E.D. Mich. 1989); *The UWM Post v. Board of Regents of the University of Wisconsin System,* 774 F. Supp. 1163 (E.D. Wis. 1991); *R.A.V. v. City of St. Paul, Minnesota,* 505 U.S. 377 (1992); *Dambrot v. Central Michigan University,* 839 F. Supp. 477, 479 (E.D. Mich. 1993), *reversed,* 55 F.3d 1177 (6th Cir. 1995); *Corry v. Stanford University,* No. 740309 (Cal. Super. Ct. filed Feb. 27, 1995).

2. *Corry,* No. 740309.

3. Kingsley R. Browne, "Title VII as Censorship: Hostile-Environment Harassment and the First Amendment," *Ohio State Law Journal* 53 (1991): 481–550.

4. *Doe,* 721 F. Supp. at 867.

5. *UWM Post,* 774 F. Supp. at 1181.

6. *Dambrot,* 839 F. Supp. at 481.

7. *Dambrot,* 55 F.3d 1177.

8. *Corry,* No. 740309, at 12.

9. Stanford University's rule, titled "Fundamental Standard Interpretation: Free Expression and Discriminatory Harassment," read as follows: "Speech or other expression constitutes harassment by personal vilification if it: (a) is intended to insult or stigmatize an individual or a small number of individuals on the basis of their sex, race, color, handicap, religion, sexual orientation, or national and ethnic origin; and (b) is addressed directly to the individual or individuals whom it insults or stigmatizes; and (c) makes use of insulting or 'fighting' words or non-verbal symbols" (Thomas C. Grey, "How to Write a Speech Code without Really Trying: Reflections on the Stanford Experience," *U.C. Davis Law Review* 29 [1996]: 948).

10. *Corry,* No. 740309, at 12.

11. Browne, "Title VII as Censorship."

12. *R.A.V.,* 505 U.S. 377.

13. Id. at 378.

14. Bradley C. Canon and Charles A. Johnson, *Judicial Policies: Implementation and Impact* (Washington, D.C.: Congressional Quarterly Press, 1999).

15. *R.A.V.,* 505 U.S. at 378.

16. William H. Freivogel, "Ruling Aimed at Hate-Speech Laws," *St. Louis Post-Dispatch,* June 24, 1992, C1.

17. Charles Krauthammer, "Annals of Political Correctness," *Washington Post,* February 8, 1991, A18.

18. *MacNeil/Lehrer NewsHour,* June 26, 1992.

19. A year after the case, Edward Cleary, the plaintiff's lawyer, published a book about the case (*Beyond the Burning Cross: The First Amendment and the Landmark R.A.V. Case* [New York: Random House, 1994]). In the book, Cleary boasts of the arguments his team used to interest the Court (Gary Jeffrey Jacobsohn, "Beyond the Burning Cross," *Washington Post,* November 21, 1994, C2).

20. "Schools Must Test Ideas, Rehnquist Says," *Los Angeles Times,* May 23, 1993, A12.

21. Michael Kinsley, "Right-Wing P.C. Is Still P.C.," *Time,* August 9, 1993, 66.

22. Charles Krauthammer, "Political Correctness is Scalia's Newest Target," *Chicago Sun-Times,* June 27, 1992, 21.

23. "Supreme Court Rules on Jury Gender Discrimination," ABC News television broadcast, April 19, 1994.

24. Nancy E. Roman, "High Court Restricts Shaping Juries, Rules Sex Cannot Be a Factor in Choices," *Washington Times,* April 20, 1994, A1.

25. Editorial, "Thought Police Disarmed; Campus Speech Codes, R.I.P.," *Arizona Republic,* March 30, 1995, B4.

26. Editorial, "Another Code Bites the Dust," *Rocky Mountain News,* April 7, 1995, A69; Nat Hentoff, "Against the Odds: A Historic Free Speech Victory," *Village Voice,* May 2, 1995, 20.

27. *Meritor Savings Bank v. Vinson,* 477 U.S. 57 (1986).

28. According to the courts, sexual harassment flows from 42 U.S.C. § 2000e-2(a), which declares it unlawful for "an employer to fail or refuse to hire or to discharge any individual, or otherwise to discriminate against any individual with respect to his compensation, terms, conditions, or privileges of employment, because of such individual's race, color, religion, sex, or national origin." At no point does this statute explicitly mention sexual harassment. Rather, the courts have read sexual harassment to be sex discrimination "with respect to [an individual's] terms . . . of employment" (*Meritor,* 477 U.S. at 63).

29. "A statute is unconstitutionally vague when individuals 'of common intelligence must necessarily guess at its meaning.' A statute must give adequate warning of the conduct which is to be prohibited and must set out explicit standards for those who apply it" (*Doe,* 721 F. Supp. at 866).

30. *Katz v. Dole,* 709 F.2d 251, 254 (4th Cir. 1983).

31. *McNabb v. Cub Foods,* 352 N.W.2d 378, 381 (Minn. 1984).

32. *Harris v. Forklift Systems,* 510 U.S. 17, 19 (1993).

33. Barbara Lindemann and David Kadue, *Primer on Sexual Harassment* (Washington,

D.C.: Bureau of National Affairs, 1992), 584, citing *Davis v. Monsanto Chem. Co.,* 858 F.2d 345, 350 (6th Cir. 1988), *cert. denied,* 490 U.S. 1110 (1989).

34. *Morgan v. Hertz Corp.,* 542 F. Supp. 123, 128 (W.D. Tenn. 1981).

35. Browne, "Title VII as Censorship," 535.

36. Ibid.

37. *Robinson v. Jacksonville Shipyards,* 760 F. Supp. 1486 (M.D. Fla. 1991).

38. Browne, "Title VII as Censorship"; Eugene Volokh, "How Harassment Law Restricts Free Speech," *Rutgers Law Journal* 47 (1995): 563–76.

39. Arati R. Korwar, *War of Words: Speech Codes at Public Colleges and Universities* (Nashville, TN: Freedom Forum First Amendment Center, 1994). Of course, many schools adopt sexual harassment rules as a defense to potential sex discrimination claims. The actual number of policies adopted is not so impressive as is their terms.

40. Elsa Kircher Cole, ed., *Sexual Harassment on Campus: A Legal Compendium* (Washington, D.C.: National Association of College and University Attorneys, 1990), 224.

41. *Cohen v. San Bernardino Valley College,* 92 F.3d 968 (9th Cir. 1996); *Silva v. New Hampshire,* 888 F. Supp. 293 (D.N.H. 1994).

42. Consider the following cases: *Rubin v. Ikenberry,* 933 F. Supp. 1425 (C.D. Ill. 1996); *Moire v. Temple University School of Medicine,* 613 F. Supp. 1360 (E.D. Pa. 1985), *affirmed,* 800 F.2d 1136 (3d Cir. 1986); *Bishop v. University of Alabama,* 926 F.2d 1066 (11th Cir. 1991).

43. Mark Bartholomew, "Judicial Deference and Sexual Discrimination in the University," *Buffalo Women's Law Journal* 8 (1999/2000): 64.

44. *Davis v. Monroe County Board of Education,* 526 U.S. 629 (1999).

45. *Doe,* 721 F. Supp. at 857–58.

46. Id. at 848.

47. *UWM Post,* 774 F. Supp. at 1168.

48. *Harris,* 510 U.S. at 21.

49. *Kishaba v. Hilton Hotels Corp.,* 737 F. Supp. 549, 555 (D. Hawaii 1990).

50. *Doe,* 721 F. Supp. at 867.

51. Id. at 869.

52. *Harris,* 510 U.S. at 22.

53. As Justice Scalia explained, these terms do "not seem to me to be a very clear standard. . . . Be that as it may, I know of no other alternative" (*Harris,* 510 U.S. at 24).

54. Under the University of Illinois Handbook of Policies and Regulations, sexual harassment is defined as "any unwanted sexual gesture, physical contact, or statement that a reasonable person would find offensive, humiliating, or any interference with his or her required tasks or career opportunities at the University" (*Rubin,* 933 F. Supp. at 1430).

55. *Kovacs v. Cooper,* 336 U.S. 77 (1949).

56. *Miller v. California,* 413 U.S. 15 (1973).

57. *Sypniewski v. Warren Hills Regional Board of Education,* 307 F.3d 243 (3d Cir. 2002).

58. *Texas v. Johnson,* 491 U.S. 397 (1989); *Bond v. Floyd,* 385 U.S. 116 (1966); *Cohen v. California,* 403 U.S. 15 (1971).

59. As one commentator rightly points out, there is "no expression that is protected or unprotected under all circumstances. A political speech may be prohibited by regulations prohibiting noise in an intensive-care unit, and obscenity may not be prohibited by a law that distinguishes among obscene expressions based upon their political content" (Browne, "Title VII as Censorship," 483). The point is that, absent a compelling basis, speech may rarely be restricted while actions are open to regulation.

60. Lindemann and Kadue, *Primer on Sexual Harassment,* 598.

61. *Robinson,* 760 F. Supp. 1486.

62. Lindemann and Kadue, *Primer on Sexual Harassment,* 598.

63. *R.A.V.,* 505 U.S. at 391.

64. Id. at 389.

65. Id. at 410.

66. Browne, "Title VII as Censorship"; Cynthia L. Estlund, "Freedom of Expression in the Workplace and the Problem of Discriminatory Harassment," *Texas Law Review* 75 (1997): 688–777.

67. The Court's reluctance is especially notable when one considers that a number of amici curiae encouraged the justices to address the First Amendment issues (Estlund, "Freedom of Expression in the Workplace," 692).

68. Browne, "Title VII as Censorship," 482–83.

69. *EEOC v. Hacienda Hotel,* 881 F.2d 1504, 1508 (9th Cir. 1989).

70. The court could hardly have been clearer in stating that sexual harassment can be founded on expression. As part of its analysis, the court observed that "Eveleth Mines' work environment was characterized by verbal statements and language reflecting a sexualized, male-oriented, and antifemale atmosphere. Language at Eveleth Mines was generally coarse; both men and women cursed and used words with a sexual referent. Strikingly, however, only men went further and used language either (1) referring to women generally in terms of their body parts, and/or (2) directing comments to or about specific women and their sex lives, including proposing sexual relationships and discussing sexual exploits. Related to this second variety of language was the use of 'pet names' and terms that persons in romantic relationships might use, e.g., 'honey' or 'babe'" (*Jenson v. Eveleth Taconite Co.,* 824 F. Supp. 847, 880 (D. Minn. 1993)).

71. Browne, "Title VII as Censorship," 483.

72. *UWM Post,* 774 F. Supp. at 1177.

73. Id.

74. *Meritor,* 477 U.S. at 72.

75. Browne, "Title VII as Censorship," 515.

76. Robert C. Post, "Free Speech and Religious, Racial, and Sexual Harassment: Racist Speech, Democracy, and the First Amendment," *William and Mary Law Review* 32 (1991): 285.

77. Browne, "Title VII as Censorship," 515.

78. Post, "Free Speech and Religious, Racial and Sexual Harassment," 289.

79. *Pickering v. Board of Education,* 391 U.S. 563 (1968); *Connick v. Myers,* 461 U.S. 138 (1983).

80. Kingsley R. Browne, "Zero Tolerance for the First Amendment: Title VII's Regulation of Employee Speech," *Ohio Northern Law Review* 27 (2001): 577.

81. *Pickering,* 391 U.S. 563; *Connick,* 461 U.S. 138.

82. Eugene Volokh, "Comment: Freedom of Speech and Workplace Harassment," *UCLA Law Review* 39 (1992): 1791–872.

83. Estlund, "Freedom of Expression in the Workplace," 715.

84. Korwar, *War of Words;* Cole, *Sexual Harassment on Campus,* 179.

85. Two notable exceptions exist, *Cohen,* 92 F.3d 968, and *Silva,* 888 F. Supp. 293. However, *Cohen* was premised less on the propriety of sexual harassment rules in the classroom than on the fact that the plaintiff had not been adequately notified that his longstanding behavior violated new collegiate rules.

86. *McClellan v. The Board of Regents of the State University of Tennessee,* 921 S.W.2d 684, 691 (1996).

87. *Parks v. Wilson,* 872 F. Supp. 1467, 1470 (D.S.C. 1995)

88. *Rubin,* 933 F. Supp. 1425; *Mann v. University of Cincinnati,* 864 F. Supp. 44 (S.D. Ohio 1994).

89. *Davis v. Monroe County Board of Education,* 74 F.3d 1186 (11th Cir. 1996).

90. 20 U.S.C. § 1681(a).

91. *Davis,* 74 F.3d at 1186.

92. *Davis,* 526 U.S. at 629.

93. See, e.g., *Doe v. Petaluma City School District,* 830 F. Supp. 1560 (N.D. Cal. 1993).

94. See, e.g., *Moire v. Temple University School of Medicine,* 613 F. Supp. 1360 (E.D. Pa. 1985), *affirmed,* 800 F.2d 1136 (3d Cir. 1986); see also *Bishop,* 926 F.2d 1066.

95. *Rubin,* 933 F. Supp. at 1429.

96. *Franklin v. Gwinnett County Public Schools,* 503 U.S. 60 (1992).

97. *Davis,* 74 F.3d at 1191, quoting *Patricia H. v. Berkeley Unified School District,* 830 F. Supp. 1288, 1292–93 (N.D. Cal. 1993).

98. Academic freedom is a widely recognized concept that nonetheless is vaguely defined. In 1940 the American Association of University Professors (AAUP) and the Association of American Colleges (AAC) issued their Statement of Principles on Academic Freedom and Tenure. As part of that statement, the AAUP and AAC said: "The common good depends upon the free search for truth and its free expression. Academic freedom is essential to these purposes. . . . Academic freedom in its teaching aspect is fundamental for the protection of the rights of the teacher in teaching and of the student to freedom in learning" (American Association of University Professors, *Statement of Principles of Academic Freedom and Tenure* [1940], online at http://www.aaup.org/statements/Redbook/1940stat.htm). The statement of AAUP and AAC is a fairly broad declaration, yet it fails to define the limits of academic freedom. Nor, for that matter, have the courts set out specific rules for its application. One commentator has argued that academic freedom has two components—a true "academic freedom" covering "the liberties claimed by professors through professional channels against administrative or political interference

with research, teaching and governance," and a "constitutional academic freedom" that insulates the university in its "core academic affairs from interference with the state" (J. Peter Byrne, "Academic Freedom: A 'Special Concern of the First Amendment,'" *Yale Law Journal* 99 [1989]: 255). In his view, the courts should only have jurisdiction over constitutional academic freedom, with true academic freedom the province of faculty interactions with administrators and outside regulators.

99. *Sweezy v. New Hampshire,* 354 U.S. 234 (1957); *Keyishian v. Board of Regents,* 385 U.S. 589 (1967); *Widmar v. Vincent,* 454 U.S. 263 (1981); *Silva,* 888 F. Supp. at 313.

100. *Sweezy,* 354 U.S. at 250.

101. *Cohen,* 92 F.3d 968.

102. Under the policy, a faculty member could be disciplined for "unwelcome sexual advances, requests for sexual favors and other verbal, written or physical conduct of a sexual nature" when "such conduct has the purpose or effect of unreasonably interfering with an individual's academic performance or creating an intimidating, hostile or offensive learning environment" (id. at 970).

103. *Cohen v. San Bernardino Valley College,* 883 F. Supp. 1407, 1409 (C.D. Cal. 1995).

104. *Morgan,* 542 F. Supp. 123.

105. *EEOC v. Horizons Hotel Corp.,* 831 F. Supp. 10, 112 (D. Puerto Rico 1993).

106. *Cohen,* 92 F.3d at 972.

107. Id. at 971.

108. See, e.g., *Jenson,* 824 F. Supp. 847.

109. See also *Silva,* 888 F. Supp. 293.

110. *UWM Post,* 774 F. Supp. at 1163.

111. *Bishop,* 926 F.2d 1066.

112. Arthur L. Coleman and Jonathan R. Alger, "Beyond Speech Codes: Harmonizing Rights of Free Speech and Freedom from Discrimination on University Campuses," *Journal of College and University Law* 23 (1996): 91, 121.

113. Cass R. Sunstein, "Words, Caste, Conduct," *University of Chicago Law Review* 60 (1993): 830.

114. Ibid., 831.

115. *Bishop,* 926 F.2d at 1073.

116. Browne, "Title VII as Censorship"; Volokh, "How Harassment Law Restricts Free Speech," "Freedom of Speech and Workplace Harassment."

117. Of course, Title VII and HWE address certain traits—gender, race, and now sexual orientation—not particular groups, for example women (*Oncale v. Sundowner Offshore Services, Inc.,* 523 U.S. 75 (1998)). Nonetheless, virtually all of the victorious HWE cases have involved men harassing women.

118. In the 1928 case, *Anthony v. Syracuse University,* 224 A.D. 487, 488 (1928), the Supreme Court of New York permitted university administrators to expel a student because "they did not think of her [as] 'a typical Syracuse girl.'"

119. See Kent Greenawalt, *Speech, Crime, and the Uses of Language* (New York: Oxford University Press, 1989).

120. See Gerald Rosenberg, *The Hollow Hope: Can Courts Bring About Social Change?* (Chicago: University of Chicago Press, 1991).

121. Patricia Smith, ed., *Feminist Jurisprudence* (New York: Oxford University Press, 1993), 211; see also Jeffrey A. Segal and Harold J. Spaeth, *The Supreme Court and the Attitudinal Model* (New York: Cambridge University Press, 1993).

122. Samuel Walker, *Hate Speech: The History of an American Controversy* (Lincoln: University of Nebraska Press, 1994), 14–15.

123. Reginald S. Sheehan, "Governmental Litigants, Underdogs, and Civil Liberties: A Reassessment of a Trend in Supreme Court Decision-Making," *Western Political Quarterly* 45 (1992): 27–39. Other recent studies show that amici are also influential in affecting decisions of the Supreme Court (Gregg Ivers and Karen O'Connor, "Friends as Foes: The Amicus Curiae Participation and Effectiveness of the American Civil Liberties Union and Americans for Effective Law Enforcement in Criminal Cases, 1969–1982," *Law and Policy* 9 [1987]: 161–78).

124. Stephen J. Morewitz, *Sexual Harassment and Social Change in American Society* (San Francisco: Austin and Winfield, 1996), 223.

125. Ibid.

126. Sheehan, "Governmental Litigants," 27.

127. Susan Estrich, "Sex at Work," *Stanford Law Review* 43 (1991): 813–61.

128. As it had at the trial level, Central Michigan University lost its appeal (*Dambrot,* 55 F.3d).

129. The ACLU brought the case in *Doe* and assisted in *UWM Post.* Attorneys affiliated with the Individual Rights Foundation assisted in *Corry.* The Individual Rights Foundation is a separate organization from the Foundation for Individual Rights in Education.

130. Walker, *Hate Speech,* 14.

131. William G. Jacoby, "Issue Framing and Public Opinion on Government Spending," *American Journal of Political Science* 44 (2000): 750–67.

132. For further discussion of these findings, consider Segal and Spaeth, *Supreme Court and the Attitudinal Model,* and Sheldon Goldman and Austin Sarat, eds., *American Court Systems: Readings in Judicial process and Behavior* (San Francisco: W. H. Freeman, 1978).

133. Alan R. Gold, "Campus Racial Tensions—and Violence—Appear on [the] Rise," *New York Times,* February 21, 1988, sec. 4, 6.

134. A year after the case, Edward Cleary, the plaintiff's lawyer, published a book about the case. In the book, Cleary boasts of the arguments his team used to interest the Court (Jacobsohn, *Beyond the Burning Cross*).

135. *R.A.V.,* 505 U.S. at 415–16, emphasis added.

136. Freivogel, "Ruling Aimed at Hate-Speech Laws," C1; Krauthammer, "Political Correctness is Scalia's Newest Target," 21; *MacNeil/Lehrer NewsHour,* June 26, 1992.

137. *MacNeil/Lehrer NewsHour,* June 26, 1992.

138. Alexander W. Astin, Kenneth C. Green, William S. Korn, Marilynn Schalit, and Ellyne R. Berz, *The American Freshman: National Norms for Fall 1988* (Los Angeles: Higher Education Research Institute, 1988), 47.

139. Jon Weiner, "Reagan's Children: Racial Hatred on Campus," *The Nation,* February 27, 1989, 260–64.

140. Telephone interview with Judge Avern Cohn, 2000.

141. One day before a House vote on the Civil Rights Act, proponents of Title VII amended the legislation to add "sex" as a protected basis. They did so with the help of Title VII's opponents, "who hoped that the inclusion of 'sex' would highlight the absurdity of the effort as a whole and contribute to its defeat" (Estrich, "Sex at Work," 816–17).

142. Lindemann and Kadue, *Primer on Sexual Harassment,* 173.

143. Lawyers Cooperative Publishing, *Handling Sexual Harassment Cases* (Rochester, NY: 1993).

144. Ruth Colker, "Whores, Fags, Dumb-Ass Women, Surly Blacks, and Competent Heterosexual White Men: The Sexual and Racial Morality Underlying Anti-Discrimination Doctrine," *Yale Journal of Law and Feminism* 7 (1995): 196–97.

145. Cole, *Sexual Harassment on Campus,* 137.

146. *Turley v. United Carbide Corp.,* 618 F. Supp. 1438, 1441 (S.D. W.Va. 1985).

147. David Cole, "Playing by Pornography's Rules: The Regulation of Sexual Expression," *University of Pennsylvania Law Review* 143 (1994): 111–78.

148. Certainly, the axiom is accepted in popular society. Consider that the A&E Television Network has even sponsored a special called "The History of Sex," which makes the same point.

149. In *Besig v. United States,* 208 F.2d 142, 145 (9th Cir. 1953), the Ninth Circuit approved the customs seizure of Henry Miller's *Tropic of Cancer* and *Tropic of Capricorn* because they lacked "the grace of purity or goodness." Also consider Anita Bernstein, "The Representational Dialectic: With Illustrations from Obscenity, Forfeiture, and Accident Law," *California Law Review* 87 (1999): 305–70.

150. Attorney General's Commission on Pornography, *Final Report* (Washington, D.C.: U.S. Department of Justice, 1986).

151. *Muller v. Oregon,* 208 U.S. 41 (1908).

152. Estlund, "Freedom of Expression in the Workplace," 717.

153. Of course, we cannot ignore *American Booksellers v. Hudnut,* 771 F.2d 323 (7th Cir. 1985), where the Seventh Circuit refused to uphold an Indianapolis anti-pornography statute championed by Catharine MacKinnon and Andrea Dworkin. Although many would disagree, I explain this decision on two grounds. First, the court framed the case as feminist activists getting too "uppity," rather than a statute that protected "average" women. Second, instead of considering pornography a protected activity, the court left open the question of how dangerous the "secondary effects" of pornography might be. To the extent that social science research can show a more direct relationship between pornography and sex crimes, the courts might be willing to reconsider and uphold a similar statute.

154. David E. Bernstein, "Trends in First Amendment Jurisprudence: Antidiscrimination Laws and the First Amendment," *Missouri Law Review* 66 (2001): 132.

155. Of course, this approach would contravene core constitutional principles under which "the government may not impose sanctions against the expression of particular

viewpoints because of the viewpoint expressed" (Browne, "Zero Tolerance for the First Amendment," 564).

Chapter Five

1. *Corry v. Stanford University,* No. 740309 (Cal. Super. Ct. filed Feb. 27, 1995).

2. Nat Hentoff, "Against the Odds: A Historic Free Speech Victory," *Village Voice,* May 2, 1995, 18; Editorial, "Thought Police Disarmed; Campus Speech Codes, R.I.P.," *Arizona Republic,* March 30, 1995, B4; Editorial, "Another Code Bites the Dust," *Rocky Mountain News,* April 7, 1995, A69.

3. See Bradley C. Canon and Charles A. Johnson, *Judicial Policies: Implementation and Impact* (Washington, D.C.: Congressional Quarterly Press, 1999).

4. See Gerald Rosenberg, *The Hollow Hope: Can Courts Bring About Social Change?* (Chicago: University of Chicago Press, 1991).

5. See William K. Muir, *Prayer in Public Schools: Law and Attitudinal Change* (Chicago: University of Chicago Press, 1967); and Kenneth M. Dolbeare and Philip E. Hammond, *The School Prayer Decisions: From Court Policy to Local Practice* (Chicago: University of Chicago Press, 1971).

6. Lauren Edelman, "Legal Ambiguity and Symbolic Structures: Organizational Mediation of Civil Rights Law," *American Journal of Sociology* 97 (1992): 1531–76; Lauren Edelman, "Legal Environments and Organizational Governance: The Expansion of Due Process Rights," *American Journal of Sociology* 95 (1990): 1401–40.

7. In the case of school prayer, a decision of the U.S. Supreme Court subjected every public school in America to prohibitions on state-sponsored prayer. So too, the federal civil rights acts prohibited a wide class of public accommodations from discriminating. However, because most of the speech code cases came from lower courts—and since the Supreme Court's decision in *R.A.V.* was not precisely on point—only a subset of colleges and universities were *absolutely* bound by the holdings.

8. Robert Mnookin and Lewis Kornhauser, "Bargaining in the Shadow of Law: The Case of Divorce," *Yale Law Journal* 88 (1979): 950.

9. Edelman, "Legal Environments and Organizational Governance," 1401–40.

10. Ibid.

11. See Samuel Walker, *Hate Speech: The History of an American Controversy* (Lincoln: University of Nebraska Press, 1994).

12. Michael W. Giles and Douglas S. Gatlin, "Mass-Level Compliance with Public Policy: The Case of School Desegregation," *Journal of Politics* 42 (1980): 725.

13. Thomas C. Grey, "How to Write a Speech Code without Really Trying: Reflections on the Stanford Experience," *U.C. Davis Law Review* 29 (1996): 891–957; Thomas C. Grey, "Civil Rights vs. Civil Liberties: The Case of Discriminatory Verbal Harassment," in *Hate Speech and the Constitution,* ed. Steven J. Heyman (New York: Garland, 1996).

14. Walker, *Hate Speech.*

15. Given the pressures they face, it is surprising that neither St. Ann's officials nor the other schools visited considered speech codes without penalties—perhaps simply a statement of college philosophy. Respondents said they were concerned about sending such a clear signal that "the policy had no teeth."

16. Michael Mintrom, "Policy Entrepreneurs and the Diffusion of Policy," *American Journal of Political Science* 41 (1997): 739.

17. Edelman, "Legal Ambiguity," 1568.

Chapter Six

1. Online at http://www.thefire.org/pr.php?doc=shippensburg_pr_042303.inc. See also *Bair v. Shippensburg University,* 280 F. Supp. 2d 357 (M.D. Pa. 2003).

2. Online at http://www.speechcodes.org/about.php.

3. Online at http://www.frontpagemag.com/Articles/Printable.asp?ID=3723.

4. Lisa Petrillo, "Reparations Ad Creates Firestorm for Student Editors. Issues of Racism, Free Speech Raised." *San Diego Union-Tribune,* April 17, 2001, B3.

5. Joan Walsh, "Who's Afraid of the Big, Bad Horowitz?" *Salon.com,* March 9, 2001, online at http://dir.salon.com/news/feature/2001/03/09/horowitz/index.html; Matt Rosenberg, "Horowitz's Journey into the Jaws of Controversy," *Seattle Times,* May 16, 2001, B7; Petrillo, "Reparations Ad Creates Firestorm," B3.

6. Beth McMurtrie, "War of Words," *Chronicle of Higher Education,* May 23, 2003, A31.

7. Ibid., A32.

8. Floyd H. Allport, "J-Curve Hypothesis of Conforming Behavior," *Journal of Social Psychology* 5 (1934): 141–83.

9. Paul J. DiMaggio and Walter W. Powell, "The Iron Cage Revisited: Institutional Isomorphism and Collective Rationality in Organizational Fields," *American Sociological Review* 48 (1983): 147–60.

10. Alexander W. Astin, William S. Korn, and Ellyne R. Riggs, *The American Freshman: National Norms for 1993* (Los Angeles: University of California at Los Angeles, 1993).

11. See Alexander W. Astin, William S. Korn, Linda J. Sax, and Kathryn M. Mahoney, *The American Freshman: National Norms for 1994* (Los Angeles: University of California at Los Angeles, 1994); and Linda J. Sax, Jennifer A. Lindholm, Alexander W. Astin, William S. Korn, and Kathryn M. Mahoney, *The American Freshman: National Norms for 2001* (Los Angeles: University of California at Los Angeles, 2001).

12. *CBS News/New York Times,* April 1–April 3, 1991.

13. *Public Opinion Online.* Accession Number 023107, Question Number 244 (1994).

14. Online at http://www.icpsr.umich.edu:8080/GSS/rnd1998/merged/cdbk/ethspkno.htm.

15. *Public Opinion Online,* Accession Number 0330081, Question Number 44 (1999).

16. Ibid.

17. *Public Opinion Online,* Accession Number 0421172, Question Number 17 (2002), and Accession Number 0436264, Question Number 16 (2003).

18. Of these, 55 percent of respondents believed hate speech on the Internet/computers was a major problem, and 26 percent saw the issue as a minor problem. Only 15 percent did not find such hate speech a problem (*Public Opinion Online,* Accession Number 0353613, Question Number 134 [2000]).

19. *Public Opinion Online,* Accession Number 0353606, Question Number 127 (2000).

20. *Public Opinion Online,* Accession Number 0328188, Question Number 30 (1999).

21. In its polling since 1999, the Freedom Forum has often asked two questions, whether respondents believe "the First Amendment goes too far in the rights it guarantees," and whether they believe that "people should be allowed to express unpopular opinions." Although there was a temporary drop in support for the First Amendment and free speech immediately following September 11, these numbers are back up to their traditional level of support, at or above two-thirds (*Public Opinion Online,* Accession Number 0330045, Question Number 8 [1999]; Accession Number 0367812, Question Number 2 [2000]; Accession Number 0384087, Question Number 2 [2001]; Accession Number 0421157, Question Number 2 [2002]; Accession Number 0436250, Question Number 2 [2003]; Accession Number 0384093, Question Number 8 [2001]; Accession Number 0421169, Question Number 14 [2002]).

22. *Public Opinion Online,* Accession Number 0384098, Question Number 13 (2001); Accession Number 0367824, Question Number 14 (2000).

23. See Doris A. Graber, *Mass Media and American Politics* (Washington, D.C.: Congressional Quarterly Press, 1980).

24. Anna Quindlen, "Getting Rid of the Sex Police," *Newsweek,* January 13, 2003, 72.

25. Keith Woods, "'Nigger': A Case Study in Using a Racial Epithet," The Poynter Institute for Media Studies (1995), online at http://www. media-awareness.ca/eng/issues/minrep/journl/nigger.htm (accessed October 2, 2002).

26. Ibid.

27. James Auer, "Newspapers Substitute 'Doonesbury' Strip," *Milwaukee Journal Sentinel,* September 6, 2003, B6.

28. Woods, "A Case Study."

29. Ibid.

30. Ibid.

31. Gina Lubrano, "Readers, Editors Respond to Issues," *San Diego Union-Tribune,* April 2, 2001, B7.

32. Michael Holley, "The Anguished Anatomy of a Slur," *Boston Globe,* March 8, 1997, C1.

33. "Native American Journalists Association "Say 'No' to Racism in the Media," 2002, online at http://aim_support.tripod.com/No-racism-in-media.htm (accessed October 2, 2002).

34. Jon B. Gould, "All the Speech That's Fit to Print: Newspaper 'Censorship' of Issue Ads." Paper presented at the Annual Meeting of the Law & Society Association, Pittsburgh, PA (2003).

35. Online at http://www.consumerdvreviews.com/news/0703/07162003_01.asp.

36. Mandi Steele, "Double Standard at AOL?" *World Net Daily,* July 20, 2002, online at http://www.worldnetdaily.com/news/article.asp?ARTICLE_ID=28338.

37. Verizon Online Policies, online at http://www22.verizon.com/ForHomeDSL/channels/dsl/forhomedsl.asp?verizon_referrer=volnet.

38. Steele, "Double Standard at AOL?"

39. Ibid.

40. "Jeannette Walls Delivers the Scoop," *MSNBC,* May 23, 2002, online at http://www.msnbc.com/news/756044.asp (accessed October 2, 2002).

41. Consider that in 1992 a German court fined British historian David Irving for claiming that the Holocaust did not occur (Jay Rayner, "Munich Court Fines Irving for Bierkeller Speech," *London Guardian,* May 6, 1992, 9).

42. *Corry v. Stanford University,* No. 740309 (Cal. Super. Ct. filed Feb. 27, 1995).

43. *R.A.V. v. City of St. Paul, Minnesota,* 505 U.S. 377 (1992).

44. Online at http://www.speechcodes.org/about.php.

45. *Wisconsin v. Mitchell,* 508 U.S. 47 (1993).

46. Id.

47. *R.A.V. v. City of St. Paul,* 505 U.S. 377 (1992).

48. *Mitchell v. Wisconsin,* 484 N.W.2d 807, 811 (Wis. 1992).

49. Laura Beth Nielsen, *License to Harass: Law, Hierarchy, and Offensive Public Speech* (Princeton: Princeton University Press, 1994). References are from the manuscript prior to publication.

50. Ibid.

51. Ibid.

52. Ibid.

53. Sally Engle Merry, "Legal Pluralism," *Law & Society Review* 22 (1988): 870.

54. Ibid., 870–71.

Appendix

1. This cut reflected both theoretical and practical grounds. On one level the cultural debate over hate speech codes played out almost exclusively at four-year colleges and universities. Because any study depends on variation in the dependent variable, the research examined the class of schools that both created *and* eschewed hate speech policies. In addition, because two-year schools are so numerous, the sample was set at four-year institutions to make data collection feasible.

2. Arati R. Korwar, *War of Words: Speech Codes at Public Colleges and Universities* (Nashville, TN: Freedom Forum First Amendment Center, 1994).

3. *Chaplinsky v. New Hampshire,* 315 U.S. 568, 572 (1942).

4. Samuel Walker, *Hate Speech: The History of an American Controversy* (Lincoln: University of Nebraska Press, 1994).

5. *R.A.V. v. City of St. Paul, Minnesota,* 505 U.S. 377 (1992).

6. *Doe v. University of Michigan,* 721 F. Supp. 852 (E.D. Mich. 1989); *The UWM Post v. Board of Regents of the University of Wisconsin System,* 774 F. Supp. 1163 (E.D. Wis. 1991).

7. Latin American, African, and Asian Studies programs were excluded from the CRS variable because they focus more on areas studies than the condition of minority groups in America.

8. Everett Carll Ladd Jr. and Seymour Martin Lipset, *The Divided Academy: Professors and Politics* (New York: McGraw-Hill, 1975).

9. Lawrence Bobo, "Group Conflict, Prejudice, and the Paradox of Contemporary

Racial Attitudes," in *Eliminating Racism: Profiles in Controversy,* ed. Phyllis A. Katz and Dalmas A. Taylor (New York: Plenum Press, 1988).

10. Again, recall that we are not simply concerned with whether a school's faculty or students are academically able. For a school to continue to attract talented faculty and students, recruits need to believe that they are joining an institution that has similarly able colleagues. Since many students and some faculty are unable to come to campus and interview a sufficient pool of their peers, they must rely on data such as standardized tests to tell them the level of a school's academic community. To the extent that a school continues to attract academically able faculty (and students), Ladd and Lipset tell us that the school will be more liberal than some of its counterparts.

11. Fred Baumann, *Fraternity and Politics: Choosing One's Brothers* (Westport, CT: Praeger, 1998); Peggy Reeves Sanday, *Fraternity Gang Rape: Sex, Brotherhood, and Privilege on Campus* (New York: New York University Press, 1990).

12. By definition, the annual budgets of research institutions include expenditures for research that teaching institutions do not. The result is to skew the data in favor of teaching institutions, making it appear that this group of schools spends a greater percentage of its funds on student services than do research institutions. Of course, there are other expenditure differences between these institutions, including numbers of professional schools and amounts spent on athletic teams (among others). However, the correlation between the number of academic programs and the amount spent on student services should be roughly constant; the more schools an institution maintains, the more it must spend for student services at each college. In addition, the budget for athletics at NCAA Division I schools is often kept separate from the university's operating budget and thus does not skew the sample too greatly.

13. African American students, faculty, staff, and administrators; female students, faculty, staff, and administrators; other racial and ethnic minorities among students, faculty, staff, and administrators; gay/lesbian groups; minority studies programs; women's studies programs; racial/ethnic incidents; *Barrons Guide; Yale Guide;* and anti-apartheid protest.

14. No speech code vs. any code; offensive speech vs. all others; offensive speech and verbal harassment of groups vs. all others; offensive speech, verbal harassment of groups, and generic verbal harassment vs. all others.

15. Dinesh D'Souza, *Illiberal Education: The Politics of Race and Sex on Campus* (New York: Free Press, 1991); Thomas C. Grey, "How to Write a Speech Code without Really Trying: Reflections on the Stanford Experience," *U.C. Davis Law Review* 29 (1996): 891–957; Thomas C. Grey, "Civil Rights vs. Civil Liberties: The Case of Discriminatory Verbal Harassment," in *Hate Speech and the Constitution,* ed. Steven J. Heyman (New York: Garland, 1996).

Index